Celebrating Spiritual Discipline

Discipline and the Western Mysteries

Walter Parrish

First Published in 2016 by
The Fraternity of the Hidden Light
P.O. Box 5094
Covina, CA 91723

ISBN 978-0-9710469-6-2

Printed in the United States of America

Cover Art: Hermes Trismegistus, floor mosaic Cathedral of Siena. Wikimedia Commons, public domain.

For Laura
My Anam Cara

Your love opened my eyes
and illuminated the path
to my Higher Soul

Contents

Prologue

The Western Mystery Tradition is a powerful and life-affirming path of spiritual transformation. It is one of the living expressions of the perennial philosophy that nurture, heal, and guide us in the search for our spiritual roots. Several traditions within the Western mysteries are based on what is called *Hermetic Qabalah*. Both Hermetic and Qabalistic philosophies play roles in shaping its practices.

Hermetic practice is composed of three sciences: astrology, *the Operation of the Stars*; alchemy, *the Operation of the Sun*; and theurgy, *the Operation of the Moon*. Many are familiar with the science of astrology. Some are familiar with or have at least heard of alchemy. Fewer know about the science of theurgy.

All three Hermetic sciences have important roles to play in the Western mysteries. Theurgy is the least understood and therefore the least practiced of these sciences. Theurgic practices are designed to train and guide our subconscious mind to act as our connection to Divine levels of consciousness. The spiritual disciplines we will be examining in this book are conscious activities that we can use to direct our subconscious mind in its interactions with these higher realms.

Even without the use of the disciplines we are subject to the forces of evolution. When we begin to understand and apply the traditional spiritual disciplines we are able to greatly accelerate the rate of our physical, intellectual, psychological, and spiritual transformation. Our communication with Divinity is improved and all areas of our lives can be transformed.

Why then is it that theurgy is not better known or more widely practiced? Part of the explanation is that communicating with our higher levels of consciousness requires knowledge of self and a desire to become a better vehicle for the Will of Divinity. Both of these require commitments of our time and efforts. We must be willing to dedicate much of our attention and our resources to these pursuits. This is not an easy task when so many of us are looking for instant gratification!

Compared to astrology and alchemy, information about theurgy is not as readily available. The ability to communicate with Divinity imparts great power and responsibility. Those who are charged with the guardianship of this knowledge choose to keep this knowledge out of the hands of the merely curious or those who would misuse it.

On the other hand, we must begin early to build a strong foundation on which we can base our future growth. The beginning of our journey is not too soon to prepare ourselves by learning about the spiritual disciplines and building up our proficiency in them. The time and the effort we invest now will be well rewarded when we find ourselves better equipped to face the tests and challenges that await us on our spiritual *Path of Return*.

This book introduces twelve traditional spiritual disciplines; theurgic tools that can be used to strengthen and clarify the connections linking the Hermetic sciences of astrology, alchemy, and theurgy. What I am proposing is the creation of correspondences for the twelve spiritual disciplines that will link them to astrological and alchemical correspondences embraced by a number of organizations that teach the Western mysteries. This is my first attempt to do this and I am merely offering it as a starting point for exploration.

This work is based on my current understanding of the three Hermetic sciences and the twelve disciplines. I hope this book will inspire a conversation about where the spiritual disciplines fit into the Hermetic Qabalah and how they can be used to improve our understanding and practice of the three Hermetic sciences. This work is not intended to be authoritative or definitive.

The Fraternity of the Hidden Light is the vehicle of the Western mysteries I have chosen for my spiritual unfoldment. When I found the Fraternity of the Hidden Light, I knew that here was a home where my spiritual longings could be fulfilled.

The Fraternity of the Hidden Light is a group of dedicated initiates and probationers that embrace both diversity and inclusiveness. Of course, any group experiences periods of peace and strife. I arrived at a time when the cohesiveness of our local group was challenged by a few individuals struggling to rise above the petty demands of personality. The success of our leaders in sorting things out was an inspiration to us all. See the chapter on the discipline of Guidance for an explanation of this process.

The commitment of the group to listen to the voice of our inner teacher helped us through this storm and created an inner strength and unity that has carried us through to the present day. I discovered within myself a resolve to rise above life's challenges and to persevere.

Soon after I entered this Path I recognized that discipline was a key that could help me work through my own challenges. I also found that discipline opened many doors to the mysteries. I resisted this knowledge at first because I grew up believing that discipline requires sacrifice. The Western mysteries taught me that only those things which hinder our spiritual progress need be sacrificed. Discipline brought me joy when I understood that it helps achieve freedom and enlightenment. That is why I celebrate the spiritual disciplines.

When I began this work I searched for material about spiritual discipline. I found only a few sources relating to the Western mysteries. This work is my attempt to reach an understanding about the role of spiritual discipline in the Western Mystery Tradition on what is called the *Path of Return.*

Discipline is part of the experience we need in order to develop a profound and lasting understanding of the mysteries. Understanding cannot be developed just by reading books or attending lectures. We live in a physical world. The actions we take and the decisions we make determine the quality and depth of our explorations of the nonphysical realms of reality.

I am by no means a master of spiritual discipline. When I first encountered the path of the Western mysteries, many areas of my life were decidedly chaotic. I was totally unaware of the degree to which a lack of discipline was keeping me from realizing my full potential.

I had previously gained a certain amount of esoteric knowledge and experience, but the work I encountered in the Western mysteries proved to be a real challenge. Entering the path of the mysteries in mid-life, I believed I was prepared to make progress on the Path of Return. I soon realized that there was much for me to learn before I could even begin. Today I appreciate the importance of the spiritual disciplines, but I still struggle to integrate them into my life.

Please take what I have to offer about the spiritual disciplines and test it in the laboratory of your own life. My hope is that some of what I offer may prove useful to you in your own spiritual unfoldment. I also hope that this work will stimulate a discussion of the spiritual disciplines that will lead to a better understanding for everyone.

If you find that some of it does not measure up after you have tested it, I encourage you to keep this conversation alive and contribute to what is now a paucity of material in this area. Be forewarned that much of this testing will require a considerable amount of time and dedication. If you persevere, the rewards will be much greater than you can now imagine.

From the beginning, my mentors gently encouraged me to look deeply into my motivations for doing the work. Shortly after I was initiated into the Western mysteries, I had a sudden flash of inspiration. This awakening was very much like the Lightning that destroys the tower on Tarot Key 16. The work I needed to be doing was not just any work; it was the *Great Work*. I needed to make a new commitment to myself and to my own Higher Soul that I would henceforth approach the Path of the Mysteries with renewed dedication and perseverance.

I understood for the first time that I would need to find the courage to try new things and to venture outside of my comfort zone. I found real wisdom in the words, *"Fear is Failure."* I discovered that it is far better to risk failure in a new venture than to accept very real failure by not trying at all.

My brothers and sisters of the Fraternity of the Hidden Light (the Fraternitas L.V.X. Occulta, or the F.L.O.) and our experiences together are treasures beyond my capacity to measure or describe. The fraters and sorors of the F.L.O. continually demonstrate for me the transformative power of Service and the other disciplines. For this and for their unfailing love and support I am ever thankful.

While the focus of this work is on the Western mysteries, I wish to acknowledge my debt to the writings of numerous Christian writers. Much of the published material on the spiritual disciplines comes from the Christian tradition. These Christian works include references to the Old and New Testaments of the Bible. I include quotes from the Christian Bible and other writings when they serve to clarify the ideas I wish to express.

As you progress through this material, you will notice many references to the work of quintessential Western adept Paul Foster Case. His contribution to our understanding of the Tarot and its use as a tool for spiritual transformation is unmatched.

Many of the books by Paul Foster Case are available through the Builders of the Adytum. The Fraternity of the Hidden Light has made available some of his early writings. The Rosicrucian Order of the Golden Dawn has made available his early alchemical teaching. I am grateful to these organizations for making them available to the public.

The early alchemical writings of Paul Foster Case found in *Hermetic Alchemy Science and Practice* seek to connect the sciences of alchemy and astrology and the Qabalah through a system of correspondences. *Hermetic Alchemy* is a treasure house of information for my explorations and the correspondences found there are invaluable. I use the symbol [††] in the text where I am relying on material from this work. This symbol will refer you to the citation at the end of each chapter.

In this present work I am relying on the correspondences found in *Hermetic Alchemy* as a starting point. I seek to expand these correspondences to include 12 traditional spiritual disciplines. As I stated earlier, one of my goals is to use these expanded correspondences to better integrate the three Hermetic sciences.

To appreciate the role of spiritual discipline in the Western mysteries we must first understand that the disciplines include practices that aid us in exploring the *"Above"* or inner planes of consciousness. These practices begin on our physical plane of reality; the *"Below."* Used consciously, these practices provide us with the tools we need to access and work with the higher realms.

For much of my inspiration in this work I am indebted to the encouragement and work of the Steward of the Fraternity of the Hidden Light and author Dr. Paul A. Clark. I thank my beloved soror Cindy Forbes of the F.L.O. for her support and assistance in getting this present work published. Barbara, also a beloved soror of mine, provided much needed clarity for many of my fumbling attempts at describing the complex material presented in this book.

From the beginning of my experiences with the Western mysteries I encountered patterns and relationships that pointed to an underlying foundation of numbers and mathematical principles. I was much influenced by what Paul Foster Case wrote about the occult meaning of numbers in his *The Tarot; A Key to the Wisdom of the Ages*. In this work he also describes a layout or tableau of the 22 Tarot major arcana that reveals how the harmonies of number found in them help us to understand the deeper meanings to be found there.

Oswald Wirth in his *The Tarot of the Magicians* demonstrates how patterns of threes and sevens within and among the Keys of the Tarot major arcana describe to us the mechanisms of creation. He shows us how these patterns reveal their wisdom and provide understanding for many of the mysteries they contain.

Frederick Bligh Bond and Thomas Simcox Lea in *Gematria: A Preliminary Investigation of the Cabala* assert that number values or powers assigned to the letters of the Greek and Hebrew alphabets reveal the wisdom hidden within ancient sacred texts. They quote the early Christian authority Saint Augustine:

> *"... numbers are the thoughts of God ... The Divine Wisdom is reflected in the numbers impressed upon all things ... the construction of the physical and moral world alike is based upon eternal numbers."*

I am also indebted to the works of Christian theologian and author Richard J. Foster; to the works of philosopher and professor at the University of Southern California Dallas Willard; to the essays of Jack Courtis of the Confraternity of the Rose Cross; and to the work, wisdom, dedication, and love of countless initiates and adepts of the Western Mysteries. Throughout all my efforts to make this work available I acknowledge the selfless contributions of many others who embody the principles of the spiritual disciplines.

Part 1
Introduction

The origin of this work is a paper addressed to my brothers and sisters in the Fraternity of the Hidden Light. For many years I have been blessed with a desire to be of service to others. I wanted to express my gratitude to the F.L.O. for opening my eyes to the value of this service. The paper was intended to help my brothers and sisters understand the power of service in their own lives. As I searched for information, I found a number of other spiritual disciplines related to service. I quickly recognized that a work on service that did not include references to these disciplines would be incomplete.

I found two essays by Jack Courtis on the website of the Confraternity of the Rose Cross at *crcsite.org* that put the interconnectedness of the spiritual disciplines into perspective. Courtis describes three branches of Hermetic science. These are the sciences of astrology, alchemy, and theurgy. The spiritual disciplines are essential practices employed in every aspect of the Hermetic sciences. These disciplines are particularly related to the science of theurgy (literally *god-working*). Courtis' descriptions of these sciences and the correspondences he used to link them together helped me to understand the role spiritual discipline plays in our spiritual unfolding.

The Emerald Tablet of Hermes Trismegistus assures us:

> *"That which is Above is as that which is Below, and that which is Below is as that which is Above, for the performance of the miracles of the One Thing."*

The alchemist works with the *Below* to balance and perfect the physical body and the personality in order to accept emanations from the *Above*. The astrologer works with the *Above* in order to understand and work with its cosmic influences *Below*. The magus or adept operates as a theurgist in both the *Above* and the *Below*. His or her spiritual operations reinforce the unity of these two worlds. Courtis asserts that the alchemist corresponds to our physical body; the astrologer corresponds to our spirit; and the magus or theurgist corresponds to our soul. The balancing and integrating of these three vehicles of our consciousness is what Courtis calls the *Great Work.*

The Great Work begins with the desire to be of service to the *One Source*, and thus to the entirety of Creation emanating from it. We are the subject of the Great Work. We serve the *Lord of the Universe* when we work to make our personalities more balanced and transparent to *Divine Will.*

At an early point on my Path as an initiate, I learned that desire alone cannot guarantee a successful spiritual quest. Desire must be followed by action. An ancient Russian proverb states: *"Pray for a miracle, but keep rowing toward shore."* Spiritual discipline leads us to the proper action. Practicing the twelve traditional disciplines discussed in this work will help us to develop the skills we need to achieve meaningful experiences as we perform the Great Work.

In a modern school of the Western Mysteries, the knowledge given to its initiates has been tested and handed down for generations. The perennial philosophy upon which the teachings of such schools are based reaches far back into prehistoric times. All initiates of a particular school or tradition study the same curriculum. However, the experiences of each initiate are deeply personal and transformative. These experiences test the readiness of each initiate to make progress in the Great Work. Seekers not affiliated with a group must find a teacher that will provide them with access to the same knowledge and experience as the initiate of a school of the Western mysteries. The greatest teacher any of us can hope to find is our own inner teacher that we access through our faculty of Intuition.

The Great Work is filled with obstacles for those who are not ready. Fortunately, we are all evolving and will one day be ready. Everyone, including the highest adept, is challenged daily with obstacles to growth. It is our willingness to push on ahead and overcome these challenges that determines our success. Spiritual discipline is an obstacle when we see it as drudgery. Here is a paradox: The work of discipline becomes joyful as we make progress in the Great Work. We begin to reap the rich rewards of spiritual living and we understand that our devotion to the Great Work is well invested.

When I discovered spiritual discipline, I knew I had found the key that for me unlocked many doors of the Mysteries. As I became more proficient in the practice of various forms of discipline, the quality of my understanding and my experiences increased. I also began to appreciate the value of perseverance in doing the work.

Paul Foster Case in an address to his fellow initiates of the Thoth-Hermes Temple in New York of the order of the Alpha et Omega said this about perseverance:

> *"You do not have to be mental giants to become practical Occultists. You simply have to do a certain amount of work every day. As* [Samuel] *Johnson says, "Yonder palace was raised by single stones, yet   you*

see its height and spaciousness. He that shall walk with vigor three hours a day will pass in seven years a space equal to the circumference of the globe."

As I made progress in my own work, I began to notice that the struggles of others were just as great, if not greater than my own. As much as we try to encourage one another, it is up to each one of us to do our own work. This book is offered to all as an encouragement to find our own unique and personal relationship with spiritual discipline.

When I became interested in spiritual discipline, I wanted to read what others had written. My search produced a few works; mostly from a Christian perspective. Being a student of the Western Mystery Tradition, my hope was to find works written about discipline as practiced in the Western mysteries. I found an article on the internet titled, *"Disciplined Action"* by Jack Courtis of the Confraternity of the Rose Cross. This provided a brief introduction to twelve traditional disciplines from the perspective of an initiate of the Western mysteries. Another article by Jack Courtis, *"Tabula Smaragdina Hermetis"* or the Emerald Tablet of Hermes, linked these twelve disciplines with twelve alchemical stages (the *Below*) and twelve signs of the Zodiac (the *Above*).

Finding these two articles was both encouraging and daunting. These articles provided a foundation for my investigation. Some of the correspondences used by Jack Courtis did not seem to work for me. I respected the fact that he had personal experience within this system, and it had worked effectively for him. Perhaps his article contained some blinds. I resolved to work out correspondences that made sense to me.

I began with the correspondences I learned in my work with the Fraternity of the Hidden Light. I gathered the works of various writers working in the Christian tradition. I compared the qualities of the spiritual disciplines as described by these authors with their qualities as I understood them.

After reading the works of the writers I had collected, I began to see that in several instances, what I thought I knew about the disciplines did not begin to describe the depth of their powers to transform our lives. This strengthened my resolve to understand them and to find a way to better integrate their practice into the tradition of the Western mysteries.

The unfoldment of this system was made possible through the guidance provided by the voice of my inner teacher or Higher Soul. My confidence in the system I was constructing grew as I worked with the correspondences. After some trial and error, I succeeded in creating a system of correspondences for the disciplines that for me appeared internally consistent.

The Hermetic Qabalah of the Western mysteries embraces a number of practices with a common goal of spiritual transformation. These practices are bound together with a system of correspondences that allow us to begin with what we know about ourselves and to expand this knowledge as we explore our inner dimensions. Intuitively I felt that there might be a way to connect the spiritual disciplines to this system.

I began with the twelve spiritual disciplines traditionally practiced in the Christian tradition, especially by the Roman Catholic Church. These were the same twelve disciplines written about by both the Protestant theologian Richard J. Foster and Jack Courtis, adept of the Western mysteries. What archetypes connected the writings and practices of these diverse traditions?

In spite of their apparent diversity and ambiguities, patterns began to emerge.

Each discipline can be practiced alone as a personal discipline. It can equally be practiced in the presence of others as an outer or interpersonal discipline. It can also be practiced with a group of others as a transpersonal discipline. However, the twelve traditional disciplines have each been placed into one of these three groups according to its most accepted mode of practice.

This system divided the disciplines into three groups of four. Looking at the four disciplines within each group, I began to notice that each discipline had qualities that associated it with the qualities of one of the four alchemical elements; fire, water, air, and earth. I began to compare the qualities of the twelve disciplines with the elemental qualities of the twelve astrological signs of the zodiac.

I was able to develop an initial set of correspondences of the spiritual disciplines with the twelve signs of the zodiac. The associations were not perfect. Some of the pairings did not appear to have very much in common.

I then compared my initial set of correspondences with the correspondences found in *Hermetic Alchemy Science and Practice.* [++] At a glance, some of Paul Foster Case's correspondences seemed obscure until I read the explanation that accompanied it. The explanation for each of his correspondences of the twelve signs of the zodiac with his twelve stages of alchemy was for me very convincing.

Scanning his explanations for connections to the twelve spiritual disciplines, I was able to resolve many of my concerns about matching the disciplines to Case's astrological and alchemical correspondences. The system I have developed is not perfect. Much work remains to be done. But I remain confident that if we begin to work with it we will eventually resolve correspondences that can consistently and confidently be relied upon. Together we can begin the process of refining this system.

This system is included here for the purposes of learning and exploration. At this point I can make no claim for its validity in wider usage. These correspondences are shown at the end of this introductory section. It is my hope is that they will provide a starting point for your own investigations. I encourage you to read Jack Courtis' articles for comparison.

From my own experience, I have come to recognize that the use of correspondences within any system can be like a double edged sword. Correspondences are meant to be memory aids that are indispensable in learning to think and act imaginatively and creatively. They help us to understand and to link ideas that might appear to be unrelated or otherwise incomprehensible.

However, once a set of symbols and correspondences has been committed to memory, it is easy to become over-reliant on it. We may forget that it is only a tool and not an end unto itself. Correspondences may lose their potency over time or take on deeper and more complex meanings for us. We must not allow the mental images associated with any set of correspondences to become so rigid that they may not be easily dissolved and transformed when they no longer serve us. This is spiritual Alchemy in a very basic form.

My experience in the Western Mysteries has made it clear that little progress can be made in the Great Work without the practices of spiritual discipline and the experiences that they bring to us. We seem to develop the use of spiritual discipline

15

concurrently with our acquisition of spiritual knowledge. This is a balanced approach and its success or failure is a measure of our readiness to take on the responsibilities that the *Great Work* demands of us.

This book was written in part to help us become more familiar with the spiritual disciplines now so that when needed, we will already have some knowledge of them and will have had some initial experience with them.

This work will show that effective use of the spiritual disciplines requires much conscious effort. Focusing on the disciplines will increase their transformative powers and can accelerate our spiritual growth. With practice and repetition, the use of the disciplines will become easier and more automatic.

Paul Foster Case in an address to his Thoth-Hermes Temple brother and sisters reminded them that the Masters of Wisdom seldom teach anything using plain and unambiguous language. They give many hints and clues, but we must take the hints and follow the clues. What we get out of them depends largely upon our willingness to work. If we approach this work in the hope of finding pre-digested truth, we will be disappointed.

The secrets of nature cannot be explained in words of one syllable. We must become serious and persevering students, who are ready and willing to go cheerfully through more or less downright drudgery to attain our ends. Only then may we hope to find the Light of Truth.

This Light is not something that can be taught or communicated to us. We will never receive it because we already possess it. In our hearts lay concealed the Summum

Bonum, Perfect Wisdom, and True Happiness. Our task is to remove the veils of illusion and ignorance.

In his address to Thoth-Hermes Case said that if our progress is tedious and uneven in the beginning, we may find comfort with the knowledge that even the greatest Adepts were once in our very same position. It has been asserted that there is no royal road to anything. We would do well to remember this. Unless we possess an unusual mind, our first steps along the Path of Return will be not only difficult, but deadly dull.

To all appearances, the dry details we must learn in the beginning seem to have no connection whatever with what we mean by "spiritual development." These details provide us with a foundation and the building blocks needed to reshape our minds and bodies into suitable vehicles for our spiritual unfoldment which is yet to come.

"Discipline" does not have to translate to *"Drudgery."* It is true that society equates discipline with work, structure, and order. But when we choose to make our spiritual life a priority, discipline becomes just another tool to help us reach our goal. The time and the work involved will be seen as small sacrifices for so great a goal. When we begin to see progress toward our goal of spiritual unfoldment, the work becomes lighter and more joyful. Later we will see that Celebration can be a spiritual discipline; one that makes all of our work more bearable.

Self-transformation is the goal of the Western mysteries. Our makeup as physical and spiritual beings involves a principle of unity known to the Greeks as *Nous* - pure mind - which includes the consciousness of our spirit, soul, and body. In our natural state, this *Nous* is often fragmented and polluted. Our whole constitution must be purified and reintegrated so that self-transformation can occur.

The spiritual disciplines are essential tools for this process of growth and unfoldment. The physical realm, the Qabalistic world of *Assiah*, is a world of action and it is here in this world of our physical senses that the Great Work must begin.

The Western Mystery Tradition is a broad collection of esoteric knowledge and practices. The Western mysteries have their roots in the ancient temples and mystery schools of Egypt, Greece, Western Asia, Africa, and Eastern Europe. Today the Western mysteries are enjoying a global renaissance. Organizations and traditions founded on principles of the Western mysteries are active throughout the world.

The modern Western Mystery Tradition received an enormous creative impetus in Alexandria, Egypt between the fourth century BCE and the fourth century CE. It is likely that the seeds of many of our modern practices and ideas were first sown in Alexandria. Scholars from all over the known world gravitated to this bustling and cosmopolitan seaport. The Libraries of Alexandria are today considered to have been one of the ancient world's greatest seats of learning up until their final destruction in the late fourth century CE.

Unfortunately the many centuries that have since passed have left us with little factual information about Alexandria. I can imagine Egyptian priests conversing with masters of the Kabballah. I can imagine philosophers from many nations debating with initiates of the Mysteries. All sorts of scholars and spiritual practitioners from around the known world met and exchanged knowledge and ideas. It was a golden age for intellectuals.

In the centuries that passed between the fall of Alexandria and today, many dedicated individuals worked to pass on the knowledge of the Mysteries. Many changes have taken place along the way. The Western Mystery Tradition did not appear in its modern form until the 19th century of our era. In the 1880's the founders of the *Hermetic Order of the Golden Dawn* did a masterful job of collecting the various threads of the Mysteries and weaving them into a rich tapestry of spiritual knowledge and practices. The Golden Dawn and the modern traditions that grew out of it are complete systems of spiritual unfoldment. These systems are united as variations of a modern spiritual tradition known as Hermetic Qabalah.

Hermetic Qabalah is a cosmopolitan and eclectic philosophy. It includes a wide range of practices that share compatible philosophies and symbolism. Hermetic Qabalah offers a complete system of spiritual and psychological development that is both structured and guided.

[††] Paul Foster Case, *Hermetic Alchemy Science and Practice.*

Hermetic Science and Practice

Tradition holds that Hermetic science was first developed in ancient Egypt. It is true that many of its root ideas come from ancient Egypt, but our modern view of it was not developed until medieval times. It was based on writings attributed to Hermes Trismegistus – Thrice Greatest Hermes. From ancient times Hermetic science has been categorized as alchemy, astrology, and theurgy.

The *Corpus Hermeticum*, fragments of a much larger ancient work, was rediscovered and translated in Florence, Italy around the year 1460. The works of other ancient writers such as Plato were also translated in this period. Some modern scholars suggest that this sudden reemergence of ancient wisdom was a factor in the flowering of the Italian renaissance in the sixteenth century.

Among the most important Hermetic works recovered was *the Emerald Tablet of Hermes Trismegistus*. Examination of the Emerald Tablet can reveal to us the relationship of these three sciences to each other and their role in connecting the *below* and the *above*.

> *"That which is Above is as that which is Below and that which is Below is as that which is Above, for the performance of the miracles of the One Thing. And as all things are from One, by the mediation of One, so all things have their birth from this One Thing by adaptation."*

These lines from the Tablet tells us that the *above* and the ***below*** are connected and that the *below* is in fact an emanation of the *above*. Theurgy, called the *Operation of the Moon*, is the science that helps us to connect the *above* and the *below* in order to become consciously involved with our own unfolding as spiritual beings. Several clues identify Theurgy as the *Operation of the Moon*.

The Sepher Yetzirah calls the Hebrew letter Gimel the *Uniting Intelligence*. On the Tree of Life the 13th Path of Gimel is located on the central pillar of Consciousness connecting the spheres of Kether and Tiphareth. Thus Gimel unites the consciousness of Ego with the highest consciousness of Divinity. In the Western Mysteries, Gimel corresponds to the Moon and to Tarot Key 2, the High Priestess. In this context the Moon does indeed connect the *above* and the *below*, the *inner* and the *outer*.

> *"The Sun is its father, the Moon its mother, the Wind carries it in its belly, its nurse is the Earth. This is the father of all perfection, or consummation of the whole world. Its power is integrating, if it be turned into earth."*

Here the Emerald Tablet with its reference to the Sun and the Moon is describing the role of astrology, called the *Operation of the Stars*, in bringing the powers of the *above* into physical manifestation in order to provide us with a spiritual roadmap and bring its perfection to the physical world *below*.

> *"Therefore am I called Hermes Trismegistus, having the three parts of the philosophy of the whole world. What I have to tell is completed, concerning the Operation of the Sun."*

22

Here the Emerald Tablet tells us that Hermes Trismegistus was master of the philosophies that became the three Hermetic sciences. The Tablet concludes by telling us that the primary subject of the Tablet is alchemy, the *Operation of the Sun*. Alchemy begins in the material world of Assiah, and its aim is to purify and transform our bodies and our personalities and elevate our consciousness in order to experience and operate consciously in the higher spiritual realms. Alchemy, spiritual unfoldment, the Path of Return, and the Great Work all refer to this process.

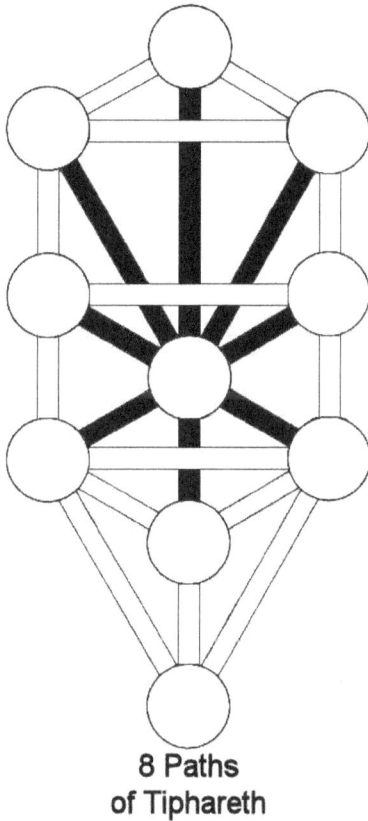

**8 Paths
of Tiphareth**

Jack Courtis in his article, *Tabula Smaragdina Hermetis*, shows us the relationship between astrology, alchemy, and theurgy as pictured on the Tree of Life. In the Tree shown above, the central sphere of Tiphareth (Beauty) is connected to eight of the remaining nine spheres via eight paths. Five of these paths enter Tiphareth from above, while three paths enter Tiphareth from the spheres below. These eight paths represent seven single Hebrew letters and one double letter. In Qabalah, a single letter has only one pronunciation while a double letter has two. Twelve single letters correspond to the twelve signs of the zodiac. Seven double letters correspond to the seven ancient planets.

Jack Courtis writes in *Tabula Smaragdina Hermetis* that of the seven single paths, three paths entering Tiphareth from Below are paths whereby Tiphareth, the sphere of the Sun and of the Christ Consciousness, may be accessed through the science of alchemy. Four of the five paths entering Tiphareth from Above are paths whereby the science of Astrology draws down into Tiphareth the influence of the fixed stars of the Zodiac.

The path of Gimel on the central pillar of the Tree of Life connects Kether (the Crown) and Tiphareth (Beauty). Gimel is a double letter and its path exerts influence in two directions. Through this path, the science of theurgy gives us access to both the *above* and the *below*.

The fact that Tiphareth is connected to all of the other spheres on the Tree of Life except for one underscores the important role Tiphareth plays in bringing the Life-Power into physical manifestation and also in maintaining the presence of the Life-Power throughout all of Creation. Tiphareth is symbolic of the Solar Logos and of the Christ Consciousness that guides and protects us throughout each incarnation.

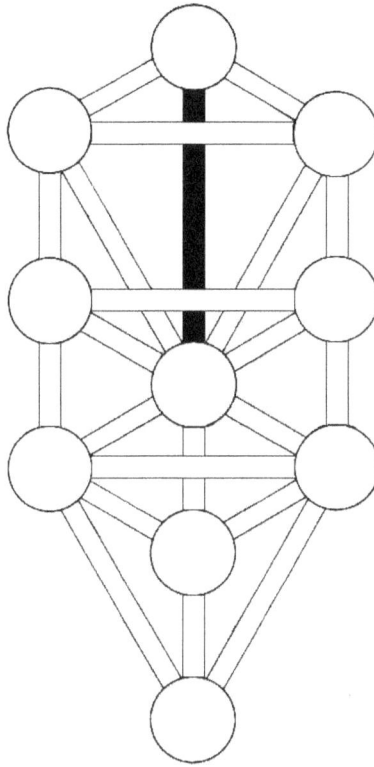

Theurgical Path
Operation of the Moon

The Tree shown above indicates the position of the theurgic path of Gimel. Its role is to connect the Christ Consciousness in Tiphareth, at the core of our physical manifestation, with Kether, the *One Source* from which all manifestation emanates. This path of Gimel is also representative of our subconscious mind. Our self-conscious aspect may direct our subconscious mind, but under the administration of Kether our subconscious mind is that aspect which actually performs the work of Creation in manifesting our desires. This relationship is masterfully depicted in Key 6 of the B.O.T.A. Tarot.

In our materialistic Western culture, theurgy is probably the least understood of the three Hermetic sciences. And yet the masters who gave us the Tree of Life placed this Path in a most prominent position. This creative aspect of the Life-force has been hidden in plain sight from those who might misunderstand or misuse its power and influence.

"Theurgy" can be translated to mean "The working of God;" the *above*. Or it can be translated "The work which takes one to God;" the *below*. Theurgic work is directed toward establishing and maintaining our personal connection to and communication with higher realms of consciousness.

The spiritual disciplines are consciously directed theurgic techniques that help us to understand the Path of Gimel and unlock its mysteries. As theurgists we approach this path with open minds and hearts, yearning to experience something greater which religion or philosophy alone cannot provide. The time and the effort we invest in learning and practicing the disciplines will be well rewarded by increasing the quality of our experiences in exploring this path.

Astrological Paths
Operation of the Stars

This Tree shows the position of the four Astrological Paths coming down into Tiphareth from the *above*. Their role as astrological paths is to bring down the influence of the fixed stars – the zodiac – into the *below* so that it can be of use to our personalities. The 16th century Danish astrologer and astronomer Tycho Brahe's motto for astrology was *"Suspiciendo despicio,"* or *"By looking up I see downward."* Through astrology the perfection of the *above* becomes imprinted on our minds and bodies.

From earliest times the stars and planets were considered to be visible images of gods. As such, they were worshipped and consulted. In the time of Alexandria in Egypt, astronomers, Neo-Platonic philosophers, and Hermeticists systemized and further developed these practices. They added features such as houses and aspects. The Greeks and later the Romans carried this form of astrology across the known world as far as the Indian sub-continent. Today we recognize that forms of astrology were already being practiced in this area and in other places scattered around the Earth.

Astrologers are fond of telling us that *"the stars impel, they do not compel."* German psychologist Erich Fromm wrote: *"Man's main task in life is to give birth to himself, to become what he potentially is. The most important product of his effort is his own personality."* We are born when and where we are born so that we may become who we are meant to become.

The stars at our birth are not responsible for all of the perceived ills and blessings in our lives. Rather, the stars function as a roadmap to lead us to the kinds of people and experiences we need in order to accomplish our life's work, mission, or purpose. The spiritual disciplines are tools available to help us interpret our own personal roadmap.

Hermetic astrology is not just a tool for divination as it is viewed today by many in the Western world. It employs stellar influences and correspondences for spiritual development in combination with alchemy and theurgy. Likewise, astrology and theurgy are dependent on astrological cycles and influences. All three sciences are dependent on the spiritual disciplines to produce the fruits of their transformative capacities in the spheres of our consciousness and our bodies.

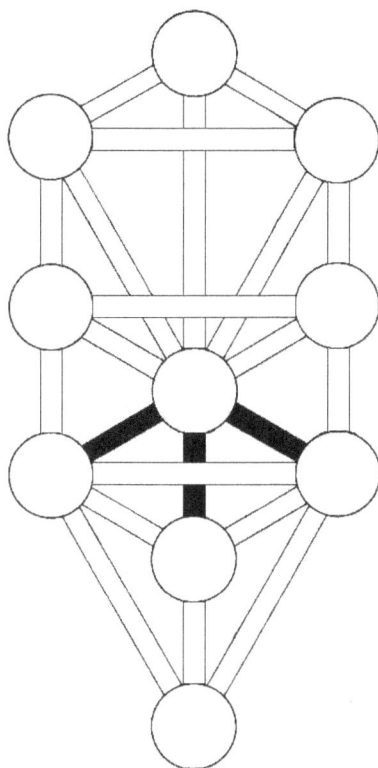

Alchemical Paths
Operation of the Sun

This Tree shows the position of the three Alchemical Paths coming into Tiphareth from the *below*. The role of the alchemical paths is to balance our minds and our bodies and transform them into vehicles for *Divine Will*. In order to accomplish this, these three paths represent the lies of materialism, limitation, and separation. These lies must be recognized for what they are and then overcome in order for our personalities to become acceptable vehicles for the work that waits ahead of us on our spiritual *Path of Return*.

Alchemy, the *Operation of the Sun,* is not just a process for changing physical lead into physical gold. Hermeticists call those who are merely trying to manufacture gold *"puffers."* These puffers are unable to understand the allegories found in alchemical texts. Behind these allegories are processes and techniques for transmutation on all dimensions of our existence, beginning with our physical bodies. Hermeticists recognize that once we have accomplished this transformation, we also have the ability to transform our physical environment; including lead into gold should this become necessary to achieve a given purpose.

Our transformation is accomplished allegorically by the creation of a powerful elixir of the Life-power often called *the Philosopher's Stone.* When we ingest this 'Stone' our physical body is transformed and purified. Knowledge of this process imparts great power and responsibility to those who possess it. For this reason, it is one of the most closely guarded mysteries of the Hermetic tradition.

Once again, we have an Hermetic mystery hidden in plain sight. In several alchemical texts we are told that the Philosopher's stone is created by the combination of the Sun and the Moon with the aid of Mercury. This is a perfectly true statement, and those with the keys to this allegory know this to be a quite literal description of the actual process.

For earnest seekers the keys to the alchemical mysteries can still be found today. Proper intentions combined with proper actions will open many doors of the Mysteries. By beginning in our material world, alchemy helps us to prepare us for our journey that will ultimately lead to a reunion with Divine consciousness.

Once again, we are reminded that the spiritual disciplines are theurgic tools that can be used to accelerate our spiritual unfoldment and better prepare us for the challenges of the journey ahead.

The Tree of Life glyph is much more than a diagram illustrating aspects of consciousness at both the cosmic and human levels. It represents Life and the Life-Power in all of its countless manifestations. The Tree of Life is symbolic of Life and is alive! If we take the time to carefully study the Tree of Life it will reward us with transformative insights into our own nature and that of the cosmos.

In the example just given we learned about the astrological, alchemical and theurgic paths on the Tree. This is but one of the potentially life-changing ideas that can be unfolded through careful observation.

The words theurgy and discipline both imply action and work. Theurgy is working with the energies of higher planes of consciousness to bring about desired change on the material plane. The spiritual disciplines are traditional practices used to facilitate such change.

When first approaching the Western mysteries, some aspirants are not prepared for the level of commitment required to make progress on this spiritual Path. Western traditions emphasize the importance of personal effort, both mental and physical, in the process of learning about oneself.

"Know Thyself, gnōthi seauton"
– ancient Greek maxim inscribed in the *Pronaos* of the Temple of Apollo at Delphi

31

Earlier I asserted that self-transformation is the goal of the Western Mysteries. We cannot hope to transform our world into a more perfect reflection of the inner spiritual realms until we have transformed ourselves. Understanding and using the principle of *As Above, So Below* begins with understanding ourselves. The spiritual disciplines help us interpret and make use of the sign-posts we encounter on our inner journey of self-unfoldment and transformation.

This *Path of Return* we have been examining is arduous but rewarding. Like any journey, it should not be undertaken without preparation. The spiritual disciplines can be a valuable aid in that preparation.

Some aspirants will look at the Mysteries and pass them by. Some will enter for a time and then retreat back to the comfortable world they knew before. A few will find the home they have been searching for. Anyone who makes use of the spiritual disciplines will find assistance in making the decisions that best suit their needs. Everyone who comes into contact with the Western mysteries will find some degree of transformation.

Twelve Spiritual Disciplines

We will focus our attention on twelve spiritual disciplines traditionally found in the Christian tradition. These are the disciplines of:

Prayer
Fasting
Study
Meditation

Submission
Service
Simplicity
Solitude

Worship
Guidance
Confession
Celebration

There are other disciplines but our focus will be on these twelve traditional disciplines. Richard J. Foster describes these twelve disciplines from a Christian perspective in his book, *Celebration of Discipline*. Jack Courtis describes these same twelve disciplines from the perspective of the Western Mystery Tradition in his essay Disciplined Action. Students of many traditions know that the number twelve possesses great symbolic importance. This will facilitate assigning to the disciplines some of the traditional correspondences used in the Mysteries.

33

Why 12? The number 12 is significant in so many ways and on so many levels of understanding. Many manifestations of the *One Source* occurring on our material plane are based on the number 12. A chromatic scale of musical tones contains 12 tones per octave spaced at half-tone intervals. The chromatic scale is related to the heptatonic scale which has 7 tones per octave spaced at whole-tone intervals.

Colors visible to our human eyes can be categorized as three primary colors, three secondary colors, and six tertiary colors adding to 12. Scientists tell us that these 12 colors correspond to the 12 tone chromatic scale as higher octaves of vibration. Many traditions make use of this correspondence in sound and color healing practices.

Astrologers in many Western traditions make use of 12 houses and signs of the zodiac in their charts. As early as prehistoric times sages identified 12 constellations in the night sky that the Sun and the other planets or "wanderers' traveled through on their journeys. They also divided up this area of the sky into 12 houses and assigned one of the 12 signs to each house. The houses represent 12 specific fields of human experience. Each house influences how we relate to our world, our interactions with others, our work, and many other areas of our lives.

The list of correspondences for the number 12 in both our inner and outer worlds is seemingly endless. A quick search for these correspondences will reveal many of these. The number 12 seems to be widespread throughout the natural world. There are many explanations for its significance in the nonphysical realms. Paul Foster Case touched on one of these in his book, *The True and Invisible Rosicrucian Order*.

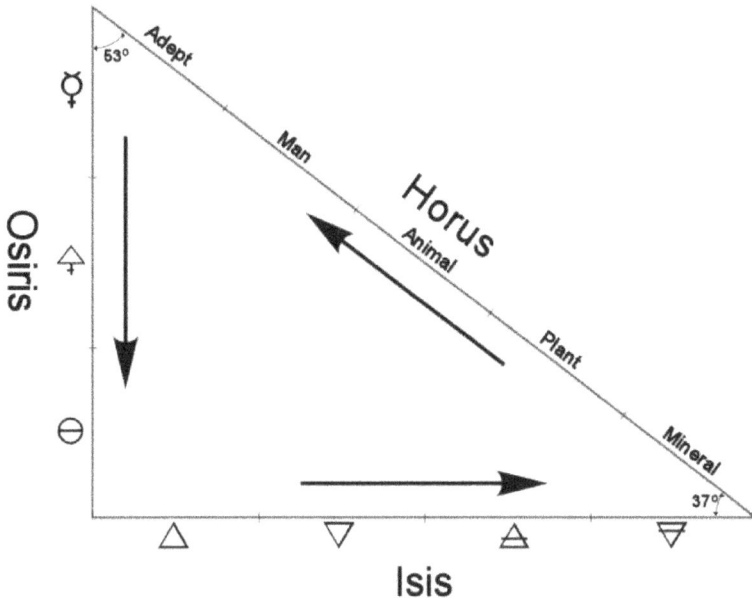

In this diagram reconstructed from Case's book, we see a right triangle with sides of 3 and 4, and a hypotenuse of 5 units. From late antiquity this has been called the Pythagorean triangle, but today we know that it was known and used long before Pythagoras' time.

An Egyptian tradition equates the 3 unit side with Osiris, ruler of their Underworld (inner world). Osiris rules our inner or spiritual realms. On this side are represented Mercury, Sulphur, and Salt, the 3 essences of alchemy. This tradition equates the 4 unit side with Isis, ruler over Nature. Here are represented the 4 alchemical elements Fire, Water, Air, and Earth. The hypotenuse of 5 units was equated with Horus, the archetypal human. Here are shown 5 kingdoms of physical manifestation. The 4th kingdom is humankind, and the 5th kingdom represents a new kingdom into which our species is evolving. This 5th kingdom is sometimes called homo spiritualis, or Spiritual Mankind. On the triangle, this kingdom is in close proximity to the 3 unit side of spirit.

Taking the numbers 3, 4, and 5, we can derive the number 12 by adding all three numbers or by multiplying the 3 by the 4. Multiplying all three numbers together yields 60, hence the number of seconds in a minute and minutes in an hour.

Deriving 12 in the manner described above takes into account our inner and outer constitutions considered as a whole.

We know that the wheel of the zodiac reflects the 3 and the 4 in the 3 tetrads of the 4 elements and the 4 triads of Cardinal, Fixed, and Mutable expressions of the elements. Other examples of 3x4 symbolisms are present as well. 12 is a well-established number in astrology.

Many alchemists recognize and use 12 stages of alchemy. The number and order of alchemical stages may vary according to the tradition we practice. Paul Foster Case uses 12 stages in his alchemical teachings and associates them with the 12 signs and houses of the zodiac.

In this work, I am presenting a system of correspondences for 12 traditional spiritual disciplines that associates each of them to one of the 12 astrological signs and to one of the 12 alchemical stages. My hope is to present an internally consistent system of correspondences that ties together the practices of the three Hermetic sciences, alchemy, astrology, and theurgy. If this system does show some merit, perhaps we can move closer to understanding how these three sciences can help us to unify body, soul, and spirit.

In keeping with the eclectic - but not arbitrary - practices of the Western Mysteries I will be proposing a number of qabalistic, astrological, alchemical, and theurgic correspondences for each of the twelve disciplines. The correspondences I am relating the 12 spiritual disciplines to astrology and alchemy are my own creations. Some of the correspondences will be easier to understand than others. Some may require some study and meditation to understand. Other correspondences may simply not be valid. Only a process of testing and discussion will determine their worth.

Students of the Mysteries know that correspondences such as these aid us in thinking critically and creatively. Learning to think in a new way opens many doors for us on the inner planes. Creative thinking leads us away from external, rational and logical sense-based thinking and helps us to turn internally toward our symbol-oriented subconscious mind.

Such thinking strengthens communication between our self-conscious, subconscious and super-conscious modes of existence. This helps us to control our subconscious impulses and to train our subconscious mind to become a powerful ally on our path of spiritual unfoldment.

Take some time to examine your beliefs about spiritual discipline. Take as much time as you need and make an earnest effort to explore your deepest feelings. It would be helpful to write down your thoughts at this point. Keeping a daily record of your spiritual work is a powerful tool that can accelerate the rate of your spiritual growth. You will find it very useful to keep a record of all of your inner experiences, including dreams.

How do you feel about the word 'discipline'? Our society engenders several unattractive misconceptions. We sometimes think of discipline as being a form of self-punishment. We may think discipline is too time consuming and involves too much work. Discipline can be perceived as an unwelcome agent of change; one which forces us to abandon our comfortable lives for ones of asceticism and conformity. We rarely think of discipline as something we can enjoy or celebrate.

Someone who clings to such beliefs will avoid the very practices that can lead to spiritual liberation. Many who do begin to practice various types of discipline may do so out of a well-intentioned but misdirected sense of duty. Some may want the benefits of living a disciplined life but are unable to commit themselves to certain changes in lifestyle.

Men and women who find themselves unwilling or unable to change are driven by the prevailing consciousness of the group mind because they have not yet developed a relationship with their authentic selves. Clinging to uninformed beliefs about discipline, we often find ourselves ensnared by behaviors and beliefs that engender the drudgery we seek to avoid!

Another aim of this work is to bring an awareness of our beliefs about spiritual discipline into the field of our self-awareness. Bringing these mental constellations into the light will help us understand the nature of the challenges that we encounter on our individual and collective Paths of spiritual unfoldment. This understanding will make working with the disciplines more comfortable and show us which areas need more work and attention. We will see that the practice of each one of the disciplines requires some degree of conscious effort on our part.

Superficiality as a social attitude is epidemic in our modern world. Technology if excessively relied upon can act as an agent of isolation, making us more reliant on our electronic devices and less reliant on personal interactions with others. Much of the media that we rely on for information about our world is aimed at our baser instincts rather than our higher human faculties. This leads to a superficial awareness of our needs arising from the animal nature within us all. This also leads to a desire for an immediate fulfillment of our perceived needs.

This expectation of instant gratification is a spiritual problem of alarming proportions. The solution to this problem is not more people of intelligence or talent. There are plenty of those to be found. The need is for people who not only 'talk the spiritual talk', but 'walk the spiritual walk.' The spiritual disciplines take us into places within our souls that we could not otherwise reach. They enable us to explore the living realms of spirit. They empower us to live authentic lives in a superficial world.

Is spiritual discipline drudgery? Only for those who decide beforehand that this must be so. Those who bring an open mind to the time and attention they devote to these practices tell us that the Path of discipline is the only one which leads to true liberation.

"and you will know the truth, and the truth will make you free."
– John 8:32

Discipline is not just for saints, or spiritual adepts, or for contemplatives who devote much of their time to Prayer, Fasting, and Meditation. Spiritual discipline is for ordinary human beings; working people, parents, religious and secular leaders, the younger generation that will take their place, and yes, even saints and adepts. The disciplines are meant to be practiced anywhere at any time by anyone; in the midst of all of our relationships with family, friends, neighbors, co-workers, and even strangers.

We should not think of the spiritual disciplines as drudgery that banishes pleasure and laughter from our lives. Joy is the sweet fruit of all the disciplines. Practicing the disciplines liberates us from fear, unhappiness, and doubt. When our spirit is transported from a world of unhappiness into a world of joy, spiritual discipline can hardly be described as drudgery. The spiritual discipline of Celebration is included among the twelve to ensure that laughing, singing, dancing, and even shouting for joy can be a part of our spiritual experience.

Saturn: Material Dominion and Slavery

This definition from the Merriam-Webster Dictionary seems to best describe the exoteric use of the word discipline when applied to a set of spiritual beliefs: Discipline is *"A way of behaving that shows a willingness to obey rules or orders."*

In this definition discipline is associated with obedience and rules. Both of these are characteristics of Saturn energy. The 32nd Path of Tav on the Tree of Life - corresponding to Saturn - is the first planetary energy encountered on the Path of Return. Saturn is also the highest placed planetary energy among the sephiroth at the third sphere of Binah. We see that we encounter Saturn energy at both the beginning and the end of our spiritual journey as it is mapped out for us on the qabalistic Tree of Life.

Actually, the Saturn energy is always present throughout our lives as are all of the other energies associated with each of the seven ancient planets and their corresponding energy centers in our physical and etheric bodies. These planetary energies are sometimes active and sometimes inactive. We can activate them consciously when we choose to work with them as we do in the spiritual disciplines.

Planet	Human Faculties
Mercury	life and death
The Moon	peace and strife
Venus	wisdom and folly
The Sun	fertility and sterility
Jupiter	wealth and poverty
Mars	grace and sin
Saturn	material dominion and bondage

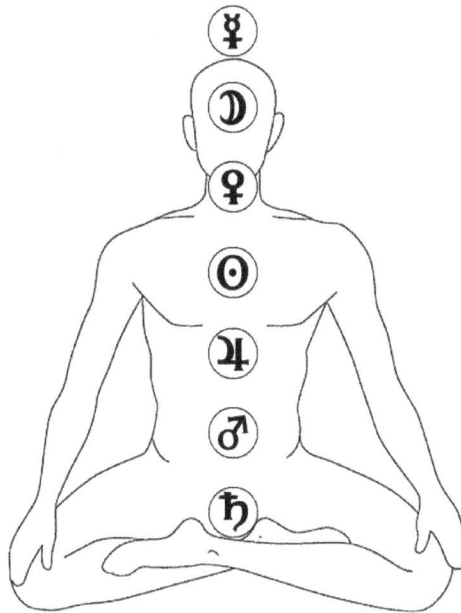

Each of the seven ancient planets is traditionally assigned two human faculties that represent polar opposites. Each planet is assigned to a Hebrew letter that has two pronunciations and the planetary energies are said to have two expressions as well. The polarities assigned to Saturn are material dominion and bondage. This polarity is expressed in Key 15 of the Tarot, associated with the sign of Capricorn. Saturn is the astrological ruler of Capricorn.

In Key 15, the Devil attempts to convince us that all that can be known about Reality is what we see, hear, smell, taste, and feel. And for a while we believe it. Still, this limited world of the senses is oddly dissatisfying and becomes unbearable, even painful over time. When the burdens and discomforts of living inauthentic and incomplete lives become too great for us to bear, we have only to call upon our higher powers of self-consciousness to discover that we can easily remove any chains that bind us. At this point we may realize these chains are self-imposed and can be removed at any time. All we need do is make new decisions. [††]

Gradually the material world is seen to be only one part of reality and therefore illusory. Sages tell us that the limitations of materialism are useful illusions available to us for the achievement of the ultimate goals of liberation and enlightenment. Formerly chained aspects of our personality are now free to become vehicles guided by our Higher Soul. This is one meaning of the image on Key 7, The Chariot. [††]

The spiritual disciplines discussed in this work are all tools to be used to guide us away from the lies of Materialism, Limitation and Separation and toward the Truth of the greater Reality that emanates from the *One Source.*

> *"I am the Alpha and the Omega', says the Lord God, who is and who was and who is to come, the Almighty."* – Revelation 1:8

and again,

> *"I am the Alpha and the Omega, the first and the last, the beginning and the end."* – Revelation 22:13 NSRV

Note that the above quotes come from the first and last chapters of the New Testament book of Revelation. Note also that Revelation contains 22 chapters. The Hebrew alphabet is made up of 22 letters. Is this a coincidence? Both verses refer to a great mystery.

Discipline and disciple share the same root word. A disciple is one who surrenders his or her personal will - which the aspirant will discover is in reality an illusion - to the will of a higher power. Initiates of the Western Mysteries understand that there is only Divine Will and that their task is to transform their personalities into transparent instruments of that Will.

[tt] Paul Foster Case, *Hermetic Alchemy Science and Practice*.

Take Up Our Cross

Then he said to them all, "If any want to become my followers, let them deny themselves and take up their cross daily and follow me. For those who want to save their life will lose it, and those who lose their life for my sake will save it." – Luke 9:23-24

The Western Mystery Tradition teaches us that Jesus of Nazareth was an avatar whose physical presence among us was as an embodiment of the Christ Consciousness that resides within us all. As such, he was speaking to us all. Regardless of our spiritual beliefs and practices, his words from Luke's gospel are directed to all of humanity. They contain a great qabalistic teaching. We should all heed these words and begin to incorporate their teaching into our lives.

What part of ourselves are we being asked to deny? We are being asked to sacrifice the supremacy of the personality which heretofore has assumed the mantle of rulership over our lives. Our task is to renounce the superiority of our personal mind in favor of the mind of our Higher Soul. This Higher Soul is none other than the Christ Consciousness that resides in the sphere of Tiphareth at the center of the Tree of Life.

The work of transforming our personalities requires more than just aligning ourselves with the *One Will*. A genuine desire to free ourselves from the conditions of bondage, which we see depicted on Tarot Key 15, is needed to initiate change. This change then needs to be reflected outwardly into some aspect of ourselves or our physical surroundings.

As beings with physical bodies, we are aware that these bodies and everything else in our material universe that we call Nature follow certain principles that we call Natural law. If we are close observers of Nature, we will occasionally notice phenomena that appear to contradict Natural law. These observations arouse our sense of curiosity. Once our senses of wonder and curiosity become engaged, we begin to take our first steps onto the Path of Return. We begin to see the workings of the higher planes of consciousness in the physical plane. We begin to get our first glimpses of the higher Worlds. When we begin to take our first steps on the Path of Return, the spiritual disciplines are there waiting to help us find our way.

Paul Foster Case explains the inner meaning of *"taking up our cross daily"* in this way: Key 16 of the Tarot, The Tower, shows the destruction of those elements of our personality that are based on illusion and falsehood. Case wrote that the Mars force or Life-power breaks down false mental images of Reality and replaces them with images of the higher planes of existence. [tt]

Recall this statement about Geburah, from Paul Foster Case's Pattern on the Trestleboard:

> *"I recognize the manifestation of the Undeviating*
> *Justice in all the circumstances of my life."*

It will be our task to gain an understanding of the cosmic laws that establish and enforce what Case calls *"Undeviating Justice."* Once understood and applied, these laws become allies on our quest to unfold the highest levels of consciousness.

A glimpse of the Reality beyond our illusions is a reversal of our former point of view. This is pictured on Key 12 of the Tarot, The Hanged Man. The Greek verb translated *"take up"* in the

46

above quotation means also, *"to keep the mind in suspense."* We are also told to *"take up our cross daily."* The cross pictured in Key 12 of the B.O.T.A. Tarot is a gallows and is shaped like the letter Tav, attributed to Saturn. To take up our cross is to raise the energy in the Saturn center of the body at the base of the spine. This is done by the denial of any personal origination for any state of consciousness, or for any aspect of our lives whether inner or outer.[††]

Raising the Saturn energy to our higher energy centers or interior stars is the practice of alchemical *Sublimation*. Sublimation is identical with the raising of kundalini energy taught by many Eastern traditions. We will encounter this practice in our discussion of the discipline of Simplicity in chapter 7.

I am associating the discipline of Simplicity with the Hebrew letter Lamed, the astrological sign of Libra, and Tarot Key 11, Justice, that pictorially represents all of these correspondences. Our achievement of liberation and enlightenment is dependent on Sublimation. We must take steps early in our paths to gradually learn about and become proficient in its practice.

Before we become proficient in the practice of Sublimation, we must begin to learn about it and experience it through all four of the inner disciplines:

Fasting helps us to prepare our bodies and personalities to be ready to work with higher levels of consciousness and begin the physical changes that will be needed.
Meditation helps us to quiet our minds to listen for instruction from our Higher Souls.

Study helps us to understand the processes that are taking place and to understand how to apply the instructions of our Higher Souls.

Prayer helps us to communicate our desires and intentions to the highest levels of consciousness and invoke their aid in carrying out our plans.

If we truly desire to commit ourselves to a spiritual path, we must be willing to relinquish our uninformed ideas about self-hood. We must be willing to *"take up"* our cross by performing the daily work of meditation and other spiritual practices that ultimately will result in the raising of our Saturn energy to the higher energy centers. The practices of spiritual discipline are an essential part of our new commitment. Understanding the spiritual disciplines and integrating them into our lives will prove to be a vital part of our spiritual growth. [††]

In Proverbs we find this rather blunt aphorism:

> *"Whoever loves discipline loves knowledge, but those who hate to be rebuked are stupid."* - Proverbs 12:1

In the Gospel of Matthew, Jesus is quoted as saying:

> *"Come to me, all you that are weary and are carrying heavy burdens, and I will give you rest. Take my yoke upon you, and learn from me; for I am gentle and humble in heart, and you will find rest for your souls. For my yoke is easy, and my burden is light."* Matthew 11:28-30

We find in St. Paul's letter to the Romans:

Do not be conformed to this world, but be transformed by the renewing of your minds, so that you may discern what is the will of God - what is good and acceptable and perfect. - Romans 12:2

These quotes all have something to teach us about practicing the spiritual disciplines. Meditate on them and take them to heart if you would seek to find joy in the work of the disciplines. They will help us to find the Will and the Strength to persevere when obstacles make the journey difficult. Remember that the obstacles we encounter temper us and make us more fit for the journey. Finally, perseverance is every bit as necessary as discipline for spiritual growth.

It must be said that knowing the mechanics and techniques of the disciplines are only part of what is needed to practice them successfully. The spiritual disciplines connect us to an inward spiritual reality. An open mind and an open heart are needed in order to make our practice of the spiritual disciplines meaningful.

Practiced properly and regularly, the disciplines do indeed produce profound changes that lead us toward enlightenment and liberation. Finally, we must always, in everything we do, recognize that the author of our life is the *One Source* residing in the highest levels of spiritual consciousness.

[††] Paul Foster Case, *Hermetic Alchemy Science and Practice.*

The Language of the Western Mysteries

The Great Work we perform in the Western mysteries is our own inner and outer unfoldment. The self-conscious and subconscious parts of our being are our agents in this work. They are pictured in the Tarot major arcana wherever we see male and female figures together. Operating at levels below that of waking consciousness, our subconscious requires guidance and training provided by our self-conscious mind.

Our subconscious mind does not fully understand the verbal and written language we use every day. Subconscious mind came into being at a time when the human race had not fully developed its faculty of self-consciousness. Our subconscious mind responds to images, shapes, colors, sounds, music, smells, tastes, physical touch, and other forms of information from our physical senses. It also responds to mental images that replicate and reinforce the input of our senses.

Long ago, sages created symbolic languages using these sensory references so that our self-conscious mind could communicate with our subconscious. The symbols we use in the Western mysteries make up one of these languages. One of the first duties of anyone new to the Western mysteries is to begin to learn this symbolic language. Early on, this will require learning and practicing the disciplines of Study and Meditation.

The Hermetic Qabalah of the Western mysteries combines qabalistic science and practice with the Hermetic sciences of alchemy, astrology, and theurgy. Each of these have specific applications in the Great Work, and may be practiced in combination with each other or singly. Quite often each of these applications may use different terms to describe identical ideas or objects or they may use a single term for several related ideas. For instance, "Mercury" can refer to a planet, a god, a metal, an alchemical essence, or an aspect of our human constitution. It is useful to create connections or correspondences between terms that refer to the same idea or archetype. Correspondences are extremely powerful when used, for example, to combine the practices of Alchemy and Astrology.

To aid in learning and applying correspondences, The 78 cards of the Tarot are indispensable. The 22 Keys of the Tarot major arcana represent cosmic influences and are most often used because of their correspondences with the 22 letters of the Hebrew alphabet. The characteristics and powers of each of these 22 letters are described in the *Sepher Yetzirah*.

Each Key of the Tarot major arcana incorporates a number of correspondences that can be used in any practice of the Western mysteries. The symbolism of the Tarot can be extended to the glyphs of the Tree of Life and the Cube of Space. Studying the placement of symbols on the Tree of Life and the Cube of Space and the implications of these placements can literally occupy an entire lifetime.

Differences in order and design exist between the many Tarot decks that exist today. Each deck reflects how its creator understands the 78 archetypes and his or her ability to express this understanding. Different people will prefer different decks. As for the symbolism of the 22 cards of the Tarot major arcana, my preference is the B.O.T.A. deck designed by Paul Foster Case and illustrated by Jessie Burns Parke. It was created specifically to eliminate errors and blinds found in the Rider-Waite deck and others. The B.O.T.A. deck performs masterfully in   representing the archetypes as I understand them. This is the Tarot deck I have chosen to illustrate the principles of the spiritual disciplines. The B.O.T.A. deck is meant to be colored by the individual as a tool for personal growth. Black and white versions of this deck and instructions for their coloring may be obtained at *www.bota.org.*

It will be helpful to have access to colored images of the 22 major arcana of the B.O.T.A. Tarot deck while studying this work. If you have not already colored your own cards, colored versions of the major arcana are included in the Paul Foster Case books, *The Tarot: A Key to the Wisdom of the Ages* and *The Book of Tokens.* Both books are available through the B.O.T.A. website.

Correspondences of the Spiritual Disciplines

Attitudes and perceptions about the spiritual disciplines are very different in popular culture than those we hold in the Western Mystery Tradition. The group mind exerts much influence over those who do not yet have a strong sense of self. The group mind or egregore for the most part has no interest in preparing us to be independent thinkers. The exoteric teachings of many mainstream traditions are designed to help us conform to their definition of spiritual followers.

Mainstream religions and philosophies have a role to play in the hierarchy of the cosmos. We need to learn to be followers before we can become leaders. This is the natural order. At some point we have learned our lessons as followers and we intuitively know that we need something more. We recognize the need to move beyond the exoteric teachings we have received. Our exoteric training has prepared us to move forward to the next level. We are ready to learn how to think, act, and express ourselves as individuals.

At this stage we are ready to begin the journey that the Western mysteries call the *Path of Return*, To do this we need to seek out a tradition that will bring us into contact with our own Inner Teacher. If we have begun at this stage to practice the spiritual disciplines, we will also have begun to develop our sense of discrimination. This discrimination is vital in helping us to discern whether a tradition can help us to navigate the next stage of our journey.

An essential part of one's lessons on the Path is learning to use the spiritual disciplines. The disciplines help us to find the portals that lead to experiences of our inner being. Once there, the disciplines help us to better understand these experiences.

The twelve spiritual disciplines can be divided into inner, outer, and group disciplines according to whether a discipline is commonly perceived to be practiced alone, in the presence of other individuals, or with a group. Historically, this is how others have grouped them. The lines of distinction between categories begin to blur at the outset because each discipline can be practiced to some degree on all three levels. These associations and the associations that follow are designed to conform to the traditional grouping of the disciplines. They are offered here as aids to the understanding and utilization of each discipline.

We will find that some of the disciplines share ideas and techniques. This is an indication of how interrelated they are. We must approach the disciplines as a whole. Various circumstances may call for specific disciplines, but no discipline is more important or more useful than any other. Experience will dictate which disciplines are more useful in given circumstances.

Traditionally, the four inner disciplines are Prayer, Fasting, Study, and Meditation.

As practiced in the Western mysteries Prayer is communicating our thoughts and desires to higher planes of consciousness. Fasting is the discipline needed to gain control over sensory and psychic distractions that impede our inner communications. Study is focused concentration of the mind on the realms beyond what is revealed to us by our physical senses. Meditation develops receptivity to the higher planes of consciousness.

The theme of inner, outer, and group orientation can be found elsewhere in our Hermetic studies. The progression of the twelve houses and signs on the wheel of the zodiac can be seen as one of these.

Beginning with the first house and the sign of Aries at the vernal equinox, we have influences such as images, appearances, and our outer personality*. These influences are inwardly oriented.

The fifth house of the zodiac and the sign of Leo reflect influences such as children, creative projects, and love affairs*. These influences involve our relationships with others and are outwardly related.

When we arrive at the ninth house and the sign of Sagittarius we see influences such as the collective mind, religion, and philosophy*. These reflect a broadening of our focus to the groups with which we identify.

With the twelfth house and the sign of Pisces we see influences such as higher ideals, spiritual values, ad selfless social service*. Here we see group involvement that reflects minimal self-interest.

The signs of the Zodiac follow a particular order of elemental associations. Beginning with Aries, the order of the elements is *fire, earth, air, and water*. This order is repeated twice more as we progress through the Zodiac. Concurrently, the elements are classified as *cardinal, fixed, and mutable*. So we have three groups of four and four groups of three. Twelve is the number that unites them in the twelve houses and signs.

It now remained for me to pair each of the four inner, outer, and group disciplines with one of the four elements. This elemental association could help strengthen their correspondence to one of the twelve signs of the zodiac.

In order to determine the best fit for each of the twelve disciplines with one of the four elements, I looked at which element was associated with each of the four qabalistic worlds. The qualities of the four qabalistic worlds could give me more correspondences to use in matching the disciplines to the elements.

I noted that fire is associated with Atziluth, the highest world and the world from which the created world is emanated. Traditionally, fire was the first element created and carries with it the ideas of both destruction and transformation. This is the world of spirit. Disciplines associated with fire would transform us in positive ways and would serve to link us to the source of our authentic Power. I chose to link Prayer, Submission, and Worship with fire.

Water is associated with Briah, the world of Creation below Atziluth. Water was the second created element. It carries the ideas of construction and preservation. This is the world of our Higher Soul. From this world the Love of our creator flows out into the entirety of its creation. Disciplines associated with water would help to reintegrate our parts of self and would serve to reconnect us to the source of universal Love.. I chose to link Meditation, Solitude, and Celebration with water.

Air is associated with Yetzirah, the world of Formation below Briah. Air was formed from the combination of fire and water. This is the world of myths and of mental images. It is in this world that the forms that become physical manifestations are created. Disciplines associated with air would bring us closer to Wisdom and nurture our faculties of reason, intuition, and discrimination. I chose to link Study, Simplicity, and Confession with air.

Earth is associated with Assiah, the lowest of the four worlds. It was formed by the combination of the other three elements and represents physical manifestation. This is the world of our physical bodies and our physical senses. Disciplines associated with earth would assist with the processes of manifestation and teach us that spiritual liberation comes from the sacrifice of our false pride and animal nature. I chose to link Fasting, Service, and Guidance with earth.

I have just described the process I used to determine the best fits between the spiritual disciplines and the signs of the zodiac. This is not a perfect system. Some correspondences are strong and some not so strong. With patience and a little imagination I believe the correspondences will become more apparent.

For the purposes of this work, I will make use of these elemental associations in examining and comparing the characteristics of each discipline. I am assigning the twelve disciplines in this way:

Aries with **Prayer**
Taurus with **Fasting**
Gemini with **Study**
Cancer with **Meditation**

Leo with **Submission**
Virgo with **Service**
Libra with **Simplicity**
Scorpio with **Solitude**

Sagittarius with **Worship**
Capricorn with **Guidance**
Aquarius with **Confession**
Pisces with **Celebration**

The wisdom or folly of these correspondences will be revealed in the pages of this work. It is hoped that these associations may shed some light on the nature of each discipline and help us to creatively integrate them into our lives.

Here are my correspondences for the three Hermetic sciences:

Alchemy (The Below) Operation of the Sun The Body	Theurgy (Above and Below) Operation of the Moon The Soul	Astrology (The Above) Operation of the Stars The Spirit
1. Calcination	Prayer	Aries
2. Congelation	Fasting	Taurus
3. Fixation	Study	Gemini
4. Separation	Meditation	Cancer
5. Digestion	Submission	Leo
6. Distillation	Service	Virgo
7. Sublimation	Simplicity	Libra
8. Putrefaction	Solitude	Scorpio
9. Incineration	Worship	Sagittarius
10. Fermentation	Guidance	Capricorn
11. Dissolution	Confession	Aquarius
12. Multiplication	Celebration	Pisces

A point of distinction is to be made between mediation as a discipline (Cancer) and meditation as a function (Aquarius), discussed in chapters 5 and 11. This particular assignment of disciplines will likely be unexpected to those familiar with the work of Paul Foster Case.

I compared the 3 cycles of the elements in the zodiac to the characteristics of the spiritual disciplines in order to determine which sign to pair with each of the 12 disciplines. Having done this, I turned my attention to the 4 sets of Cardinal, Fixed, and Mutable elements in the zodiac. How did these qualities match up to the disciplines? If my choices of correspondences of the signs with the disciplines were valid, the ternary energies of the elements within the zodiac should also be compatible with them.

In *The Tarot of the Magicians** Oswald Wirth writes this about the Law of the Ternary:

> *"Everything inevitably comes from 'three' which makes but one. Within every act, single in itself, these factors can indeed be distinguished:*
> *1. The active principle, causes or subject of the action.*
> *2. The action of this subject; its verb.*
> *3. The object of this action, its effect or its result. These three terms are inseparable and rely on each other. Hence this 'tri-unity' which one finds in everything."*

> *"In a general way, in the elements of the ternary, the first is above all active, the second is intermediary, active as seen with the following, but passive as seen with the preceding one; whereas the third is strictly passive. The first corresponds to the spirit, the second to the soul and the third to the body."*

Compare this to the *Tao Te Ching* of Lao tzu:

> *"Tao generates one, one generates two, two generates three, and three generates all things."*

We need look no further than the qabalistic Tree of Life to see the Law of the Ternary in the supernal triad of Kether, Chokmah, and Binah; the ethical triad of Chesed, Geburah, and Tiphareth; and the astral triad of Netzach, Hod, and Yesod.

Looking at the correspondences used by Paul Foster Case in *Hermetic Alchemy,* it seemed possible to group his 12 stages of alchemy in groups of 3. Case characterized the basic nature of each alchemical stage in a single keyword. The first 3 stages of Calcination, Congelation, and Fixation had natures of analyzing, synthesizing, and balancing. The separation of analysis and the building up of synthesis result in a third condition of balance.

Among the disciplines, Prayer can be said to be analyzing if we understand that it helps us to understand how our desires (the causes) manifest themselves in our lives (the effects). Fasting can be said to be synthesizing if we understand that it improves the metabolism of the body by eliminating toxins and excess fuel. Study can be said to be balancing if we understand that if it is done effectively, it produces a balanced picture of the object of our study.

Looking at the remaining 3 ternaries of disciplines, similar patterns of correspondences can be found with the remaining 3 ternaries of alchemical stages.

Alchemical Stage	Basic Nature	Spiritual Discipline
1. Calcination	Analyzing	Prayer
2. Congelation	Synthesizing	Fasting
3. Fixation	Balancing	Study
4. Separation	Defining	Meditation
5. Digestion	Extracting	Submission
6. Distillation	Assimilating	Service
7. Sublimation	Exalting	Simplicity
8. Putrefaction	Disintegrating	Solitude
9. Incineration	Purifying	Worship
10. Fermentation	Inspiring	Guidance
11. Dissolution	Combining	Confession
12. Multiplication	Increasing	Celebration

One of the purposes for using the spiritual disciplines is to help us transcend our material awareness and to reconnect with our higher realms of existence. They help us to know ourselves and to reclaim our birthrights as sons and daughters of *The One*.

We can only accomplish this when we venture into these realms and discover for ourselves the treasures that await us there. Using as a roadmap the fixed stars of the zodiac, we use the spiritual disciplines to help us unfold our hidden spiritual natures. When we arrive at our spiritual home after journeying afar into material reality, *The One* will welcome us and, paraphrasing the parable of the Prodigal Son, will say, *"These children of mine were spiritually dead and are alive again; they were lost and are found!"*

In a work such as this, there is a reliance on material that is too voluminous to be included. Much of this material is publicly available. Some material requires a certain amount of inner work to be properly understood. None of this material is completely inaccessible. As Michael Schneider writes in *A Beginner's Guide to Constructing the Universe*, "The universe may be a mystery, but it's no secret."

* George Demetra and Douglas Bloch, *Astrology for Yourself.*

Part II
the Inner Spiritual
Disciplines

Prayer	1st house	Aries	cardinal fire
Fasting	2nd house	Taurus	fixed earth
Study	3rd house	Gemini	mutable air
Meditation	4th house	Cancer	cardinal water

1st house influences*

> how others see me
> images, appearance
> outer personality

2nd house influences*

> personal resources
> money
> possessions
> material attachments
> earning and spending habits

3rd house influences*

> networking
> communications
> learning and exchanging information
> making connections in immediate environment

4th house influences*

    private self
    home and family
    psychological foundations
    nurturing parent

*from *Astrology for Yourself,* by George Demetra and Douglas Bloch

Astrologically, I am associating the four inner spiritual disciplines with the first four houses and signs on the wheel of the zodiac. We see from the influences of these houses that they affect us in personal ways. Beginning with Aries and the 1st house, we see a progression from purely personal concerns to our identity within our family environment.

The four disciplines of Prayer, Fasting, Study, and Meditation are all included as traditional disciplines by the Christian tradition; particularly by the Roman Catholic Church. Modern Christian authors such as Richard Foster and Dallas Willard have also embraced this classification. In the Western Mystery Tradition, authors such as Jack Courtis have accepted this division of the disciplines.

The four inner disciplines help us to communicate with and understand our inner planes of consciousness. These skills are needed to make progress on our spiritual path. Spiritual growth requires us to *"know ourselves."* Early on, we begin to train our subconscious mind to be a loyal and obedient companion accompanying us on our journey. Over time we will find that our subconscious becomes a loving and willing partner. We will discover that our subconscious is the channel through which we communicate with the higher realms.

The Inner disciplines are primarily interior exercises involving the three parts of self pictured on Key 6 of the Tarot, the Lovers. These are our subconscious, self-conscious, and super-conscious minds. Shown separately, they are but three aspects of our *One Reality*.

While the inner disciplines may be practiced in the presence of or in concert with other people, their effects are deeply personal and are experienced on the inner planes. In the New Testament, Jesus instructs his followers to pray and fast in private. The outer and group disciplines by definition are practiced with others, or at least may be witnessed by others.

The inner disciplines are for the most part practiced alone and thus we do not usually draw attention to ourselves when we practice them. If someone were to observe us, they would be hard pressed to identify the discipline we are practicing based on our outward appearance.

The discipline of Prayer has a transformative and fiery nature and thus we will associate it with the fiery sign of Aries. Fasting has an earthy nature and has profound effects on our physical bodies. We will associate it with the earthy sign of Taurus. As a mental activity, Study has an airy nature. We will associate it with airy Gemini. Meditation engages our subconscious mind and has a watery nature. We will associate it with watery Cancer.

As a practical matter, we may find that using two or more disciplines together will produce the best results for a given circumstance. In time, we will be able to intuitively understand which ones are required. Each discipline produces a different kind of result. Fasting is the discipline needed to gain control over sensory and psychic distractions that impede inner communications. Study is focused concentration of the mind on the Reality beyond that which is revealed to us by our physical senses. Meditation develops receptivity to communications from higher planes and helps us to build a working relationship with our subconscious. Prayer is communication and cooperation between the material and the spiritual planes.

A working knowledge of the inner disciplines is most helpful when we begin working with the outer and group disciplines. Thus we will begin by investigating the inner disciplines.

Chapter 1
Prayer

Correspondences for Prayer

Qabalah:

the Hebrew letter Heh, meaning "Window"
the Constituting Intelligence
Reason
the function of Sight
the North-East edge on the Cube of Space
the 15th Path of Heh on the Tree of Life

Astrology:

the sign of Aries (1st house, cardinal fire)
Rulership: Mars (Key 16 the Tower)
Exaltation: the Sun (Key 19 the Sun)

Alchemy:

Calcination (the 1st Stage) – Analysis - Removing the Volatile (non-physical) with Heat (Analysis) - Breaking Down

Theurgy:

the discipline of Prayer

Tarot:

Key 4, the Emperor
Key 19, the Sun
Key 16, the Tower

Prayer is one of the most deeply felt and personal of the disciplines. Because Prayer is so intimately connected with our relationship to Divinity, it is an emotional subject for many. Most people will have an opinion about it. It is difficult to reach a consensus on a definition for Prayer because our experiences are so different. When emotions predominate, it is difficult to approach Prayer in a balanced way. Balance is the Key to all of our work in the Western Mysteries and the aim of this work is a balanced approach to the study of spiritual discipline.

Our personal experience with Prayer is typical of the personal nature of the Aries experience. Aries is native to the first house of the zodiac and is the most self-oriented of the twelve signs. Paul Foster Case associates the alchemical stage of Calcination with Aries. Disagreement over the definition of Prayer is due in part to the fact that in Calcination, the first of twelve stages of alchemy, the illusions and the false impressions of Reality that reside in our personalities have yet to be completely removed ††.

Other than the correspondence of the spiritual disciplines with the signs of the zodiac, there is no intrinsic importance given to the order of the inner disciplines. However, spiritual progress would be impossible without developing relationships with higher realms of consciousness. These relationships are made intimate through the discipline of Prayer.

It is fitting that Prayer corresponds to the alchemical first stage of Calcination with its fiery and active removal of mental images that would impede inner communication. The Emperor of Tarot Key 4, with his correspondence to the Ancient of Days, is present to preserve order and reason throughout the Calcination process. Notice that the Emperor sits with his ear toward us, always ready to hear our petitions. Aries with its initiatory energies of both Mars and the Sun assures us that our communications will result in a response from the *One Source* in answer to Prayer.

The inner disciplines of Prayer and Meditation both require a quieting of the mind and the body for us to be able to practice them effectively. Outwardly, it would be very hard for someone to determine whether we were praying or meditating. Prayer and Meditation do share many of the same techniques. However, each discipline is used to achieve different goals. Meditation is passive receptivity of communications from the inner realms. Prayer actively engages the energies of both worlds.

Meditation as practiced in the Western Mysteries usually begins by focusing the mind on a particular question or mental image. This is seeded meditation. The goal of Meditation is for us to listen for a response from the *One Source* – through the channel of our subconscious mind – to the question or image with which we began our meditation. These messages from the *One Source*, if recorded and acted upon, greatly expand our knowledge of the Reality beyond the limits of our five physical senses.

> ". . . *work out your own salvation with fear and trembling; for it is God who is at work in you, enabling you both to will and to work for his good pleasure.*"   - Philippians 2:12-13

> *The fear of the Lord is the beginning of knowledge; fools despise wisdom and instruction.*   - Proverbs 1:7

Prayer creates change in our outer world by communicating and interacting with the inner worlds. This is one aspect of theurgy, or God-working. The fiery energies of the Sun and Mars, through their association with the astrological sign of Aries, are available to help us perform our God-working.

Prayer can be practiced as an inner, outer, or group discipline. Because our relationship with the realm of spirit through our Holy Guardian Angel, or Higher Soul, is paramount in the Mysteries, the focus here will be on the inner aspects of Prayer. All of the other disciplines rely on the inner communications established by the disciplines of Prayer and Meditation.

Prayer is the ability to communicate with levels of consciousness higher in vibration than that of the body and of the personality. Therefore, a thorough and honest effort to ameliorate the distractions of the mind, the body, and the demands of daily life is required. When we seek to communicate with the higher realms, we must learn how to silence the loud voice of our personality and know with confidence that our petitions can be heard above the noise created by our everyday lives. We must consciously work to become a clear channel of communication. The self-conscious aspect of the Emperor Tarot Key is vital to this effort.

The energies of the Sun and Mars are active and initiating. Clues to their association with Key 4 of the Tarot, the Emperor, are found throughout the image on the Tarot Key. The Emperor is positioned so that his upper body and arms form an upward pointing triangle. His legs form a cross. Together, the cross and the triangle form the alchemical symbol for sulphur, the active essence in alchemy that corresponds to self-consciousness.

The Emperor shines the bright light of Reason onto our thoughts, beliefs, and actions and begins the process of elimination of those that are based on illusion and false assumption. These are immediately replaced with mental images that are based on the Reality of the higher realms of consciousness.

Tarot Key 3, the Empress, is the consort of the Emperor. She represents our subconscious mind (Key 2 the High Priestess) after self-consciousness (Key 1, the Magician) impregnates her with a suggestion. The Magician becomes the Emperor when the High Priestess becomes the Empress. The Empress takes that suggestion and produces mental imagery appropriate to the suggestion. The Emperor then imposes order on this imagery and places his attention on the most promising ones. This is the process whereby the personality is purged of false images and is provided with new ones that reflect our better understanding of Reality.

Many times when we practice a particular discipline, we call upon other disciplines for support. The disciplines of Fasting, Study, and Meditation are essential to the practice of Prayer. To quiet the mind and the body is one goal of Fasting. Study opens the self-conscious mind to the Reality beyond the five physical senses. Meditation as a discipline involves specific practices that establish and strengthen communication with the *One Source*. Effective Prayer is the result of effective Fasting, Study, and Meditation.

> *Then Job answered: "Today also my complaint is bitter; his hand is heavy despite my groaning. Oh, that I knew where I might find him, that I might come even to his dwelling! I would lay my case before him, and fill my mouth with arguments."* - Job 23:1-4

We might think that if anyone had a right to be bitter, it would be Job. But instead of rejecting God or complaining about God's injustice, Job first seeks to be in the presence of God so that God might hear his case. Job knew that God would hear him if he were in God's presence. Effective Prayer can only happen when we are certain that the *One Source* is present and listening. This is a confidence that can only be achieved when the fire of Spirit has burned away the illusory mental images created from our physical senses by our personality..

There are innumerable forms of Prayer being practiced around the world. Prayer to one's particular form of Deity is a fundamental aspect of both exoteric and esoteric spiritual practice. When Prayer is mentioned, almost everyone thinks about the particular form that they are accustomed to using.

Although the focus here is on Prayer as it is used in the Western Mysteries, the principles behind the discipline of Prayer are universal in application. Since the dawning of mankind's spiritual impulses, sages have developed the principles of Prayer based on their own personal experiences. Prayers based on these universal principles are effective regardless of their outer form.

Written from a Christian point of view, the 6th chapter of the Gospel of Matthew contains an excellent primer on the art of Prayer. This is the passage that contains the Lord's Prayer. It contains much more than that. If we truly understand its contents and practice them, we shall be well on our way to developing a Prayerful attitude.

Mystics tell us that the mind and the soul are headquartered in the body in the forehead, immediately behind and above our two eyes. This center is known as the *Brow or Moon chakra*. It is also called *the inner or single eye*. It has also been called by some *the center of consciousness* and *the thinking center*.

> *"The eye is the lamp of the body. So, if your eye is healthy* [single], *your whole body will be full of light; but if your eye is unhealthy* [not single], *your whole body will be full of darkness. If then the light in you is darkness, how great is that darkness!"*

Mathew 6: 22-23

This 'singleness of the eye' can be taken to mean a number of things. We have already mentioned the inner eye. It can mean to give our undivided attention when we focus. It can also mean that to succeed in life we must have singleness of purpose.

The inner light is to be seen at the level of the eyes, but only when *"our eye is single"*; only when the attention is single-mindedly and entirely focused at this point. If our mind is full of negative thoughts and worldly tendencies, then all that we see inside is darkness. And if we, as beings of light, are full of darkness - *"how great is that darkness!"*

When we begin to pray we create a mental image in the eye of our mind. It may appear to us as if it were an image on a screen. A little imagination can add the dimension of depth as well. This is where we focus our attention. But if we lose our focus, our attention drops down into the body, spreading out and scattering into the world through the sense organs and the organs of activity. We lose track of the mental image and our Prayer comes to naught.

The gospel of Matthew is telling us that if we want to bring light – spirit - into our body, we must remain focused on our inner eye. If we do not, we will continue to be enslaved by our physical senses and the falsehoods of our personality. Followers of the Western Mysteries are taught to focus on the image of Tarot Key 2, the High Priestess rather than on the brow chakra itself.

When speaking of spiritual matters, there are really only two orientations. We can turn our backs on spirituality, orienting our lives toward the pleasures and rewards of physical existence, or we can choose to focus on the spiritual truths that exist beyond this physical world and live our lives according to these truths.

> *"You cannot serve God and Mammon".*
> Matthew 6:24

The fact is that our choices in life are rarely ever that simple or easy. Once we gain a glimpse of the Reality behind and within our physical existence, we may begin to understand that changes need to be made in our lives. But in the beginning we are not sure of the path that leads to making spiritual practice and philosophy a part of our everyday lives. We are faced with many confusing choices.

At this point we may turn to the discipline of Prayer to help us sort through our choices and receive insight from higher planes of consciousness which points us to our best courses of action. †† Paul Foster case tells us that Tarot Key 4, the Hebrew letter Heh, and the sign of Aries are all related to the aspect of self-consciousness called *Reason*. Reason helps us to bring order and definition to the mental images produced by our Creative Imagination brought about when self-consciousness gives a suggestion to our subconscious. In this way we make a start in expanding the spiritual dimensions of our lives. In later chapters we will explore the roles that our faculties of intuition and discrimination play in bringing even more depth to the spiritual dimension of our lives.

Our human faculty of self-consciousness is a marvelous wonder. To the best of our knowledge, no other species on Earth has yet developed it to the extent that we have. Without it, spiritual growth would not be possible. We cannot divide our attention between two choices if we wish to be successful in manifesting our desires. If our desires be for the pleasures of physical existence, that is what we will manifest. If our desires be for closeness to the *One Source*, that is what we will manifest. The manifesting abilities of Prayer won't work as effectively if our attention is divided.

Do we need to forego the pleasures of the physical world in order to lead a spiritual life? Definitely not! But we must make sure that our highest priorities are centered on spiritual concerns and not material ones.

> *"Therefore do not worry, saying, "What will we eat?" or "What will we drink?" or "What will we wear?" For it is the Gentiles who strive for all these things; and indeed your heavenly Father knows that you need all these things".*   Matthew 6:31-32

By pursuing a spiritual life and claiming our birthright as children of the *One Source*, cosmic law is arranged so that our material needs and desires are fulfilled. If we are honest, most of us would say that we do not manifest the faith in the *One Source* necessary to receive these blessings consistently.

> *"But strive first for the kingdom of God and his righteousness, and all these things will be given to you as well".*   Matthew 6:33

Many people would say they understand the meaning of Prayer. For most of us, however, our understanding is faulty or incomplete, if we have thought about Prayer at all. We may not have been exposed to the principles that produce effective Prayer. This can result in Prayer that is unfocused, lacking in direction, or even misdirected. The sages assure us that all Prayer is answered, often in unexpected ways. Depending on the level of our understanding or lack of it, Prayer can bring unforeseen and undesirable consequences.

Exoteric religion has quite a lot to say about Prayer. Prayer to one's particular form of Deity is a fundamental part of exoteric religious practice. Every form of exoteric religion teaches its adherents how to pray according to its doctrines.

To pray effectively, we must learn to do it properly. Exoteric religion as a rule does a poor job of teaching effective Prayer. And my personal opinion is that any religion which insists that an intercessor is necessary between the *One Source* and its creation is being at best disingenuous.

Everyone has their own thoughts about the nature of the *One Source*. We all imagine it in ways that make sense to us and make us comfortable. How we imagine that highest level of consciousness is less important than knowing that the *One Source* is a mystery and its true nature is essentially unknowable. Fortunately, the axiom of *"As Above, so Below"* allows us to construct ideas and images of our Creator based on the qualities we observe in the created universe that surrounds us.

What is effective Prayer? Simply stated, it is any Prayer that leads to the manifestation of what we consciously desire to manifest. Effective Prayer is more than reciting words out of a book or demonstrating one's piety by making a show of praying in public:

"⁵Whenever you pray, do not be like the hypocrites; for they love to stand and pray in the synagogues and at the street corners, so that they may be seen by others. Truly I tell you, they have received their reward. ⁶But whenever you pray, go into your room and shut the door and pray to your Father who is in secret; and your Father who sees in secret will reward you. ⁷When you are praying, do not heap up empty phrases as the Gentiles do; for they think that they will be heard because of their many words. ⁸Do not be like them, for your Father knows what you need before you ask him."   – Matthew 6:5-8

When we pray in public places, whether in a synagogue, a church, a temple, a mosque or on a street corner, we are conscious of those around us and we are usually unable to forget our outer selves and to concentrate entirely on the Divine, the recipient of our Prayers. This is one reason Prayer is traditionally thought of as an inner discipline. Jesus tells us that when we pray in public we may be interested in receiving the praise of men. We may want to be seen as holy and spiritual people. When this occurs, that is the reward we will get and that is usually the limitation of such Prayers.

Our most effective Prayer is done in private to insure the clearest possible communication with the *One Source*. Establishing this communication requires time and a real desire to be heard. It requires a commitment to releasing attachment to thoughts, beliefs, and actions that are based solely on our material world. The elimination of illusions such as these is alchemical Calcination. Once the Calcination process has begun, we must make a commitment to learn about the Reality within and then begin to manifest a life based on that Reality.

We might expect our Prayers to be not quite as effective in the beginning of our spiritual practice as they will become later when we have gained more experience and more confidence. Patience is indeed a virtue, and a willingness to persevere in the face of difficulty and disappointment will make the difference in our success.

What about the content of our Prayers? If the purpose of our Prayer is material gain, for an advantage over another person, or for any other purpose that is personality driven, our Prayers will come to naught. That is not to say that these types of Prayers are not answered. We may indeed receive what we ask for, but our answer will inevitably come with unintended karmic debt attached.

The ideal content of our Prayers will be for knowledge and experience of ourselves or of the spiritual realms. The best motive for receiving this knowledge is to improve our ability to be of Service to the world, to humanity, and to the *One Source*. Prayers of this type can be very effective, if made with a sincere and humble heart.

It is best if we treat our spiritual practice with the same open-mindedness and curiosity as befits any good scientist. Both mundane and spiritual scientists are driven by a desire to discover the truth behind whatever they are investigating. Both are intensely curious and are willing to ask questions. Consciously, we use our inductive reasoning to form a hypothesis about the inner realms of spirit. It is best to formulate this hypothesis with as much specific detail as is possible.

Then we test our hypothesis against the Reality of the spiritual realms. We give a suggestion to our subconscious mind to use this hypothesis in manifesting something in our outer world. Prayer is what sets this process in motion. We can determine the validity of our hypothesis according to the results that are manifested.

We must also be willing to change or even reject our hypothesis if the results are unexpected. And then we test again. As we gain in experience and confidence we build up a picture of our inner Reality. We begin to develop a solid philosophy of life based on our experiments (experiences) with the inner realms of consciousness.

Instinctively we understand that to pray effectively is to initiate change. The personality is often resistant to change and thus may block attempts at effective Prayer. Conversely, we may rationalize that Prayer is ineffective if not done properly. We may tell ourselves that we do not know how to pray properly. We may become convinced that Prayer does not work. The personality is capable of manufacturing a multitude of excuses, and so we do not pray.

Effective Prayer is transformative because it puts us into direct contact with the hidden processes and laws of the cosmos. When this contact is established, the experience is vivid and overwhelming. No external verification is needed. Sages have tried to describe this experience for centuries, but there are no words that can do it justice. Prayer, then, leads us to a form of inner gnosis.

Even if it were possible to adequately describe our inner experiences to someone, the description can never match the personal impact of the experience itself. And why would we want to deprive anyone of partaking in their own transformative inner experience?

Paul Foster Case writes that the alchemical stage of Calcination employs what a Hindu yogi would call Tejas or Agni, the element of fire, and it makes particular use of the currents of energy which originate in the Mars center, just below the navel, and in the Sun center, above and behind the heart. The matter which is the agent of Calcination is a radiant energy, invisible to the ordinary physical eye, which produces all the manifestations of light on this planet. From this energy all forms are made manifest, for it is their root substance. [tt]

Case goes on to tells us that this is the alchemical Sol, or Sun, that is exalted, or lifted up in the work of the later stage of alchemical Sublimation. This Sublimation requires the action of fire, and the cooperation of Mars, the astrological ruler of Aries. Remember that the Mars force represented by Tarot Key 16 the Tower breaks down man-made images of Reality and replaces them with images of the higher planes of existence. [tt]

Psychologically, the process of Calcination is that which drives out from consciousness the volatile or changeable elements of emotion, personal bias, erroneous opinion, etc. [tt] Case tells us that the figures falling from the tower in Key 16 show the expulsion of these volatile substances from our personalities.

This description of the process of Calcination is in agreement with the ultimate goal of Prayer: to purify the mind and the body so that we may become better servants of the Light. This purification allows us to see the physical plane with vision that is clearer and better than that of most persons. Case associates the faculty of Sight is with Aries and with Calcination. [tt]

Most people see the world through the distorted lenses of false interpretations and assumptions. But occasionally we find a knower of Reality who sees the world as it really is, and rejoices in that vision. This is how we make the world a better place to live, one person at a time.

A rather curious aspect of Prayer is described in the words of St. Paul of Tarsus:

> *"Rejoice always, pray without ceasing; give thanks in all circumstances; for this is the will of God in Christ Jesus for you. Do not quench the Spirit. Do not despise the words of prophets, but test everything; hold fast to what is good; abstain from every form of evil."*
> 1 Thessalonians 5:16-22 NSRV

What does St. Paul mean – to *'pray without ceasing'*? Is Paul saying to pray in every waking moment? That would certainly not be practical, even if we were to somehow able to train ourselves to do so. When our thoughts turn to worry, fear, discouragement, and anger, we are to consciously and quickly reject the negative thought and replace it with a Prayer of thanksgiving, a positive affirmation, or a positive mental image. It is a natural response to give thanks for the ability to restore peace and balance to our lives. Over time, it becomes easier to invoke a Prayerful attitude whenever we desire.

In this passage, St. Paul is endorsing the quest that ultimately leads to personal contact and experience with the *One Source*. When Prayer without ceasing becomes second nature, we become co-workers and co-creators with the *One Source* in manifesting our future.

When we have succeeded in adopting a Prayerful attitude, Prayer should be like breathing. We do not have to think to breathe because it is a subconscious process. The air pushes on our lungs and forces us to breathe. It is harder to hold our breath than it is to breathe. When we place ourselves on the *Path of Return*, we enter into a spiritual atmosphere where the presence of the *One Source* exerts influence on our lives. Prayer is response to that presence. Praying is as natural as breathing.

How do we make this Prayerful attitude a way of life? Repetition and perseverance! We formulate in our mind a detailed image of what we desire. Then we release the image and await the outcome. We should not worry if our first few attempts do not match our expectations. Our meditations may help us to make changes to the mental imagery we present to the *One Source*.

We can use the image of Key 6 of the Tarot to reinforce the proper relationship between our self-consciousness mind, our subconscious mind, and the mind of our Higher Soul. This process is explained in chapter 3 as we examine the discipline of Study. Once our self-conscious mind has chosen new mental imagery, we try again! Since antiquity, sages have agreed that this process does produce results, so we persevere. Eventually we will learn to use Prayer effectively to manifest what we truly desire.

Through the symbols associated with the astrological sign of Aries and the alchemical stage of Calcination, I have attempted to illuminate the theurgic aspects of Prayer as a discipline. The fiery energies of Mars and the Sun, and that of the Mars and Sun centers of our bodies initiate our spiritual transformation. In our investigation of the discipline of Fasting in the next chapter, we will examine how the energies of Venus and the Moon counterbalance these Martian and Solar influences and begin to create a firm foundation upon which our spiritual unfolding can find support.

I should mention here that our spiritual unfoldment usually does not occur at the level of our self-conscious mind unless we *desire* to change. We will see in the next chapter how Venus, associated with our desire nature, opens doors for us that will allow our spiritual transformation to proceed.

†† Paul Foster Case, *Hermetic Alchemy Science and Practice.*

Chapter 2
Fasting

Correspondences for Fasting

Qabalah:
the Hebrew letter Vav, meaning "Nail or Hook"
the Triumphant and Eternal Intelligence
Intuition
the function of Hearing
the South-East edge on the Cube of Space
the 16th Path of Vav on the Tree of Life

Astrology:
the sign of Taurus (2nd house, fixed earth)
Rulership: Venus (Key 3 the Empress)
Exaltation: the Moon (Key 2 High Priestess)

Alchemy:
Congelation/Coagulation (Stage 2) - Synthesis - Changing from a Liquid to a Solid by removing Heat - Building Up

Theurgy:
the discipline of Fasting

Tarot:
Key 5, the Hierophant
Key 2, High Priestess
Key 3, the Empress

"And whenever you fast, do not look dismal, like the hypocrites; for they disfigure their faces so as to show others that they are Fasting. Truly I tell you, they have received their reward. But when you fast, put oil on your head and wash your face, so that your Fasting may be seen not by others but by your Father who is in secret; and your Father who sees in secret will reward you." - Matthew 6:16-18

"So, whether you eat or drink, or whatever you do, do everything for the glory of God."
1 Corinthians 10:31

We learned in the chapter on Prayer that mental imagery which does not serve our awakening interest in spirituality must be replaced with more appropriate mental imagery in order for Prayer to manifest what we truly desire. Clear communication with higher realms of consciousness is a necessary requirement for Fasting as it is for all of the other spiritual disciplines. In this work, Prayer is associated with Calcination which applies heat, or analysis, to unproductive mental imagery. This cleansing is a vital process that makes the other disciplines more effective.

The spiritual discipline of Fasting is associated with the second alchemical stage of Congelation. Paul Foster Case associates Congelation with the zodiacal sign of Taurus, the Hebrew letter Vav, and the function of hearing. Venus is the planetary ruler of Taurus. The Moon finds its highest expression – its exaltation - here as well. Case writes that the exaltation of a planet in a particular sign imparts significant potency to its alchemical effects. Case also writes that the body's function of hearing is associated with receiving the "still, small voice" of our inner teacher, so the auditory center of the brain is active in Fasting as well. [tt]

The receptive energies of Venus and the Moon both contrast and complement Mars and the Sun whose active energies were at work in Calcination and Prayer. Despite the outward appearance of denying food or anything else to the body, the feminine and receptive energies of Fasting promote building and preserving.

Paul Foster Case associates Congelation with Key 5 of the Tarot – the Hierophant. The Hierophant represents that portion of our subconscious mind through which the voice of our inner teacher, or higher self, may be heard. This voice is always present but cannot be heard until the loud voice of our personality has been reduced. This reduction begins with the elimination of the personality's fallacies and misconceptions by alchemical Calcination and by Prayer. [tt]

The Venus, Moon, and hearing centers are all activated by consciously taking the receptive and devotional attitude illustrated by the two men kneeling before the Hierophant in Key 5. Thomas Norton says, in his 1477 Ordinal of Alchemy:

> *"The science of this Art has never been fully revealed to anyone who has not approved himself worthy by a good and noble life, and who has not shewn himself to be deserving of this gracious gift by his love of truth, virtue, and knowledge. From those who are otherwise minded this knowledge must ever remain concealed. Nor can anyone attain to this Art, unless God send a Master to teach him."*

This Master is what Tarot pictures in Key 5 as our inner teacher, the Hierophant.

In some Tarot decks, another name for the Hierophant is *The Pope*. This title is also given to the head of the Roman Catholic Church. In *Hermetic Alchemy*, Paul Foster Case tells us that in the Hierophant Key, this title is reserved for the universal Wisdom (Chokmah) which is called *"AB,"* the Father of Lights.[tt]

Knowing that this Wisdom is within each one of us, we reach out to understand this connection. The result is a teaching that comes from within. This inner instruction forms the basis for alchemical Congelation. It reveals to us the secrets of the Great Work that are written upon our heart.

The voice of the Hierophant, our intuition, will never try to compete with the voice(s) of our personality. Because it speaks to us through our subconscious mind, it communicates through symbols for our self-conscious mind to interpret. The voice of the Hierophant has no need try to persuade through logic or attempt to flatter us or coerce. Any voice that does this is not our intuition. Paul Foster Case tells us that the voice of our Higher Soul associated with the Hebrew letter Vav – the Triumphant and Eternal Intelligence – was, is, and always will be forever victorious.[tt]

Vav means *nail* or *hook*; something to join things together. Its energy is associating like the Hebrew letter Gimel, the High Priestess Tarot Key, and the Moon. It can also denote something that supports hanging objects. Vav is therefore something on which other things depend. A nail is a fastener, a link, a means of union. As a means of support, it is linked in thought and language with concepts such as aid, assistance, sustenance, furtherance, ministry, and similar ideas. Paul Foster Case tells us that these ideas are not only connected with the meanings of Vav, but also with the symbolism of the Hierophant.[tt]

The Hebrew letter Vav is the equivalent of the English "*and*." Its literal meaning and grammatical use are the same. The conjunction "*and*" links together a series of nouns describing various objects such as "lions and tigers and bears." "*And*" also joins dependent clauses to a sentence. In Hebrew, the letter Vav is used exactly the same. Like a nail, it binds the parts of a sentence together. Clauses or phrases introduced by it hang from it, like pictures supported by hooks driven into a wall.

The main idea of Vav is *union*. Paul Foster Case tells us that this is the English translation of the Sanskrit noun *yoga*. The same Sanskrit noun is the root of our word *yoke*. Some scholars are of the opinion that the original hieroglyphic symbol for Vav was a picture of a yoke such as is used for harnessing oxen.[tt]

These words from Matthew's gospel that we looked at in the introduction are again brought to mind:

> *"Come to me, all you that are weary and are carrying heavy burdens, and I will give you rest. Take my yoke upon you, and learn from me; for I am gentle and humble in heart, and you will find rest for your souls. For my yoke is easy, and my burden is light."*   - Matthew 11:28-30

This suggests an interesting connection between the letters Aleph *(ox)*, Vav *(yoke)*, and Lamed *(ox goad)*. The Hebrew alphabet contains a number of letter groups that have particular associations. For example, the letter Teth has the shape of a coiled serpent, Lamed has the shape of an active serpent, and Samekh has the shape of a serpent biting its tail. Study and meditation on these connections will provide much illumination.

Case further tells us that Yoga is a system of practice where personal consciousness is linked (yoked) to the universal mind. Its object is direct, personal experience of those phases of reality from which religions spring. The founders of religions are persons who have had such experiences.[††]

Occultists tell us that this sort of experience may be produced whenever conditions are favorable. It is not miraculous. It is perfectly natural, and if we address ourselves earnestly to preparing for this kind of experience we will find what we seek. As we have seen, the Hierophant of the Tarot is a symbol of the mode of subconscious activity which takes form in such experiences.

It is important to impress upon our subconscious mind a set of symbols that we can easily understand. There are several of these symbol sets to choose from in the Western Mysteries. These are the symbols found in Qabalah, astrology, alchemy, theurgy, and the Tarot. The glyphs upon which these symbols may be found are the wheel of the zodiac, the tree of life, and the cube of space.

The supreme glyphs upon which all of these symbols are written are the twenty two Keys of the major arcana of the Tarot. The 22 Keys of the B.O.T.A. Tarot were created to include as many symbols as possible and to eliminate the blinds found in previous versions of the Tarot.

One way to reduce the size of a fire is to take away some of its fuel. With alchemical Congelation and with Fasting we want to move away from the influence of the Sun and of Mars and focus on the building powers of Venus and the Moon. Venus and the Moon correspond to the throat center and to the pituitary body just above and behind our physical eyes. Fasting is one method of reducing this fuel. Proper fasting calms the processes of the physical body so that they may be more easily brought under control.

Now that we have determined to remove false and illusory mental images from our personality, new mental images must be created to replace them. Key 2, the High Priestess, represents the Moon (memory and the passive subconscious mind). Key 3, the Empress, represents Venus and the subconscious mind after it has been impregnated with a suggestion. Venus generates new mental images. †† The symbolism of the Empress Key suggests fertility, fecundity, and the development of form. The Creative Imagination of Venus is the active principle in alchemical Congelation, and Creative Imagination is the embodiment of clearly conceived desires. The Hierophant instructs us in the principles which enable us to bring into manifestation those forms which we desire.

Here in the initial stages of alchemical transformation we must be careful to not allow this congealing process to harden the new images. Further work may reveal to us the need to replace or to modify them. The images must remain malleable enough to allow us to alter them if necessary. We would do well to begin to adopt an attitude of humility at this stage.

Memory, represented by Key 2 the High Priestess, also plays a part in Congelation and Fasting. We use memory to recall - time and again - the truth that the power of *the One* is always present in everything. We use it to remind ourselves as often as necessary that our senses report to us nothing but the <u>fact </u>of the Eternal Presence of the *One Source.* ††

Paul Foster Case tells us that Memory, the Moon, reaches its highest manifestation in Intuition, because what we learn   from our inner teacher is what our Higher Soul has known from the beginning. What we call intuition is in reality participation in the perfect memory of the *One Source*. [††]

We tend to think about Fasting as a sacrificial act of denying food to the body. Taken to extremes, this can be detrimental to our health. Careful consideration must be given to the details of any fast. An average person in one of the more prosperous countries of the world consumes more calories in a day than the amount needed to maintain the health and well-being of the body. A well planned fast can help us to determine whether we are indeed consuming too much.

For many of us, the effects of a well-planned fast would be mostly beneficial. Those of us with health issues should consult with a medical professional before undertaking any significant change in diet. Those of us new to Fasting would do well to start by Fasting for short periods – perhaps a day or two – and pay attention to how our body reacts. Due to differences between male and female bodies, the two sexes may react differently to the same set of Fasting conditions.

If, against all advice to the contrary, some of us should want to begin with a more severe regimen, we should consult with a medical professional in order to design an individual program that would follow the most optimal set of conditions.

When our bodies are faced with the task of digesting more food than needed or if we provide them with poor choices of nutrition, metabolic imbalances are created and must be dealt with. Our nervous and glandular systems are affected along with every other part of the body, and so our thoughts and emotions are also affected.

When well planned, a physical fast can help our bodies to eliminate much of the excess and unwanted material moving through our digestive systems. We will discover in a later chapter that Digestion is one of the 12 alchemical stages. With Fasting and the second stage of alchemical Congelation our bodies can begin to devote more of their resources to bringing balance back to their digestive processes.

If a fast is accompanied by an honest examination of our eating habits, we may able to reverse some of the damage created by our poor choices. We may find that the amount of available physical energy increases, as does our mental and emotional perceptivity. This is due in large measure to the building and preserving qualities of the Venus and Moon centers of the body.

Before we undertake any fast, we need to be certain that it is an entirely voluntary act. It must be our own personal choice and must be based on our own convictions. We must be certain that we are not fasting to gain approval from others. We must be certain that we are not fasting to punish ourselves for perceived sins.

Other common sense precautions apply as well. We should not fast if we are pregnant or breast-feeding. If we are on medication, we should not fast without first consulting with our physician. If we are not in good health, or suffer from any illness, physical or psychological, we should consult our doctor before fasting. We should not fast if we have ever suffered from diabetes, epilepsy, anorexia, bulimia, psychological disorders or mental illness.

We should approach fasting carefully, if at all, when doing so could put other people's lives at risk - if our occupation is for example a surgeon or a bus driver. Fasting is recommended only for reasonably healthy, mature adults. We should not fast if our body is still developing or if our body has become debilitated with age. If we are in doubt, we should consult our physician. These proscriptions may sound elitist and severe,   but generations of fasting have proven their value.

Obviously, withholding nutrition from the body is going to produce physical and mental changes. We need to be certain that we provide the proper conditions for these changes to be beneficial in nature. The purpose of the two stages of alchemy that we have looked at so far is to begin to restore balance to all parts of our being. We are preparing solid foundations from which to reconstruct our personalities into vehicles for the expression of the Will of the *One Source,* emanating from our Higher Souls. If our foundations be faulty, the houses that we build will also be faulty and will not stand.

Paul Foster Case warns us about the potential dangers of performing any kind of magical work if one is ill or has any kind of physical imbalance. He tells us that it is far better to defer our work to a later time than to perform it in an unbalanced state. At this stage of the work this is sound advice because we are preparing our bodies and minds for even greater changes yet to come. [††]

The power of consciousness on the higher planes is greater than what our bodies and minds in their natural state are capable of sustaining without damage. Some of us may be tempted to move forward in our work without bringing into our lives all the balance that is possible. The result will be that whatever imbalances we carry forward with us will become magnified when we encounter the powerful energies of the higher realms.

The spiritual discipline of Fasting involves much more than a food fast. By lowering the amount of heat normally generated by digestion, a moist heat, we are temporarily reducing the effects of the Sun and Mars centers of the body. Receptive centers such as the Venus and Moon centers can now be worked with more efficiently. In a manner of speaking, the waters of the mind have been stilled and the process of forming mental images becomes easier. Thus one purpose of Fasting is to prepare our bodies and minds to be capable and willing partners in the creation of new and useful mental imagery.

Another effect of Fasting is a renewed receptivity to the consciousness of the higher realms. When our subconscious mind no longer feels the satisfaction of a full stomach, it searches for something else to fill the void. That something else can be the Reality that is found in these higher realms.

This experience is particularly heightened in shamanic cultures where seekers are subjected to such rigors as physical exertion, pain, sensory deprivation, and even the ingestion of entheogens in combination with Fasting to produce visions of spirit. Most teachers of the Western Mysteries discourage the use of entheogens because these chemicals are capable of forcing open psychic gateways in chaotic and unregulated ways.

So far, we have only considered the food related aspects of Fasting. A look at the origins of the word and its uses will shed some light on other ways we may look at Fasting. According to the *Online Etymology Dictionary*, "To fast" is derived from the Old English *fæstan* "to fast" - as a religious duty. The original meaning was hold firmly, or to abstain. The sense evolution is from "firm control of oneself," to "holding to observance." Compare Gothic *fastan* "to keep, observe;" also "to fast." To be "steadfast" is to be firm in Fasting or abstaining. Originally,

Fasting also referred to other observances such as abstinence and continence or self-control.

Abstinence is self-enforced restraint from indulging in bodily activities that are widely experienced as giving pleasure. Most frequently, the word refers to sexual abstinence, or abstinence from alcohol, tobacco, caffeine, certain foods, drugs, etc. Abstinence may be considered to be a partial or selective fast as compared to a complete fast. Reasons for abstinence vary as widely as the object of the abstinence and the people who practice it.

Sexual abstinence or chastity is encouraged by many traditions and institutions as an alternative to birth control or as a means to purify the body in order to enhance spiritual experience. Opponents of abortion and birth control often champion the use of abstinence. At the same time, many traditions view sexual activity as a form of spirituality and do not promote abstinence. There is no consensus on this matter.

The benefit or detriment to our health of abstinence versus sexual activity is widely debated as well. Science has yet to produce an objective or definitive study on this subject. As spiritual scientists, the best answers will come from the experiments we perform on ourselves. An ancient maxim states *"Moderation in all things."* It may be that results will show that a middle road is best. Perhaps short periods of abstinence may produce better results than long term abstinence. Personal experience remains the best mediator in this debate.

Before we make a personal decision about whether or not to pursue sexual abstinence, we should consider this: Does the Divine really forbid this highly pleasurable gift that was bestowed upon us? Or are beliefs that condemn sexuality the result of outdated religious edicts that neither reflect nor respect our sexual human nature?

On the other hand, many people throughout history have achieved spiritual transcendence through sexual abstinence. This was achieved either through rigorous religious doctrine, or achieved through an unbreakable discipline and an unyielding will power emanating from their own personal convictions. In the end, each of us must rely on our own experience to attain a personal resolution to this question.

Another observance that may be considered a type of Fasting is continence. This is a term more familiarly used in connection with our ability or inability to control the elimination of waste from the body. In relation to moral or ethical behavior, continence - self-control or mastery - is adherence to what we know to be virtuous or correct. Continence is acting on our convictions in resistance to passion. Incontinence is yielding to passion where we know it to be wrong, and may also be indulged in the pursuit of vengeance, honor, or gain.

Continence is really more of a character trait than a practice, although by definition it involves the participation of our self-conscious mind. We may deliberately practice continence during such times as purity or singleness of mind or purpose is required in order to make a particularly important decision or to take decisive action.

Most people think of Fasting as being a withholding of nourishment from the body. We have seen this is not all that can be said regarding the discipline of Fasting. Without a spiritual component to fill the emptiness created by the lack of food, Fasting would be just an exercise in cleansing the body. The discipline of Fasting is really about adding to our spiritual experience and enhancing all parts of our being.

The discipline of Fasting does not require us to give up things that we love, use or need. All of our relationships, our possessions, all of our activities, all of our passions need to serve these ends. The mental images created during the Fasting process can help us to make better decisions and make it easier for us to know what it is that we truly desire.

We are only asked to sacrifice those things which bind us to the material world and make it more difficult to follow our spiritual longings. Those of us who pay little or no attention to our food choices may benefit by becoming more conscious about our eating once the fast is over. Those of us who do not pause to think about our sexual activities may need to determine whether our sexual life serves our spiritual life. Those of us who are too easily persuaded to bend to the will of others may need to look within and discover the true source of our own will.

We need to be more intentional about what we keep. This is true for both the disciplines of Fasting and Simplicity. What brings us joy? What motivates us to give our best efforts? What is it that we are most passionate about? Retain what brings us these things and get rid of what makes them harder to attain. Be aware of what fills one's life. Fill it with what brings joy and empty from it what brings stress. We are only restricted in what we can accomplish by the limits we place on our Creative Imagination.

Today in the Western world people are addicted to instant gratification. Because the spiritual disciplines require our attention, time, dedication, and effort, many people find them to be tedious and unrewarding. That being said, there is probably no discipline more unpopular or misunderstood than Fasting. In contrast to earlier times, today's exoteric religion places little emphasis on the importance of Fasting, if it is mentioned at all. It is seen as atonement for sins or as a means of bringing our animal passions under control. We have seen that Fasting is much more complicated than that.

Contrary to the group mind's definition, Fasting is not dieting. Dieting is about losing weight, improving our waistline or improving our desirability to others. Fasting is not going on a hunger strike. A hunger strike is used to force others to bend to our will. Fasting is not about denying nutrition to the body. A healthy and balanced body is an absolute necessity for the physiological changes taking place as we make progress on the Path of Return. Any dietary change that denies proper nutrition to the body for extended periods of time is counter-productive.

There is much more to Fasting than food or drink. Fasting is about establishing control over all areas of our lives. It is about establishing conscious control over decisions that impact the directions of our lives. It is equally important to exercise control over what we see, hear, think, read, write, and speak as it is to control what we eat.

Fasting on a deeper level is about the acquisition and use of self-knowledge. The more we know about ourselves and the more we are able to eliminate false images from our consciousness. This gives us greater ability to create images that reflect our growing awareness of inner Reality. Eliminating many of the voices that compete for our attention makes it easier to listen to the voice of our inner teacher. Going deeper still, Fasting leads to an understanding and knowledge of the *One*

Source. This is precisely the rationale and the goal of the maxim *'Know Thyself.'*

Once mastered, Fasting prepares us for and facilitates the exercise of the other inner disciplines of Prayer, Study, and Meditation. Done properly, Fasting aids in making discipline acceptable, and perhaps even desirable, to the mind and to the body. Fasting helps us place everything in our lives into proper perspective.

As we noted earlier, the energies empowering the disciplines of Prayer and Fasting both counterbalance and complement one another. The fiery energies behind Prayer are initiating and analytical in nature. We shall see in the next chapter that the airy energy of Mercury gives the discipline of Study a balancing nature. In Study we see a balance established between the analytical nature of Prayer and the synthetical nature of Fasting.

> *"Tao generates one, one generates two, two generates three, and three generates all things."*
> – Lao tzu, Tao Te Ching

Here we have a group three disciplines, a triad that fits the creative role of triads discussed by Oswald Wirth in his book, *The Tarot of the Magicians.* Wirth writes that the creative principle behind triads consists of a creator, the action of creating, and the thing created. In our case, we have the initiating action of Prayer acting together with the synthesizing action of fasting to create through Study the ability to bring balance and objectivity to our studies.

In similar fashion the remaining nine disciplines form three more creative triads to aid us in our journey of spiritual unfoldment.

Here is another look at the creative triads we first examined in the introduction:

Alchemical Stage	Basic Nature	Spiritual Discipline
Calcination	Analyzing	Prayer
Congelation	Synthesizing	Fasting
Fixation	Balancing	Study
Separation	Defining	Meditation
Digestion	Extracting	Submission
Distillation	Assimilating	Service
Sublimation	Exalting	Simplicity
Putrefaction	Disintegrating	Solitude
Incineration	Purifying	Worship
Fermentation	Inspiring	Guidance
Dissolution	Combining	Confession
Multiplication	Increasing	Celebration

The defining nature of Meditation and the extracting nature of Submission lead to the assimilating nature of Service. The exalting nature of Simplicity and the disintegrating nature of Solitude lead to the purifying nature of Worship. The inspiring nature of Fermentation and the combining nature of Confession lead to the increasing nature of Celebration.

Perhaps one reason why Prayer and Fasting are so often mentioned together in the sacred texts of many traditions is that they are complementary and form the bedrock of the foundations upon which our spiritual unfoldment is built. Together they create balance. As we will see in the next chapter, balances found in the effective practice of Study form the basis of the *Great Work* itself.

†† Paul Foster Case, *Hermetic Alchemy Science and Practice.*

Chapter 3
Study

Correspondences for Study

Qabalah:

the Hebrew letter Zain, meaning "Sword"
the Disposing Intelligence
Discrimination
the function of Smell
East-Above edge on the Cube of Space
the 17th Path of Zain on the Tree of Life

Astrology:

the sign of Gemini (3rd house, mutable air)
Rulership: Mercury (Key 1 the magician)
Exaltation: none

Alchemy:

Fixation (Stage 3) - Fixing the boundaries between self-consciousness, sub-consciousness, and super-consciousness – Balancing

Theurgy:

the discipline of Study

Tarot:

Key 6, the Lovers
Key 1, the Magician

"Study to present yourself to God as one approved by him, a worker who has no need to be ashamed, rightly explaining the word of truth". - 2 Timothy 2:15

In our Western world, society rewards intellectual achievement. Study is probably the most socially acceptable of the disciplines Most of us are familiar with the time and effort that Study demands. Every school child knows the rigors of keeping up with one's studies. As students we know the rewards of Study, and dread what might happen if we do not. Many of us probably think of studying as a chore, something we want to be done with so we can concentrate on something more pleasurable.

Studying comes more naturally for some than it does for others. Often we struggle to learn the basic information we are expected to learn. If we are fortunate, a parent or an educator will spend time with us teaching us good study habits. Unfortunately, most of our educational institutions are not designed to devote very much time on individual students. Time and resources spent generating high test scores are often greater than for those spent in creating individually optimized educational experiences.

All of us have the ability to concentrate – at times. Think of the times when we are "lost" in something we enjoy: a sport, playing music, a good game, a movie. We are devoting our total concentration to that activity. The Key to transforming Study from a chore into an enjoyable experience is to find something pleasurable – something that we really want, that gets us excited – about whatever we need to focus our attention on. Perhaps this might be found in the knowledge that the next piece of information we receive might hold a Key to a part of our inner world that we have yet to discover. The possibilities are limitless.

We have all had to face the prospect at some time in our lives of needing to study in order to be promoted or to become better prepared for the next stage in our lives. The Western mystery tradition is no different in this respect. Most traditions have their own system of "grades" that must be navigated in order to make spiritual progress. The Mysteries have their own vocabularies, buzz words, and symbols that must be mastered. There is just no escaping the fact that the discipline of Study is one of the first that must be undertaken. Why not search for a personal and pleasurable goal that will make this part of our journey more pleasurable and worthwhile?

The ability to focus or concentrate is one of the Key aspects of Study. Concentration is needed to make the inner journey to self-knowledge possible. To encounter concentration and to begin practicing it at the beginning of our journey is right and proper. In Key 1 of the Tarot we see the Magician standing in his garden in deep concentration. Eyes closed, he holds his wand high in order to draw down the mysterious forces of the Life-power to be directed by him for his use and for the use of his subconscious mind.

All of the spiritual disciplines are interconnected and contribute to the actions of one another. It is natural for the four inner disciplines to resemble each other in certain ways because they all produce their effects in the same internal and external environments. Through their astrological and alchemical correspondences the disciplines all participate in the great hermetic cycles of transformation we experience and use in the accomplishment of the *Great Work*.

With Prayer, we saw that through the sign of Aries and the alchemical stage of Calcination, one aspect of Prayer is to alter or replace images that prevent us from communicating with the *One Source*. With Fasting, we saw that through the sign of Taurus and the stage of Congelation, the energies of Venus and the Moon create a calmer atmosphere and new mental images are created to form a deeper understanding of the inner realms. With better images to work with and a calmer environment in which to work, a sense of balance between our inner and outer realities begins to develop.

Now as we take a look at the discipline of Study, we see that establishing balance connects Fasting and Study. Fasting eliminates toxic substances from the body and begins to create new and healthier mental images for the mind. The different parts of self could are able to repair themselves and move toward a more balanced state of being. This new sense of balance now helps us to better see the inner relationships of our super-conscious, self-conscious, and subconscious minds. These three are the essences that alchemists call *Mercury, Sulphur,* and *Salt*.

We see their proper relationships illustrated on Key 6 of the Tarot. Alchemical Fixation is the creation – or fixing - of absolute certainty in our minds as to the proper relationships existing between these three aspects of consciousness.

Through Gemini, the element of Air - manifested as mental activity - predominates in alchemical Fixation as it does in the discipline of Study. Alchemical Air has a middle nature between Fire, the element active in Calcination and Prayer, and the element of Earth, which is active in Congelation and Fasting. The ruling planet in Gemini is Mercury. No planet is exalted in Gemini. †† Paul Foster Case tells us that Fixation is described as the perfect balance of elements in which nothing predominates over anything else. Study involves the stability - or fixity - of perfect balance.

Case tells us that this perfect balance in which nothing predominates over anything else also applies to the three alchemical essences. This balance or fixity is governed by Mercury, the Magician of the Tarot, representing self-consciousness. This tells us that the process of fixing the relationships between the three parts of self is a fully conscious one. The scene depicted on the Lovers Key of the Tarot is the result of self-consciousness working with sub-consciousness to place it in right relation to super-consciousness. [††]

The situation depicted in Tarot Key 6, The Lovers, is the result of the initiative of the man (self-consciousness) shown in that Key. It is self-consciousness that, by giving a suggestion, emancipates our subconscious mind, and puts it in contact with the angel. This is one way for us to interpret the symbols of Key 6. [††]

Paul Foster Case writes that an alchemical interpretation of Tarot Key 6 imparts the same meaning. Alchemists call the man *our Sun* and the woman *our Moon*. They become alchemical Sulphur and Salt. The angel becomes alchemical Mercury. [††]

The symbolism of Mercury is easily confused because it is the name of a planet, a Roman god, a metal, an alchemical essence, and an interior star or chakra, When we come across the name 'Mercury' in our studies, we need to know which of these correspondences is being referenced. It will help our understanding of the material tremendously. One way to begin to understand the subtle differences between them is to meditate using the Tarot Key corresponding to Mercury: Key 1 the Magician.

Mercury corresponds qabalistically to the Hebrew letter Beth. It represents both the planet and the god. A *god* in this context is understood to be a personified aspect of universal consciousness. The *gods* are understood to be the Elohim of the Hebrew Torah.

Then Elohim said, "Let us make [humankind] in our image, according to our likeness; and let them have dominion over the fish of the sea, and over the birds of the air, and over the cattle, and over all the wild animals of the earth, and over every creeping thing that creeps upon the earth."　　Genesis 1:26

In astrology, Mercury can represent the planet or it can represent intellect. To Mercury, called Hermes by the Greeks, was attributed the authorship of forty-two books, embracing astronomy, astrology, mathematics, geometry, medicine, logic, rhetoric, music, magic, and other subjects.

Mercury or Hermes was the great magician and transformer, bearing the caduceus which we know today as a symbol of the healing arts. Mercury was only the messenger of a higher Deity. He was the channel not the source. In the same fashion, our faculty of self-consciousness is a channel for higher wisdom, not its source.

Beth is one of the seven double letters of the Hebrew alphabet. Double letters are so called because they have in Hebrew two pronunciations. Every double letter is assigned a pair of opposites. Because the consciousness attributed to both Beth and Mercury has the ability of both destruction and creation, the pair of opposites assigned them is Life and Death.

To make matters more confusing, alchemical Mercury represents the spiritual or super-conscious aspect of our being. We just discussed Mercury's qabalistic connection to self-consciousness. This seeming contradiction reveals to us that self-consciousness is none other than super-consciousness being expressed on the material plane. Our self-conscious personality in its natural state is unaware of this fact, but our self-conscious aspect balanced by our super-conscious and subconscious becomes an active agent for the Will of the Lord of the Universe.

Mercury is one of three alchemical essences along with Sulphur, or self-consciousness, and Salt, or subconsciousness. These can be interpreted on both the physical and spiritual levels. While there is much interest in alchemy performed in a physical laboratory, our primary interest here is in the spiritual and psychological aspects of alchemy.

The Intelligence of Transparency is the mode of consciousness assigned to Beth and to Mercury.. Transparency is a physical characteristic in which no resistance to light is offered. Light can thus shine through. Here we have the same idea of transmission that is suggested by Hermes as the transmitter of the messages (or light) of the higher realms. In like manner, our personalities must become transparent channels for the light of our higher selves to shine through. The Transparent Intelligence provides a channel of communication, which permits the free passage of the super-conscious Light. [††]

Let's take a look at the Hebrew letters Vav (Congelation) and Zain (Fixation). [††] Paul Foster Case writes that both Vav and Zain promote balance but create it in different ways. The name of the letter Zain means "sword". This suggests the opposite of Vav, the nail, which connects or fastens together. A sword cuts, divides, separates, and etc. Diversity, analysis, contrast, antithesis, distinction, and therefore discrimination, are implied.

Discrimination means clear perception, acuteness, sharpness like a sword's edge, a sharp wit, etc. Vav and Fasting create balance by making new connections and providing a space for Creative Imagination to produce appropriate mental imagery.

We will see in the next chapter on the discipline of Meditation that Vav and Zain combine to produce the letter Cheth, meaning "fence" or "enclosure." This enclosure provides a space for discrimination and other spiritual activities can take place.

Zain and Study create balance by giving the creative parts of self (the subconscious, self-conscious, and super-conscious minds) clear boundaries and definitions.

Although not referenced here, boundaries and definitions are clear references to Saturn. This is a good example of the ubiquity of Saturn's influence in all areas of our life. The very existence of boundaries and definitions in our lives is what creates the space for liberation and illumination to unfold.

Qabalistically, Key 1 the Magician, represents the human faculty of self-consciousness. The concentration of the Magician is necessary for Fixation. In the image for Key 1 the conscious action taken by the Magician is the raising of his wand toward the super-conscious level. †† Paul Foster Case tells us that this wand is a symbol of the secret force which is sublimated in the alchemical process. The Magician points toward the garden, just as the man in Key 6 looks toward the woman. The woman and the garden are both symbols of our subconscious mind.

Gemini is the sign of mutable air. Alchemical Air is closely related to concentration, and to the *Disposing Intelligence*, or discrimination, which results from concentration. There is a connection between our breathing and concentration. During concentration, breathing becomes slower and more rhythmical. The conscious creation of a pattern of slow rhythmic breathing aids our concentration. Paul Foster Case writes that Breath-control facilitates mind-control.

Breathing is also connected to our sense of smell. The act of breathing brings air into our nostrils where it then comes into contact with the odor sensors in our nose. Our sense of smell is a marvelous faculty that can be activated by very small amounts of molecules in the air. When combined with our sense of taste, we can be said to have a discriminating palate.

Smell is attributed to the letter Zain in the *Sepher Yetzirah* or *Book of Formation*. Our sense of smell is associated with keen perception and sagacity. Everyday speech has a number of phrases like "smell a rat" or "something smells fishy" to say that our inner senses detect a falsehood. [††]

Gemini means *the Twins* and its sign approximates the Roman numeral II. The sign is also said to represent the pillars of Hermes and Solomon that are found in several Western traditions. This gives a clue to the Hermetic doctrine that states that all opposites are really but different aspects of the One Thing, and that they are complementary. Mercury the Messenger carries this message from the supernal world through the letter Zain on the path from Binah to Tiphareth on the Tree of Life. The Sun in Tiphareth is a symbol of enlightenment and represents One Force which is differentiated into pairs of opposites. [††]

If taken literally, the name The Lovers and the image on Key 6 can be misleading. †† Paul Foster Case writes that esoterically this Key does not represent the love of two persons. It is, rather, the dualities of a single individual, willfully united in pursuit of Divine Love. The dual energies which the Lover proposes to unite are equal and opposite. The uniting of these twins is a major step forward on the Path of Return.

At the moment of Creation, Divine consciousness cascaded across the Abyss from Binah into physical manifestation. Dualities were created. †† Paul Foster Case writes that the *Great Work* is a union or wedding of these dualities. He tells us that this path of Zain may be considered the aspect of the Garden of Eden from which mankind was expelled, but to which it may gain re-entry by consciously uniting our inner Sun and Moon. The whole Key to the Great Work is said to be the uniting of the Sun and the Moon under Mercury. To better understand this, take a look at the locations of Solar, Lunar and Mercurial influences on the Tree of Life.

The Key to good discrimination is the ability to see Unity behind the appearance of opposites or differences. This ability to perceive Unity in diversity is intuitive in nature. True Discrimination depends upon true intuition (Tarot Key 5 the Hierophant, and Vav). Harmonious reciprocity between opposites (Love) depends upon our faculty of discrimination.

How do we learn discrimination? †† Paul Foster Case writes that physical sensations lead to desire. Desire leads us to temptation. Temptation leads us to action. Through trial and error, by reaping the results of our actions we eventually learn to discriminate. Eventually this brings us inner harmony and then outer harmony, or Love.

East-Above is the location on the Cube of Space assigned to Zain. It is the edge along the Eastern side of the top of the Cube. It joins the top face (Mercury) to the Eastern face (Venus). Through our system of correspondences, this edge also joins the top of the North-Eastern edge (Heh) to the top of the South-Eastern edge (Vav). The combination of East and the Above suggests the working together of creative imagination and the self-conscious faculty of discrimination.

Gemini is the zodiacal sign corresponding to Zain and thus to Study. This sign suggests duality, division, and other ideas related to the sword. This also relates Gemini to the idea of discrimination. Gemini is ruled by Mercury (Key 1 the Magician). In Egyptian mythology the jackal headed Anubis had a keen sense of smell and was sometimes substituted for Mercury or Hermes.

The *Disposing Intelligence* is assigned to Zain and Study. The act of disposing is to place apart and by doing so to separate or divide. This also implies analysis. These characteristics show up in our 'disposition'. Discrimination affects our disposition.

When we understand our self-conscious and our subconscious powers and can guide them in performing their proper duties, we say that these *'volatile'* entities are now *'fixed'* or defined. They can now be intelligently merged with super-consciousness. The delusion of our separateness is now at an end. We can be participants in the eternal NOW. Imagine what a powerful tool we will have when we combine the discipline of Study with this state of consciousness. We are beginning to see that the discipline of Study involves far more than learning from a book or from nature.

As we noted earlier, Gemini and Fixation are associated with our sense of smell. When the qualities of a substance harmonize with our nature, the odor will be pleasant; but if the substance be of a kind that does not sympathize with our nature, we will be disagreeably affected by the odor. This is discrimination. Smell will also enable us to distinguish between a subtle and a gross substance. It is by smell that the alchemist accomplishes this part of the Emerald Tablet:

> *"Thou shalt separate the earth from the fire, the subtle from the gross."*

Smell in relation to discrimination refers to our non-physical faculty of smell that represents direct experience of frequencies and characters of vibration in octaves of manifestation beyond the range of our physical senses. All of our inner senses gradually unfold in this manner as a result of our progress in the *Great Work.*

The above sentence from the Emerald Tablet is, in part, telling us that we must discriminate between the input of just our physical senses and the input from our non-physical senses. We begin with what our physical senses tell us about our world, and then add to that what our non-physical senses are telling us. We begin to understand the limitations of our physical senses and we separate out and discard any information that is of little or no use to us. What remains is a much more accurate picture of our world and the non-physical realms higher in vibration.

Study as a Spiritual Discipline is a left-brained, intellectual, analytical, and objective type of experience. This discipline engages the self-conscious mind after the discipline of Fasting has placed some degree of control over the psychic and physical demands of daily living. Contrast this to the discipline of

Meditation, which is a right-brained, devotional, and subjective experience in which the subconscious mind is engaged. Study provides the self-conscious framework within which the subconscious mind can function during Meditation.

When we are studying something that really interests us, concentration comes easily. At times, despite our best efforts, our minds tend to wander. Our worries distract us. Outside influences and activities divert our attention. Despite our best efforts, we may find the material difficult, or uninteresting. Here are a few suggestions to help us to get ourselves centered and focused on the subject of our studies:

Find and dedicate a suitable space for our studies. This might include adequate lighting, a chair that is both comfortable and supports the body in an upright seated position, adequate space for reading and writing, and convenient storage for our books and other study materials. Music is acceptable as long as it is not loud or distracting. Avoid the use of cell phones and other means of communication during our period of study. This is a time we dedicate ourselves to study alone.

Maintain an atmosphere conducive to studying by performing a banishing ritual or by creative visualization. This will clear our immediate area of unwanted or distracting energies. We need to study in ways that are suited to our style of learning. We process information in one of four ways. We process through our inner sight, inner hearing, inner feeling, or through intuition. Usually one or two of these inner senses will be dominant. If we process visually, it is good to focus on images, shapes, colors, and other visual symbols in our study material. Whichever of our senses dominates, we should honor that and provide input for that sense.

Take notes as we study. This can help to simplify complex ideas and put them into words of our own understanding. We may find that coming back to these notes at a later time will provide material that would be profitable for us to meditate on.

We should set aside a regular time for study and be sure to keep that appointment. Take note what time of day our energy is at its highest and we are most alert. This will be our best time for Study. If possible, we should arrange our schedules for it. Frequent and regular study periods will eventually make Study into a habit – a good one.

Create an objective that we would like to accomplish for a particular session. Focus on that objective until it is completed. Once we accomplish our objective, we should reward ourselves with something we enjoy, such as talking to a friend, a food treat, playing a game, etc. If we accomplish a big objective such as finishing a paper, we should reward ourselves proportionately.

Perhaps it has been a while since we have studied on a regular basis. We will find that there are periods of ups and downs and plateaus. Perhaps we find our minds wandering a bit too much. This is normal in the beginning and will correct itself over time. When our minds begin to wander, we gently remind ourselves what our purpose is in studying and bring our focus back to our subject. Eventually our subconscious minds will get the message about what we expect them to be doing.

So far we have only considered the discipline of Study in a controlled environment. It is important to know that anytime, anywhere we can find opportunities to study, especially when we are outdoors. Nature herself is perhaps the best teacher about us and our world. Direct observation of Nature in the outdoors makes a wonderful laboratory.

We must train ourselves to be good observers – to be able to take note of the tiniest, seemingly insignificant details – and to use these observations to learn about nature's laws. Once Mother Nature begins to reveal herself to us, we can use the Hermetic principle of Correspondence – *"as above, so below; as within, so without"* – to expand our understanding of ourselves and of our Cosmos.

We only have to venture as far as our own bodies to observe nature. As human beings we represent the universe – on a smaller scale – and everything in it. So far as we are aware, we are the only species on Earth that has evolved a highly functioning abstract consciousness. We contain within our being the consciousness of all the kingdoms – mineral, plant, animal, human, and even an emerging super-human. We have the needs, desires, and urges of the lower kingdoms constantly struggling for our attention. We have all of the potential awareness and abilities of the super-human – homo spiritualis – waiting to be unfolded.

We remain in bondage to the lies of materialism, limitation and separation while we do not make the effort to study information available to us about the Reality beyond our five physical senses. Until our self-conscious mind focuses on this greater Reality, our subconscious mind has no alternative but to act on the illusions of a sensory world.

> *"…and you will know the truth, and the truth will make you free."* – John 8:32

Only the truth of the Reality beyond the material world can bring freedom from its illusions. Good intentions, good feelings, and good acts alone will not free us. Freedom will come only when these are combined with knowledge of the Truth. Right knowledge must then be followed by right action.

Look at the way most people live their lives. Expectations of instant gratification have reduced the attention span of an average person to no more than a few minutes. Television and radio take advantage of this by inserting commercial messages every few minutes. Study as a spiritual discipline requires focused attention for longer periods than this. We must learn to exercise our mental muscles as well as our physical ones. Study is indeed a discipline. It is no surprise that most people would prefer to play computer games or watch television.

> *"Finally, beloved, whatever is true, whatever is honorable, whatever is just, whatever is pure, whatever is pleasing, whatever is commendable, if there is any excellence and if there is anything worthy of praise, think about these things."*
> Philippians 4:8

With the creation of balance between our aspects of consciousness, we can now begin to develop the indispensable faculty of discrimination. As we shall see in the next chapter, discrimination will aid us in making better use of our meditations.

[††] Paul Foster Case, *Hermetic Alchemy Science and Practice.*

Chapter 4
Meditation

Correspondences for Meditation

Qabalah:
  the Hebrew letter Cheth, meaning "Fence or Enclosure"
  the Intelligence of the House of Influence
  Receptivity to the Will of the One
  the function of Speech
  the East-Below edge on the Cube of Space
the 18th Path of Cheth on the Tree of Life

Astrology:
  the sign of Cancer (4th house, cardinal water)
Rulership: the Moon (Key 2 High Priestess)
Exaltation: Jupiter (Key 10 Wheel of Fortune)

Alchemy:
  Separation (Stage 4)- Formulating a goal – Moving Forward

Theurgy:
  the discipline of Meditation

Tarot:
  Key 7, the Chariot
  Key 3, the Empress
  Key 10, Wheel of Fortune

"but their delight is in the law of the Lord, and on his law they meditate day and night." - Psalms 1:2

"Let the words of my mouth and the meditation of my heart be acceptable to you, O Lord, my rock and my redeemer." Psalms 19:14

Through the discipline of Study, associated with alchemical Fixation, we saw that we are able to establish firmly in our minds the bounds and functions of the super-conscious, self-conscious, and subconscious aspects of our being. These are the *Mercury, Sulphur*, and *Salt* of the alchemists. We can begin to develop the very useful faculty of discrimination at that stage. Self-consciousness through the rulership of Mercury is the guiding principle of Study.

We now take a look at the spiritual discipline of Meditation and the alchemical stage of Separation. †† Paul Foster Case associates the zodiacal sign of Cancer with Separation. In Cancer we have the additional correspondences of cardinal water, Tarot Key 7, the rulership of the Moon (Key 2), the exaltation of Jupiter (Key 10), the *intelligence of the House of Influence*, the function of Speech, and the direction East-Below on the Cube of Space.

Paul Foster Case writes that if we wish to understand the relationship of Meditation with these correspondences, it is helpful to examine the placement of Cheth on the Tree of Life and the symbolism that makes up the image of Key 7, the Chariot. The path of the Charioteer begins with his crown in the sphere of Binah and his feet in Geburah. A traveler on this path must reconcile the fiery Mars energy of the sephirah of Severity with the watery energy of the sephirah of Understanding. ††

On the Path of Return, Cheth is the first path that crosses the Abyss. The Abyss is the veil between Atziluth – the world of Emanation – and Briah – the world of Creation. It veils the brilliant light of the Supernals from the rest of creation. It is because of the Abyss that it is written, *"The light* [of the above] *shineth in the darkness, and the darkness* [of the below] *comprehendeth it not."*

Paul Foster Case tells us that Tarot Key 7 the Chariot represents mastery on all planes of existence and refers to the descent of Spirit into the lower manifested universe. One purpose of this path is to illustrate that whatever our personal beliefs, we need to remain receptive to the influence of the *One Source* moving through the vehicle of our body and personality in its own unique way. We must recognize Spirit behind all form. Our form must be directed towards the ultimate reunion with our source. [††]

The symbolism in the Chariot Key indicates that this path is an important connection. It represents a reconciliation between the *above* and the *below*. The stone body of the chariot is covered by a starry canopy. The two sphinxes are black and white and wear two different expressions. The chariot sits on low ground in front of a higher walled city with a stream flowing between. The Chariot is shown as intermediary. It participates in both the above and the below. It is perfect control on more than one plane of existence. At the same time it protects the sanctity of the Supernals by maintaining the necessary separation of those planes which it affects. [††]

Much of the same symbolism can be applied to Meditation. It too is a mediator between the *above* and the *below*. Although we cannot establish a direct self-conscious connection, we can consciously place our subconscious mind into the flow of the cosmic Meditation and receive the wisdom coming from the higher realms. We saw in the last chapter that this is the relationship illustrated by the Lovers Key of the Tarot.

Many schools of the Western Mysteries, including the F.L.O. and the B.O.T.A., assign the function of Meditation to the sign of Aquarius and the alchemical stage of Dissolution. There is a distinction to be made between Meditation as a *function* and Meditation as a *discipline*. For the purpose of this work we will associate the discipline of Meditation with the function of Speech in Cancer and we will associate the function of Meditation with the discipline of Confession in Aquarius. We will explore the connection between the discipline of Meditation and Speech in this chapter and examine how the function of Meditation relates to the discipline of Confession in chapter 11.

Many of us practice Meditation simply as a means to an end. That is, we use it to gain knowledge or a deeper understanding of a subject. This is the use of Meditation as a function. Meditation is a Cosmic Process. Subconscious mind on the cosmic level (Key 2 the High Priestess) is a never-ending stream of consciousness. The image on Key 2 shows this stream flowing from the bottom of the robe of the High Priestess.

When we meditate, we simply enter into this constant stream of mental activity. This implies that self-consciousness must step aside once the subject of our meditation has been chosen. It is a hermetic axiom that *"We do not unveil Nature. Nature unveils herself to us."* It is not we who meditate. By entering into meditation, we immerse ourselves into the stream of cosmic meditation. This is Meditation used as a function.

Under the direction of our self-conscious mind, The Moon or subconscious mind is the ruler of the body. It is she who creates changes in the body, establishing new neural pathways and enabling new behaviors. It is she who works tirelessly to eliminate sense-based mental images in order to replace them with mental images provided by our inner teacher. It is she who must gain control over the elemental forces of our lower nature.

These elemental energies are much like wild creatures and cannot be tamed by force. They must come to love their master. Through the normal functions of the High Priestess the body is tamed. And this can only be accomplished when the Magician gives the High Priestess the proper suggestions in the form of good mental images. For an elaboration on this idea read Chapter 5 where we discuss the discipline of Submission.

Meditation as a discipline makes use of the function of Meditation. The function of meditation is a subconscious process and the information we seek is returned to us with very little conscious effort on our part. As a discipline, we make a conscious effort to determine what it is that we most want and whether receiving it will bring us closer to our ultimate goal of unity with the *One Source*. Then we give a suggestion to our subconscious to manifest our desire or to bring us information on how to manifest it.

As a discipline, the subject of Meditation is the establishment of our personal objective in life and the formulation of our definition of that objective. This is a much broader goal and one that will require multiple meditations over a period of time. As a discipline, Meditation becomes a tool for fundamental change at the very core of our being. We begin to make use of the faculty of discrimination that began to develop with the discipline of Study. We learn to carefully distinguish essence from appearance; spirit from body; the subtle from the gross; the *I*

AM from its personality. This is the alchemical Separation associated with the sign of Cancer and with Meditation.

The work of alchemical Separation demands stillness of body and is aimed at silencing the mind. Its technique is described in all the books of the wise. The essence of the practice is in this:

"Be still, and know that I am God! I am exalted among the nations; I am exalted in the earth."   Psalms 46:10

The Moon rules alchemical Separation through its rulership of the sign of Cancer. Through this sign Jupiter is also active. The High Priestess holds a scroll in her lap, upon which is printed *"TORA,"* or Law. This is the scroll of cosmic memory. It is the Book of Life. The surface of the scroll has written on it the details of our personal lives. On the interior of the scroll is written the cosmic record of the *One Life*. It is written in a magical language of pictorial symbolism. The images of the twenty two Tarot major arcana were produced using this magical language.[††]

According to Paul Foster Case, our subconscious mind contains these records written in the magical language. It is stored in our Jupiter center, a great complex of nerves and ganglia often called the *"abdominal brain."* Here in our DNA is written the entire story of physical life on Earth. In the etheric substance surrounding the Jupiter center is written the complete story of the Life-power's unlimited manifestations.[††]

Case tells us that regardless of our own unique objective in life, the objective of everyone on the Path of Return is to establish within ourselves the Truth that *"that which is below is truly as that which is above."* In other words, the canopy and the base of the Chariot are different in appearance and function, but they are *ONE*. Our task is to free our minds from the illusions of the material world. When we see with our eyes and with our mind that all things regardless of appearance are manifestations of the *One Source*, then the work of Separation is complete. ^{††}

In order to experience the deep transformation available at this stage, we must use all of the inner disciplines. We use Prayer to ask for the aid of the *One Source* to produce inner transformation. We use Fasting to cleanse and balance ourselves in preparation for transformation. We use study to help us come to a conscious understanding of what is needed for transformation to occur. We use this understanding to formulate the suggestions we give to subconscious in order to initiate the process of transformation. What Meditation brings to us is an understanding of the objectives required to achieve transformation.

"My mouth shall speak Wisdom [Chokmah]; *the meditation of my heart shall be Understanding* [Binah]. *"*
Psalms 49:3

Speech is the physical function attributed to Cheth, and thus to the discipline of Meditation. Speech defines. Words take on the function of fences that enclose separate fields of consciousness. The association of Speech with Cheth tells us that words are imbued with the preservative power of Cheth. This means that the right choice of words can protect us. Extend the meaning of speech from the spoken word to the unspoken words of thought, and we can understand why the wise have always attached so much importance to right speech.

Speech is the utterance of our own Magical Word. Magical words are used to produce specific vibrations and mental images for specific purposes. Paul Foster Case writes that each of us has a unique Magical Word given to us on the inner realms for protection and for the accomplishment of our own spiritual purposes.

Paul Foster Case writes that this magical word is identical with the "new name," written on a white pebble, spoken of in Revelation 2: 17. Case states that this white stone is given to "him that overcometh," and that in the passage mentioned it is associated with eating the hidden manna. This is a clear reference to the sign of Cancer, which rules the breast and stomach, and is predominantly the sign of nourishment.[tt]

Case states that the white pebble is a symbol of the Stone of the Sages, and in Key 7 of Tarot there is a direct reference to that same Stone. The body of the chariot is a cubical made of stone. The new name is known only to the recipient. It is a new personal definition, marking a new phase of our life activities.[tt]

Although the position of the personality must be sacrificed so that our higher Soul may ascend to the throne of our lives, the personality does not undergo a complete destruction. Our self-conscious and subconscious minds are indispensable in spiritual growth. Our goal is not the destruction of the personality, but its complete transformation. Even the highest adepts find the personality to be a valuable ally.

While we are subject to the wheel of Karma, we never completely release all of the illusions of the personality. But the adept knows them to be illusions and sees their usefulness and necessity in completing the *Great Work*. [tt] Paul Foster Case tells us that the objective of the Work at the alchemical stage of Separation is the establishment of a clearly defined spiritual identity.

With the discipline of Fasting and its association with Key 5 the Hierophant we learned the importance of listening to the voice of our inner teacher. With Study and Key 6 we began to learn the symbolic language of our subconscious mind. With the discipline of Meditation and Key 7 we learn that this symbolic language is a magical language that existed before human speech. This Magical Language is introduced to us when we receive our Magical Name and will be used in later stages to communicate with the deepest levels of our being.

This magical language is related to the concept of the *Solar Logos*, or the *Word* of the *One Source*. Mystics have reported that the experience of the Logos includes inner light, sound and music. These are our soul's guides and constant companions on the inner planes. The *One Source* continually creates and maintains its creation through an emanation. In very simplified terms, this emanation can be described as the *Logos*.

From our limited human viewpoint, the most significant characteristic of the *Word* of the *One Source* is that it can be seen and heard from within during our spiritual exercises or perhaps even spontaneously for brief periods when the mind is quiet. We hear the most beautiful music. It is primal and pristine and sings to us of our creation at the dawn of time. It resonates without end within every particle of creation and within every fiber of our being. It is awe-inspiring, breath-taking and supremely blissful. It instills in its listeners a sense of true Worship (see chapter 9). This is the Music of the Spheres which keeps the universe and all of its souls in existence. Using the discipline of Meditation, we can experience the *Logos*. Through this encounter, the Magical Language becomes our constant companion and interpreter on the inner planes.

Paul Foster Case tells us that Tarot Key 7, which represents Cheth, is one of seven Keys which represent various aspects of self-consciousness. The meaning of Cheth as a 'fence or enclosure' is similar to Beth meaning 'house' Both letters convey the idea of 'location.' Beth is the letter assigned to self-consciousness itself. The enclosure of a particular area by a fence is what happens in the mental realm when we define anything, so that Cheth is also related to Heh, considered as the definite article *'the.'* Heh is also a letter corresponding to an aspect of self-consciousness. We have already seen how speech defines. This is another connection of Cheth with our self-conscious mind. [††]

'Intelligence of the House of Influence' is the name given to the energy of Cheth. It is "consciousness of that which is the abode of inflowing power" according to the Sepher Yetzirah. This is awareness of the fact that human personality resembles an enclosed area where universal forces are at work. Taking form as thought and finding expression in the spoken word, these universal forces flow through our personalities into manifestation.

Paul Foster Case writes that *Influence* carries the meaning of "something flowing in from above." This implies that of ourselves we do nothing. All of our inner life comes from the Higher Soul, whose mental image we are. *"Of myself,"* Jesus is quoted, *"I can do nothing."* Thus it is with Meditation. We place ourselves in the ever-flowing stream of cosmic consciousness, and become receptive to the influx of images flowing to us from the higher realms of consciousness. [††]

If we accept that all of our thoughts originate in higher levels of our consciousness, we must accept that our only choice comes in the way we express those thoughts in our words and deeds. If we heed the voice of our inner teacher, we place ourselves in the current of the *Will of the One Source* and we make progress on our spiritual path. If we choose to ignore the voice of our inner teacher, we reap the pain that comes from struggling against the currents of this cosmic flow. Either way, we learn.

Meditation begins by making a conscious effort to create a space, mentally and physically, where subconscious forces can be productive in their assigned task. The self-conscious mind steps aside and takes on the role of an observer. While not active during the meditation, self-consciousness is able to intervene if our subconscious mind becomes distracted or rebellious. The subconscious mind must be trained to carry out our suggestions. This is especially true when we are first learning to meditate.

Cheth is located on the East-Below edge of the Cube of Space. The Eastern (Venus) and Below (Moon) faces of the Cube are joined at the East-Below edge. This is an indication that most of the work of Meditation is done by subconscious forces. Paul Foster Case writes that a bit of introspection will show us that thought and speech are largely subconscious in origin. Our vocabulary depends on subconscious associative processes. All of our sentences, our style, our figures of speech originate below the self-conscious level - all the more reason to train our subconscious and clear out all of the non-productive bits of consciousness that reside there. [tt]

The shape of the Hebrew letter Cheth suggests two explanations that are equally valid.

In the first case, the shape of Cheth is that of a Vav and a Zain joined together. The Vav is on the right and the Zain is on the

131

left. The feminine Vav and the masculine Zain combine in a symbolic of marriage in which masculine and feminine unite for a Godly purpose and protection. Cheth takes the form of a wedding canopy. This idea of the union of our masculinity and femininity is reflected in the glyph for the sign of Cancer. We see two circular currents of consciousness united in a single symbol. [tt]

Qabalists tell us that the secret of Cheth is the idea of "hovering" – touching but not touching. This is seen in Genesis 1 where the Elohim hovered over the face of the waters. God hovers over his creation in order to keep from overpowering or destroying it. By hovering over created reality, God continues to sustain and nourish His Creation. Simultaneously this allows each creature to grow and develop "independently". Cheth hints at the balance between the creative and sustaining powers of Vav and the destructive and potentially life threatening powers of Zain. [tt]

In the second explanation, the shape of Cheth is similar to that for Heh, but the line at the left is carried up into the top. Heh is the same shape as Daleth, with a Yod added to it, and this Yod is extended up to the top to make the letter Cheth. Thus the letter Cheth is composed of a Daleth (4) and a Vav (6). This gives Cheth a secret value of 10, the same as Yod. [tt]

Yod is the nucleus of the sacred Flame alphabet of the Hebrews. Yod is the letter which stands for Spirit. The various components of Cheth tell us that when we use our Creative Imagination in the same way as The *One Source* does, we become reasonable beings. Reason is used to bring order and balance into our lives. This transforms our bodies to receive the consciousness of our Higher Selves. We then are able to become co-creators with the *One Source*. [tt]

The numerical value of Cheth is 8, which as the symbol of infinity represents equilibrium and dominion. This symbol is seen above the heads of the figures in Key 1 and Key 8 of the Tarot. Key 7 which represents equilibrium. †† Paul Foster Case writes that Cheth depicts equilibrium in several ways: the result of equilibrium, what equilibrium can achieve, and the equilibrium of self-consciousness with subconsciousness. Case is saying that Key 7 reveals that the basis of the Great Work is equilibrium.

Without a properly trained subconscious mind in control of the sub-human forces within its makeup, the physical transformations of the body which enable it to become the Chariot of the Higher Soul cannot occur. We must conquer our moods and emotions – our internal phases of the Moon . The Moon rules Cancer, and we must rule the Moon if we wish to transform our bodies.

The Charioteer in Key 7 wears moon-shaped epaulets on his shoulders. These represent the waxing and waning of the Moon, two aspects of emotion which can be creative or destructive. Our shoulders telegraph the state of our emotions to others; we square our shoulders, we droop our shoulders, and we shrug our shoulders. Epaulets were designed to protect the shoulders. As the Charioteer, we are protected from the effects of our changing moods. Our head sits squarely and erect between them indicating a state of emotional equilibrium. Our Higher Soul is now the driver of our Chariot.

Meditation is that faculty which enables us to listen to the *One Source* when it speaks to us through the Magical language. We place a suggestion into the field of our subconscious mind and then confidently await the response. Sometimes we get an answer immediately; sometimes it is delayed. Sometimes the answer comes to us after we re-enter the world of waking consciousness.

In terms of an ancient magical formula for manifestation, we do our best to align our personal WILL to the *Will of the One Source*. We then gather all of what we KNOW about what we want in the form of mental images. Then we DARE to give our subconscious suggestions in the form of appropriate mental images. Finally, we are to REMAIN SILENT. We release our subconscious mind to perform the work assigned to it.

Put into the simplest of terms, the discipline of Meditation in the Western Mysteries is the ability to hear the voice of the *One Source* and to obey its Word. The process of Meditation creates an interior mental, emotional, and spiritual 'space' that allows inner communication to occur. All we are consciously doing is suggesting to our subconscious mind that it enter the stream of cosmic consciousness and retrieve for us certain information or manifest for us a certain outcome.

Many Eastern meditation practices such as Samadhi seek to empty the mind, making it passive and receptive to realms of higher conscious. Samadhi is an example of unseeded meditation. Its ultimate goal, Nirvana, is release from the limitations of personality and thus from suffering. Meditation in the Western mystery tradition is usually focused and seeded, filling the mind with truth about the Reality that leads to physical manifestation. This takes us farther down the path that leads to unity with the *One Source*.

The time and effort involved can be daunting and results can be limited when first learning how to meditate. This can be discouraging in a society that creates expectations of instant gratification. This is where devotion to the *One Source* is essential. Patience is a virtue in the discipline of Meditation. Perseverance will greatly reward our practice of Meditation as it will reward our practice of the other disciplines as well. . The discipline of Meditation will bring us into the presence of the *One Source,* but the process requires effort and the sacrifice of our false pride and control over one's vital soul or animal nature. This is discipline indeed!

[††]Paul Foster Case, *Hermetic Alchemy Science and Practice.*

We take a look at the discipline of Submission in chapter 5. The negative aspects of Submission greatly overshadow its positive qualities in the collective mind of Western culture. We will see that the discipline of Submission is ultimately empowering. With Meditation we establish our personal goals for our journey on the Path of Return. We gain information and we make plans for the road ahead.

With Submission and its associations with the sign of Leo and alchemical Digestion, we raise or sublimate the energy of our Saturn center which rouses the energy of our Mars center. The Saturn/Mars energy then rises to the Jupiter center in the area of our stomach to create energy with a moist heat, mimicking physical digestion.

The Saturn/Mars/Jupiter combined energies are the subhuman forces referred to in Paul Foster Case's writings on Tarot Key 8 and on alchemical Digestion. These subhuman forces representing the mineral, plant, and animal kingdoms then rise to the Sun center where they combine with solar forces to become the red lion pictured on Tarot Key 8.

It is this red lion that is worked with by our subconscious mind in the discipline of Submission. Our authentic power to be whom and what we were created to be resides within the energies of the red lion. It must be tamed and directed by our subconscious mind. Its power can then be extracted and the discipline of Submission becomes empowering rather than debilitating.

Part III
The Outer Spiritual Disciplines

Submission	5th house	Leo	fixed fire
Service	6th house	Virgo	mutable earth
Simplicity	7th house	Libra	cardinal air
Solitude	8th house	Scorpio	fixed water

5th house influences*

> creative self-expression
> children
> creative projects
> love affairs
> risk taking

6th house influences*

> physical and psychological health
> day-to-day work and duties
> personal service

7th house influences*

> significant one-to-one relationships
> husband/wife
> mate
> business partnerships
> therapist-client

8th house influences*

> shared resource
> financial
> psychological
> sexual and emotional
> intimate unions
> depth interactions

*from *Astrology for Yourself,* by George Demetra and Douglas Bloch

Astrologically, I am associating the four outer spiritual disciplines with the 5th through the 8th houses and signs on the wheel of the zodiac. We see from the influences of these houses that they affect how we express ourselves creatively in ever-expanding areas of relationships with others.

As disciplines, these four differ from other interactions with others in that they are intentionally created by the actions we take. We choose to practice the disciplines and so we can anticipate the effects they will have on ourselves and others. Submission balances perfect order with perfect discipline. This facilitates a balanced use of power in our relationships. Our devotion to service purifies our desires and intentions. Simplicity allows us to re-prioritize everything in our relationships according to our spiritual needs. Solitude breaks down old patterns and beliefs in our relationships so that new spirit based relationships can be created.

The outer disciplines affect our relationships with our outer world. Their associated behaviors and practices can differ noticeably from the norms of our modern Western society. They set us apart and can increase our visibility to those who do not practice the disciplines. At times, this extra visibility can bring negative and even hostile reactions. This does not have to affect us in a negative way. We simply create and manifest positive mental images in reply to external resistance.

Submission has a fiery nature because of its power to transform. I am associating it with fiery Leo. Service has an earthy nature both because of its practical qualities and because service is performed in the material world of Assiah. I am associating it with the earthy sign of Virgo. Simplicity has an airy nature because it requires us to make conscious choices. I am associating it with the airy sign of Libra. Solitude has a watery nature because it brings us in close communion with the love of our Higher Self. I am associating it with the watery sign of Scorpio.

The outer discipline of Service is the ground from which the other disciplines sprout. Service is the reasoned concern for the well-being of all. Progress on the Path of Return is virtually impossible without the spiritual discipline of Service. Simplicity places material concerns in perspective with spiritual truths. This produces inner unity that manifests as outward liberation. With liberation, Solitude allows us to see and hear with control. Words and interactions with others become meaningful. Strengthened communication facilitates the discipline of Submission which, along with Service, places the well-being of others first.

Chapter 5
Submission

Correspondences for Submission

Qabalah:
  the Hebrew letter Teth, meaning "Snake"
  the Intelligence of the Secret of all Spiritual Activities
  Suggestion
  the function of Taste
  the North-Above edge on the Cube of Space
  Teth connects Chesed (Key 10 Wheel of Fortune) to Geburah (Key 16 the Tower)
  the 19th Path of Teth on the Tree of Life

Astrology:
  the sign of Leo (5th house, fixed fire)
  Rulership: the Sun (Key 19 the Sun)
  Exaltation: Neptune (Key 12 Hanged Man)

Alchemy:
  Digestion – (Stage 5) - Exposure of a substance to the action of a liquid with the aid of heat (Analysis)

Theurgy:
  the discipline of Submission

Tarot:
  Key 8, Strength
  Key 10, Wheel of Fortune
  Key 16, the Tower
  Key 19, the Sun
  Key 12, Hanged Man

"In the same way, you who are younger must accept the authority of the elders.* And all of you must clothe yourselves with humility in your dealings with one another, for 'God opposes the proud, but gives grace to the humble.' Humble yourselves therefore under the mighty hand of God, so that he may exalt you in due time. "   1 Peter 5:5

With Submission we move from inner spiritual disciplines to outer ones. We are now doing the work of self-transformation through our relationships with other individuals as well as through the inner realms. A good foundation in the practice of the inner disciplines is helpful in understanding the practice of the outer ones.

Four inner disciplines took us through one cycle of the four elements on the wheel of the zodiac. Having worked with the watery energy of Cancer, we now return to the element of fire in Leo.

With the sign of Leo and alchemical Digestion we are working with the fire of the Life-force (Mars) and the water of cosmic mental energy (Jupiter). These two are combined through the nineteenth Path of Teth on the Tree of Life which connects the sephiroth of Chesed and Geburah. In the human energy system, the Life-force from the Mars center rises to the Jupiter center where it combines with and is transformed by the watery consciousness of Jupiter. Soluble parts are separated from the matter, allowing the mental analysis of a situation to take place. ††

Fire is a transformative element and we will see that the discipline of Submission is a transformative practice. Associated with Leo and Digestion, it is an active process that requires thoughts and actions which often contradict social norms and expectations. With this association we are given our first clue that submission is not an abdication of authentic power. Also, the outgoing personality of the Leo native would not allow themselves to submit without good reason. Submission requires the courage of a lion and a willingness to follow the counsel of our inner teacher.

Paul Foster Case writes that the alchemical stage of Digestion begins with a blending of the Mars force with the Jupiter force in the area of the stomach. This mirrors the physical process of Digestion. As the Mars force, or kundalini, rises to the Jupiter center moist heat is generated in both the physical and alchemical digestive processes. The subhuman elemental energies of the Mars center can be tamed as they submit to the authority of the higher Jupiter center. This is another hint that Leo is associated with Submission. [tt]

But there is more. The Mars/Jupiter energy is then combined with the solar energy of Leo in the Sun center. Case writes that this creates the red lion of Tarot Key 8, Strength. This is the fiery energy that combines with the watery energy of Jupiter in alchemical Digestion. It is this fiery and moist elemental energy that submits to the direction of the subconscious mind, depicted by the woman in Key 8. *The secret of all spiritual activities* is the combination of the energies of the Mars and Jupiter centers. This combination is the foundation of all subsequent activities of spiritual unfoldment. [tt]

Paul Foster Case tells us that the nineteenth path of Teth, connecting Chesed to Geburah on the Tree of Life, is the highest path encountered that is completely within the Microprosopus, or manifested universe. It begins and ends below the abyss. This path balances the perfect order of Chesed with the perfect discipline of Geburah. [tt]

Case writes that this balance is expressed as perfect control. It is the mediator between two types of power: the power to destroy and to eliminate, and the power to create and to sustain. The destructive power is manifested in processes such as catabolism and entropy. The creative power is manifested in processes such as catabolism and negative entropy.[tt]

It is said that unbalanced Severity is but cruelty. Tyranny and oppression are its result. Unbalanced Mercy is but weakness. To remain passive in the presence of evil is to be an accomplice of that evil. Chesed or Geburah alone will move us to one extreme or the other. Balanced thought, words, and deeds require that the two forces be used together in balanced disposition. And where is this balance found? On the 19th path of Teth and Leo that connects Geburah and Chesed.

The discipline of Submission teaches us this balanced use of power. The balance point between Mercy and Severity shifts from moment to moment and from situation to situation. The discipline of Submission temporarily withdraws our active use of power. We may then determine where the balance point is to be found. From this we may know the most appropriate circumstances for the expression of our power. This power is authentic and includes the ability to express what we were created to be or to do. It is not a power *over* anything or anyone.

Exoterically, we might think that the gregarious and often very public nature of the Leo personality would be a poor fit for the discipline of Submission. The Leo native need have no fear of giving up power. We will see that true Submission is not the negation or suppression of our authentic power. Only the false perceptions we have concerning power need be relinquished. The esoteric teaching is that true Submission is ultimately empowering. This is completely contradictory to how the great majority of humanity defines Submission.

The esoteric definition of Submission is eloquently illustrated in Tarot Key 8, Strength. Here we see a red lion docilely submitting itself to the direction of our subconscious mind. ††
Paul Foster Case tells us that the chain of roses the woman uses to lead the lion indicates a relationship forged by mutual desire and respect. This is not a forced relationship. The red lion represents all of the sub-human elemental forces and their expressions. In the relationship pictured here, the forces act in concert with and become a part of our human consciousness. They are working with us rather than against us.

As the intelligence assigned to the letter Teth and thus to Leo, the *intelligence of the secret of all spiritual activities* is active in the discipline of Submission. It is helpful to remember that *all* activities are spiritual. One key to the operation of this intelligence is that all forces and activities everywhere are expressions of the *One Source*. When we submit ourselves to the authority of anyone or anything deserving of our obedience, we do not lose power. We actually regain a sense of our own authentic power by our act of submission. We also partake in the beneficence and protection of the power to which we submit.

We saw in chapter 3 the Fixation of the three aspects of our consciousness. In Key 6 the Lovers we see our self-conscious mind giving a suggestion to our subconscious mind. Our subconscious then submits to the self-conscious mind and enters the stream of cosmic consciousness. There it interacts with our super-conscious mind in order to act on the suggestion of our self-conscious mind. At this point the High   Priestess becomes the Empress, the consort of the Emperor. The Empress produces mental imagery appropriate to the suggestion.

The fixation of these three aspects of our consciousness establishes a hierarchy in which our subconscious mind submits to our self-conscious mind, and both submit to our superconscious mind or higher soul.

Just as we establish a productive relationship with our subconscious mind, Subconscious establishes a relationship with all sub-human manifestations of cosmic energy. In this relationship she is able to influence and direct these energies. Every force in nature down to atoms and sub-atomic particles is under the control of the subconscious mind. This is the arcanum of *the intelligence of the secret*. Through this we are able to extend our dominion over all of the forces within our internal and external environments.

For those who do not understand the principles behind cosmic law, such willful dominion over nature might seem miraculous. We must recognize that no laws of the universe are overwritten or suspended in the process of creating conscious changes in our environment. A person able to do this understands cosmic law and works with higher levels of consciousness to manifest desired changes on the lower levels.

The Tree of Life diagram used in Hermetic Qabalah shows us the relationship of all levels of consciousness from pure undifferentiated spirit in Kether to completely differentiated spiritual matter in Malkuth. The Tree is made up of four qabalistic worlds from the spiritual and emanating world of Atziluth to the physical and manifesting world of Assiah. What is shown as we go from the top of the Tree to the bottom is a decrease in vibration rates and a veiling of the higher vibrations from the lower ones.

Another qabalistic idea related to the discipline of Submission is that on the Tree of Life, every sephirah has a feminine quality compared to the sephirah directly above it. It is receptive to the masculine powers of the higher sephirah. In this sense, each sephirah is subordinate or submissive to the one above it.

Two processes are active on the Tree of Life. The first one is *involution*, an emanation of Kether consciousness all the way down to physical manifestation in Malkuth. The second process is *evolution*, also called *the Path of Return*. Matter is manifested spirit, and spirit longs to return to spirit.

Our consciousness, as manifested spirit, recognizes aspects of its Creator at each level of *the Path of Return*. We understand that each level is higher in vibration and consciousness than the one below it. There are veils between the levels that prevent the ill-intentioned or the merely curious from gaining access. Coming from the dense level of physical manifestation, we understand that each of the higher worlds has dominion over the ones below. Our qabalistic model of the cosmos is a beneficent hierarchy, not a democracy.

Even our inner makeup is hierarchical. Our higher Soul is super-consciousness, our human consciousness is self-consciousness, and our animal, plant, and mineral consciousness constitute our subconscious mind. The hierarchy of the cosmos was put into place at the instant of Creation. Wise men and women affirm that it brought order and discipline to the primordial Chaos and has guided the operation of the cosmos even to the present day.

The discipline of Submission helps us to recognize and make use of this Divine order of Creation. Submission is not an abdication of our power or our responsibilities. It is recognition of the Divine order and a willingness to work within that order to serve the *One Source* and to manifest our desires. To a personality that has not yet been trained, submission to a higher power may seem servile and demeaning. For one that has been trained, it is empowering and liberating.

The personality that insists on controlling every detail in life takes on an awesome responsibility. It quickly tires and becomes unable to carry the entire load. Once it accepts the existence of the cosmic hierarchy and understands how useful it can be, it can be easily convinced to set down its burden and begin to work in concert with the natural order of nature and the cosmos.

The untrained personality seeks power. It does not yet have a sense of its own innate power and looks for it externally. Often we seek power over others or over the events of our lives. This is based on illusion. We begin our search for authentic power when we embrace the Reality beyond our material world. Our search for authentic power is a search for the power that resides within every atom of the created universe. This is the power that frees us to be who we were created to be and to do what we were created to do. Once we have seen a glimpse of this Reality and the awesome power available to us through the cosmos, it becomes easier to understand and accept our position in the hierarchy of creation.

Submission, then, is the recognition and acceptance of our true position within the hierarchy of the manifested universe. Our present position was never intended to be our permanent one. All of creation is constantly evolving, moving ever closer to its creator. However, the rates of evolution vary from one kingdom to another. The mineral kingdom is the slowest, followed by the plant and animal kingdoms. The human kingdom is the quickest to evolve, aided by the capabilities of self-consciousness. It is awesome to consider that one day on our evolutionary paths, each one of us will take our places as star beings in the administration of the universe!

If we take *"nature"* to mean the kingdoms below the human level, the saying, *"Nature unaided fails,"* begins to take on more meaning. As the fastest evolving kingdom of our physical world, we humans have a responsibility to assist nature in its evolution rather than using our power to dominate and destroy it.

We use our intellect and imaginations to create new alloys, composites, and other materials. Instead of simply taking from the Earth, we work to identify renewable resources. We identify the useful characteristics of plants and create plants that will produce those characteristics. We work to preserve habitats for all of the species that inhabit this planet. We domesticate certain animal species, creating animals that can willingly work alongside us. Working closer with humanity speeds up the evolution of those animals which are chosen.

We can also speed up the rate of our own evolution by becoming aware of levels of consciousness higher than that of physical manifestation and interacting with them. We start by training our own subconscious and establishing a productive relationship with it. This gives us a solid and balanced foundation from which to work.

Our subconscious mind is our channel of communication between all other levels of consciousness. It performs our work for us on the inner planes as we seek to learn about and work with them. If we are wise, we submit to those individuals who have already traveled the path ahead of us and who have much to teach us about the journey of our spiritual unfoldment.

The word Teth, name of the ninth Hebrew letter, translates to "serpent" in English. *The Intelligence of the Secret of All Spiritual Activities* involves the raising of the serpent-power, Life-force, or kundalini. In alchemy, the serpent is transformed into the eagle, a symbol of the Jupiter power. †† Paul Foster Case writes that the eagle pictured in the upper right corner of Tarot Keys 10 and 21 is a representation of the Mars energy of Scorpio that has been sublimated and transformed.

This transformation is depicted in the Tarot when the burning tower of Key 16 is transformed into the wheel of Key 10. This is the destructive power of the Mars force in Geburah becoming the perfect understanding of Reality in Chesed that leads to the perfect fulfillment of our desires. The eagle in the upper right corner of Keys 10 and 21 depicts the Scorpio energy after this transformation has taken place. ††

Paul Foster Case notes that the number of Key 16, Mars, is numerically the square of 4. Chesed, the fourth sephirah on the Tree of Life, is the sphere of Jupiter. Case tells us that 16 is the number of cells in the 4x4 magic square of Jupiter, Key 10. We begin to see hints of a relationship between Keys 16 and 10. Also, 16 = 1 + 6 = 7, and the sum of the numbers from 1 to 7 is 28 = 2 + 8 = 10. This demonstrates that there is indeed an esoteric mathematical correspondence between 16 and 10. The correspondences do not end here. I encourage you to study Keys 16 and 10, and work them out for yourself. ††

Submission corresponds to Teth, the ninth letter of the Hebrew alphabet. Look at the shape of Teth. It is similar to the shape of Cheth, but it is inverted with its opening at the top. It reminds us of a container for something. †† Paul Foster Case writes that Teth contains the unrealized potential of the kundalini energy, or Life-force.

Teth translates to "serpent" and is associated with the kundalini coiled at the base of the spine. When fully raised, kundalini enables us to eventually partake of all of the levels of consciousness on the Tree of Life from Malkuth to Kether. But with Teth and alchemical Digestion, the kundalini energy has far to go before it can achieve its full potential.

Teth, with a power or numeration of 9, is the highest of the single digit archetypal letters in the Hebrew alphabet. As the serpent of kundalini, Teth has the ability to put into activity all of the archetypes within us. The next letter is Yod, whose power is 10. Yod begins a new series whose power is expressed as two digits. The tenth through the eighteenth letters of the Hebrew alphabet are the nine archetypes as they are expressed in the world of the microcosm.

With the letter Teth, an act of submission allows us to go within, as if going back to the womb. Indeed, the shape of the letter Teth is suggestive of a womb. When we enter the spiritual womb of Teth we are able to explore all of the unmanifest possibilities which are yet open to us.

In spite of outward appearance, Submission is a very empowering opportunity. We can deliberately choose how to manifest our power in such a way as to include rather than exclude, to love rather than hate, to serve rather than to be served, and to take our proper places within the hierarchy of Light. We can fulfill our destiny to become co-creators of Paradise on Earth.

We can now better appreciate that the discipline of Submission is very transformative. We have associated it with the letter Teth, the sign of Leo, the element of fixed fire, alchemical Digestion, and the forces of the Sun and of Jupiter. Taken together, how could Submission not be transformative? The discipline of Submission is effectively working with the *Secret of All Spiritual Activities*.

It is a common misconception, especially among religions such as Christianity, Islam, and Judaism, that the discipline of Submission is primarily intended for married couples and children, or people of lesser rank or status. As a spiritual discipline, Submission is intended to be practiced by everyone, whether great or small, old or young, male or female. If our situation dictates that Submission is the best course of action, we must submit. To act otherwise would be to deny the cosmic principles that apply to all.

> *"Do not speak harshly to an older man,* * *but speak to him as to a father, to younger men as brothers, to older women as mothers, to younger women as sisters—with absolute purity."*   - 1Timothy 5:1-2

This passage tells us that we are to treat everyone with all due love and respect. When we submit to the authority of the *One Source*, we are duty bound to treat all of humanity as we would treat our family because they <u>are</u> our family. We are all sons and daughters of the *One Source*.

The act of Submission, then, is recognition of the fact that everything in the cosmos is a unique expression of the *One* and <u>is</u> the *One*. Thus, Jesus said, *"I and the Father are one,"* and *"I can of my own do nothing."*

To practice Submission is not to relinquish our rights or our responsibilities. Though outer appearances may be altered and we may be called upon to sacrifice certain prerogatives cherished by our personalities, Submission never requires us to compromise our inborn power as children of Spirit. In today's society many people think and act as if they have rights but no responsibilities. The prevailing inclination is to submit to no one. Submissive action is viewed as weakness and cowardice. Most do not see how Submission can be transformative. And yet, Jesus is quoted as saying:

> *"If any want to become my followers, let them deny themselves and take up their cross and follow me."*
> Mark 8:34

Submission is the denial of our false pride and the baser instincts of our animal nature. Most despise the concept of self-denial. Many would put self-fulfillment and self-actualization before self-denial. We can now see that self-fulfillment and self-actualization are products of the discipline of Submission.

Self-denial is equated in the popular mind with self-hatred and self-rejection. Paradoxically, the degree to which we practice self-denial is the degree that we are able to experience liberation and enlightenment. Individuals are free moral agents and have personal moral responsibility. Submission bestows the freedom to act responsibly. Submission means reordering our relationships according to spiritual principles. Using our faculty of discrimination, we place the interests of others ahead of our own wherever it is practical. Esoterically, we know that the well-being of one is identical to the well-being of all. Practicing the discipline of Submission strengthens all of one's relationships; with self, with others, and with Spirit.

"But when you are invited, go and sit down at the lowest place, so that when your host comes, he may say to you, 'Friend, move up higher'; then you will be honored in the presence of all who sit at the table with you. For all who exalt themselves will be humbled, and those who humble themselves will be exalted." - Luke 14:10-11

When we are called to humble ourselves before the *One Source*, we are practicing Submission. The Gospel of Luke tells us that when we humble ourselves in this way, *the One Source* will elevate us. We will also be elevated when we practice humility in our dealings with people in our lives. When we allow elements of our personalities to be exalted, they will surely fall as they do in Tarot Key 16. When our personalities submit to higher realms of consciousness, our Higher Soul can take control as is shown in Tarot Key 7. We also see a numerical connection between these two Keys: 1 and 6 sum to 7.

Submission does not debase, it exalts! Submission elevates us to our proper position within the hierarchy of the cosmos. When we know Truth and live our lives according to Truth, we are liberated to be the people we were created to be. The illusions of this world will always be with us and we will always be tempted by the ways of this world, but now we know we have the power to overcome them. No longer can we be content with chasing after baubles in the gutter. As children of the *One Source* it is time for us to take our places at the table of the celebration of our homecoming.

In the next chapter we take a look at the discipline of Service. It is the culmination of the second triad among the twelve disciplines; Meditation, Submission, and Service. We will see that its nature is assimilating, resulting from the defining nature of Meditation and the extracting nature of Submission. In physiology, assimilation is the conversion of absorbed food into the substance of the body. This is in keeping with the earthy nature of Virgo and Service.

†† Paul Foster Case, *Hermetic Alchemy Science and Practice.*

Chapter 6
Service

Correspondences for Service

Qabalah:
the Hebrew letter Yod, meaning "Open Hand"
the Intelligence of Will
Response
the function of Touch/Coition
the North-Below edge on the Cube of Space
the 20th Path of Yod on the Tree of Life

Astrology:
the sign of Virgo (6th house, mutable earth)
Rulership: Mercury (Key 1 the Magician)
Exaltation: Mercury (Key 1 the Magician)

Alchemy:
Distillation – (Stage 6) - Fixing the Volatile - Extracting the Divine Essence from the gross physical, making it available to the entire body

Theurgy:
the discipline of Service

Tarot:
Key 9, the Hermit
Key 1, the Magician

"Like good stewards of the manifold grace of God, serve one another with whatever gift each of you has received." 1 Peter 4:10

In all this I have given you an example that by such work we must support the weak, remembering the words of the Lord Jesus, for he himself said, 'It is more blessed to give than to receive.'" Acts 20:35

After the transformative power of fire in Submission the experience of the manifesting and assimilating power of earth is evident in Service. We are assigning the astrological sign of Virgo and the alchemical stage of Distillation to the discipline of Service. Alchemical Distillation is largely a physiological process, taking place in the small intestines. Medieval alchemists described this area of the body as a dark cave in the bowels of the Earth. The earth connection continues with the function of touch or coition. Also, acts of service are performed in the physical realm. These are some of the reasons why the element of earth has been associated with Service.

The element of air is also active in Distillation and in Service. We note that in the sign of Virgo, Mercury (Tarot Key 1, the Magician) is both the ruler and has its exaltation. *The Intelligence of Will* is assigned to Yod. These correspondences reveal that our faculty of self-consciousness plays an important role in both Service and Distillation.

Alchemically speaking, we take the physical elements of earth, water, air, and fire into our bodies as food, water, breath, and sunlight/heat. They carry their living substances within us as we incorporate them into our bodies. As they make their way through our bodies, their spiritual essences become mixed in our small intestines with an oily white milky liquid called chyle.

Paul Foster Case tells us that chyle is a physical substance but it contains the living essences of the four elements. This living essence called chyle is volatile (easily separated) and contains several components that are vital for life. In this form, the volatile essences can be quickly distributed to all parts of the body. Distillation is the extraction of this Divine Essence from the gross physical forms that we eat, drink, and breathe. Case tells us that one of these Divine Essences is called by the alchemists *"Aurum potable,"* or liquid gold.[††]

The Divine Essence found in chyle is actively assimilated by everyone all the time or we would not be alive. In most people, only a small portion of the available Divine Essence is assimilated. [††] Paul Foster Case tells us that a spiritual adept who has been trained to efficiently use the faculty of concentration is able to assimilate much more. His or her circulatory and nervous systems accumulate an abundance of the Divine Essence. This brings about physical changes to the adept's body which facilitate the use of the very potent energies of higher levels of consciousness. These same energies in the body of an ordinary person could cause severe damage and perhaps death of the physical body.

Service and Distillation correspond to the sign of Virgo. In Greek mythology, Virgo is Demeter, the mother of the harvest. During the time of harvest, grains, fruits, and vegetables are reaped in order to sustain life throughout the winter. She also presided over sacred law and the cycle of life and death. Demeter and her daughter Persephone were the central figures of the Eleusinian mysteries.

Paul Foster Case tells us that esoterically, Virgo is also the mother of the harvest of our Higher Souls. He says that the forms of our bodies were created to be a temple of the soul. Our personality begins to unfold and reach a high degree of development in Leo. In Virgo the personality prepares to become the mother of the inner *"Christ consciousness"* which is our indwelling Higher Soul. Here the personality assumes the role of nurturer and protector of our Higher Soul which remains in the background until we are ready to 'give birth' to it. [††]

In Virgo we begin to make changes to our personality that better equips it to work with our indwelling Higher Self. We purify our desires and intentions. We devote our minds and our talents toward service. Gradually our personalities become more balanced and achieve a higher level of consciousness. This facilitates our communications and interactions with our Higher Souls.

The body and the soul which are given separate and distinct definitions in Gemini, begin to be recognized as unified in Virgo. The relationship of our personality with our Higher Soul is still being developed here. This relationship will achieve its fullest manifestation in the sign of Pisces. No wonder Pisces is assigned to the discipline of Celebration!

Virgo has been called the *"womb of time."* When we harvest crops, we put them away for a period of time until they are needed. In Virgo, the Higher Self lies hidden in her womb. During this period of time we have the opportunity to reap wisdom from our experiences in this physical realm. We also learn to repay the unconditional compassion of our Earthly Mother and Divine Father with loving service. [††]

A Virgo native ruled by personality might say: "I'm adaptable. I will go anywhere and do anything to survive." A Soul-centered Virgo might say: "I want to experience things that encourage my creative self-expression, and serve others at the same time." As

Virgo grows spiritually, the need to be of service also grows. This niche is perfectly suited for Virgo.

Yod, corresponding to Virgo and to Service, is assigned *the Intelligence of Will.* The Sepher Yetzirah says, Yod is

"...so called because it forms the patterns of all bodies; and by this intelligence, when it is perceived, the pre-existent Wisdom is discovered."

Paul Foster Case tells us that Tarot Key 9 illustrates this point. The Hermit personifies Universal Wisdom. The power that forms patterns on the physical level is represented by the star in his lantern. The light shining from his lantern is *the Intelligence of Will.* [tt]

Will power and the *power of Light* are both descriptions of the emanations originating in the Ain Soph Aur, or Limitless Light above the Tree of Life. The cosmos is a single living organism. Every part of the cosmos is related in some way to every other part. The power which forms the patterns of bodies is the Universal Wisdom, a power of the *One Source.* All of the forms in our physical world are manifestations of it, but the forms veil this power until we are ready to experience it. [tt]

At the level of mental activity, alchemical Distillation clarifies and purifies our consciousness. *Cosmic Truth* is extracted from our mental and emotional constructs. We can see the truth behind any event. We become less and less identified with our bodies and personalities. In doing this we are not only serving The *One Source.* We also serve by being examples for others to follow. This service is depicted by the figure of the Hermit on Key 9 of the Tarot. [tt]

The direction on the Cube of Space of Yod, and therefore to Distillation and to Service, is North-Below. This is the intersection of the North (Mars) face with the Below (Moon) face. These correspond to the Mars center just below the naval and to the Moon center just above and behind the eyes. We are unable to recognize the Wisdom symbolized by the Hermit of Key 9 until we have utilized the Mars power to break down our illusions of separateness and have achieved some measure of success in uniting our personal subconsciousness with the vast universal subconsciousness.

Through the discipline of Submission, raw elemental power is transformed into the power and freedom to act responsibly. Service is that discipline which grounds this newly unfolded power in the arena of physical activity. The physiological processes of Distillation separate spiritual essence from gross matter and speed its delivery to all parts of the body. Parts of the old personality dominated body start to go away and are replaced with cells and components more capable of working with the higher vibrations of the Higher Soul.[††]

The food, water, breath and light that we take into our bodies are combined in the previous process of Digestion. In Distillation the spiritual components of these nutrients are extracted and transformed into chyle that becomes available for use by the body. This is one meaning of the term *'fixing the volatile'*. The custom of blessing our food before a meal serves the very practical purpose of accelerating the production and use of the spiritual components of chyle.

Both Virgo and Gemini are ruled by Mercury. Because of this, we might expect to see similarities. Gemini with its discipline of Study, and Virgo with its discipline of Service both require the use of concentration by our self-conscious mind. However,

Gemini is an air sign and uses analysis to break down information into smaller pieces. Virgo is an earth sign and uses synthesis to build a more suitable temple for the Soul. Gemini is electric and masculine. Virgo is magnetic and feminine. Together, they embody the alchemical formula *Solve et Coagula*, Dissolve and Reform.[††]

We have seen the importance of Mercury and the self-conscious mind in alchemical Distillation. The discipline of Service requires a conscious decision to be of service and a plan to carry it out. In the beginning, it may take some effort to identify opportunities for service, but once we begin looking, we find them everywhere. In a society where self-promotion and the accumulation of wealth are encouraged and rewarded, there are plenty of opportunities to be of service to our Creator, our community, and our loved ones.

Service is one of the most important lessons learned on our spiritual path. It is difficult to make significant spiritual progress without practicing it. If we are fortunate, we learn this lesson early in our journey. If we study those individuals that we have come to regard as truly spiritual people, we will see that every one of them has found a way to incorporate Service into their daily practice.

Dr. Paul A. Clark, Steward of the Fraternity of the Hidden Light, tells us in his book, *"The Hermetic Qabalah"* that the 32nd Path on the Tree of Life, situated just above the 10th Path of Malkuth, is the first path in our journey of awakening. It corresponds to the Hebrew letter Tav, Key 21 of the Tarot, and the planet Saturn. He writes that the 32nd Path

> *". . . is associated in the Qabalistic classic "The 32 Paths of Wisdom" with the title, the Administrative*

Intelligence. This path is also designated as, the Serving Intelligence. The desire to serve permeates all true Mystery Schools at all levels, from the humble Neophyte to that of the highest Magus. It is this Key quality that opens the door of the Temples of Initiation. It is, indeed, the only safe and effective motive for traveling the ancient Path of Return."

We have seen that the twentieth path of Yod (Virgo and Tarot Key 9) is related to Service. The Hebrew letter-name Yod, means an open, creative or helping hand. Associated ideas are giving, receiving and reciprocal action. We give freely and unconditionally. When we are receptive, we open ourselves to receive love and other gifts. When we open our minds and hearts we are open to the free exchange of these things. Our hands serve our minds and hearts. In time, we will learn that we are serving the *One Source* as well. Everything we do, say, write, or think will be seen as serving the *One Source*. Bringing this to mind in the midst of our everyday existence makes life joyful.

Many of us don't have a full appreciation of the transformative power behind even the simplest acts of service. We learn of the importance of service at the very beginning of our path when we come from the darkness of the outer into the light of spiritual awareness. From that moment forward each one of us creates our own personal definition of service and determines how it best fits into our daily life. Practiced daily, Service soon becomes a way of life.

In the beginning it is easy to view service as more of a chore; something we do to justify the knowledge that we gain along our spiritual path. We learn about service through many of our other practices and gradually develop a deeper appreciation for it as we make progress on our path. Gradually we begin to recognize that Service is a joyful and rewarding way to connect with our inner awareness, with humanity, and with higher planes of consciousness. We never stop learning about the joys of Service. Let us never forget that we and our world both benefit from every act of service performed.

Note that one of the magical tools on the Magician's table in Key 1 of the Tarot major arcana is a cup or chalice. This chalice corresponds to the element of Alchemical Water and the Qabalistic world of Briah. This is called the World of Creation. On the Microcosmic Tree of Life, the Briatic triangle of Chesed, Geburah, and Tiphareth constitute the realm of the Higher Soul. The cup on the Magician's table is reminiscent of the one described in the stories of the Holy Grail. We can profit in exploring this relationship. Among the many possible correspondences for the Grail, one of the most intriguing for spiritual seekers is between the Grail and the Higher Soul.

Service plays a prominent role in the legend of the quest for the Grail. According to one version of the story, a Grail Seeker named Perceval finds the wounded Grail King and is allowed to hold the Grail. Perceval must then ask a question such as "Whom does the Grail serve?" If the question is asked, the quest is successful and Perceval becomes the Guardian of the Grail. Perceval's failure to ask a question in his first encounter with the Grail causes the Grail to disappear and Perceval's quest begins afresh. In most versions of the Grail legend the Grail Knight must prove his worthiness. Perceval does get a second chance and ends up years later achieving the Grail.

It has been said that the Grail is all things to all people. There are probably as many definitions for the Grail as there are Grail questers. The Grail might be a physical object or it might be something ethereal. It might be a holy relic or even a descendant of Jesus of Nazareth. It is almost always claimed to have spiritual or magical powers. It is reputed to heal or transform anyone who succeeds in achieving it. One thing is certain: it has excited the imaginations of many generations of Grail questers.

Whom does the grail serve? The best answer I have found is, "The Grail serves those who serve."

To whom do we offer our service? We know that both Humanity and our Higher Self emanate from the *One Source*, so that service in any capacity serves the All.

> *"There are those who seek knowledge for the sake of knowledge; that is Curiosity.*
> *There are those who seek knowledge to be known by others; that is Vanity.*
> *There are those who seek knowledge in order to serve; that is Love."* - St. Bernard of Clairvaux

"I seek to know in order to serve." This should be the declaration of those who approach the portal of initiation of a school of the Western mysteries. These words, or words like them, are impressed upon all candidates when they knock on the portal because they are words of power. They hold the Key for the candidate's advancement. For as long as the candidate takes these words to heart and begins to live according to their meaning, no door will remain closed to him or her.

Let us take a closer look at the words:

"I"

"I" refers to a conscious identification of the higher ego of self-consciousness with the *One*. The *One* is the Eheieh or *"I Am"* of Kether. Note that the title given to an Adept who has attained to the grade of 10=1 is Ipsissimus, or *"One Who is Most Himself."* Meditation on this can yield much understanding of the relationship of the *"I"* of Malkuth with the *"I"* of Kether. There is something healing and profound in the knowledge that the ultimate goal of the *Great Work* is to be and to become our True Self in body, in mind, and in spirit. Remember the words of the Master Jesus:

> *"The Father and I are One."* – John 10:30

"SEEK"

The Great Work is a quest to remember and to unite with who and what we truly are. This quest takes place on many levels. We seek ourselves, we seek our place in the world, and we seek the *One*. We seek to know ourselves and others as unique expressions of the *One*. The Master Jesus said:

> *"Ask, and it will be given to you; seek, and you will find; knock, and the door will be opened for you."*
> – Matthew 7:7

"TO KNOW"

Knowledge refers to Unity, Wholeness, and Love. On the Tree of Life, Knowledge or *Da'ath* represents the unity of Chokmah, or Wisdom, with Binah, or Understanding. Unity or *Achad* and Love or *Ahbah* are connected gematrically by the number 13. Knowledge of Self ultimately leads us to the *Knowledge and Conversation of the Holy Guardian Angel* (our Higher Soul). St. Paul of Tarsus wrote:

> *"For now we see in a mirror, dimly, but then we will see face to face. Now I know only in part; then I will know fully, even as I have been known."*

1 Corinthians 13:12

"IN ORDER TO SERVE"

Service is one of the most important Keys that open the portal leading to one's Higher Soul. Service must always be among our highest motivations and intentions. Service brings us closer to our Higher Soul and actually allows our Higher Soul to express itself through that Service. In the parable of the talents (Matthew 23: 14-30), the Master of the house says:

> *"Well done, Good and trustworthy servant; you have been trustworthy in a few things, I will put you in charge of many things; enter into the joy of your master."* – Matthew 25:23

In the quest to connect with our Higher Soul it seems logical to begin by trying to define it. We soon realize that we are trying to define something which cannot be defined. Any attempt to name it or to put a label on it or to define it in any other way is an attempt to put limitations on that which has no limits. This will not yield very satisfactory answers. Only by going within using meditation and other techniques will we be able to begin to understand the nature of our Higher Soul. Here is a profound Truth: Every conscious act of service gives expression to our True Self.

Remember the words of the Master Jesus from the Gospel of Thomas:

> *"The kingdom of God is not coming with things that can be observed; nor will they say, 'Look, here it is!' or 'There it is!' For, in fact, the kingdom of God is among* [or within] *you."*   - Luke 17:20-21

This Kingdom of Heaven includes the triad of our True Self on the Tree of Life.

If this Kingdom of Heaven is present within us here and now, how can we begin to recognize it?

Only by humbly offering ourselves up for what is called "*the Knowledge and Conversation of the Holy Guardian Angel*". Initiates are fortunate to have been given instructions on how to accomplish this in a gradual and methodical manner through their grade work. But it is up to each one of us to understand the lessons and to internalize them so that the necessary preparations will be made and the requisite changes will take place. This can be accomplished whether or not one is an initiate.

Remember Key 17, The Star. Tzaddi is a Hebrew word meaning 'fish hook'. But who is doing the fishing? Certainly we are when we open ourselves up in quiet expectation during our meditations. But by opening up, we become receptive to our Higher Soul and find that our Higher Soul is also fishing – for *US!* An excellent way for us to become even more receptive is for us to humbly offer ourselves in Service.

We now know WHOM we serve; But WHY do we serve? Is it because we believe it is the right thing to do? Are we just trying our best to fit into someone's definition of what it means to do good? This rationale is reasonable up to a point, but it can also fit into the category of doing the right thing for the wrong reasons.

Ultimately we seek to serve simply because it is a vital part of who we are. The desire comes from deep within us and we are merely expressing that desire. Remember, when we serve, we are giving expression to our Higher Souls!

This next bit is a paraphrase of comments made by the French Cabalist Carlo Suarez in his book "*The Second Coming of Reb YHSHWA – The Rabbi Called Jesus*." Suarez believed that the second coming of Jesus is happening right here, right now, as our consciousness is raised to the awareness that we are each in Him (or at least in His archetype). He states:

> *The easiest way to do this is to put ourselves at the service of our natural talents. If we do so without exploiting our talents for personal profit, then those talents are at the service of the One - Ourselves, our True Selves, all of humanity, and the One Source which is their origin.*
>
> *By becoming the humble servant of our natural talents, we open up channels that our True Selves will use. Gradually, we discover much more within us than we ever knew we had – more intelligence, more capacities, more inner gifts, and wider horizons. Our soul prospers, growing richly and vigorously.*
>
> *So let us never limit ourselves to what our environment has made us. We are much more than the labels that we and others use to define who we are. The more open our viewpoint, the greater our soul's harvest.*

Service is a deeply personal experience. Service can take on many forms and can be performed on many levels, often simultaneously. Each of us must go within and listen to our inner teacher as to how and where it can best be manifested.

When we first set out on the Path, we often have little idea what form our service will eventually take. Many of us do not recognize that the conscious act of placing ourselves on the Path of Return is itself an act of service.

We may not realize it at the time, but our mere presence is a service to ourselves and others. John Milton wrote these words in his poem titled On His Blindness: *"They also serve who only stand and wait."* What he is telling us is that regardless of our abilities or challenges, we all have a purpose that we unfailingly serve whether or not we are consciously aware of it. One of my F.L.O. fraters once said, *"Some of the most precious gifts we can give to one another are our time and our attention."*

Service does not involve sacrifice. We can give to others only what we ourselves possess. The Will to be of Service comes from the Will of the *One Source*. If we place ourselves in the cosmic stream of consciousness, this Divine Will becomes part of whom and what we are. Hidden forces of the cosmos become our allies when we offer ourselves for Service. Our pathway to Service becomes clear. We discover hidden talents within ourselves and reap unexpected benefits as a result of our Service. Service is one of the most noble and rewarding of the disciplines.

From the assimilating nature of Service we now move to the exalting nature of Simplicity. The result of the practice of Simplicity is the raising or exaltation of the Saturn energy to higher energy centers. This is the process of alchemical Sublimation.

[††] Paul Foster Case, *Hermetic Alchemy Science and Practice.*

Chapter 7
Simplicity

Correspondences for Simplicity

Qabalah:
the Hebrew letter Lamed, meaning "Ox Goad"
the Faithful Intelligence
the function of Work or Action
the North-West edge on the Cube of Space
the 22nd Path on the Tree of Life

Astrology:
the sign of Libra (7th house, cardinal air)
Rulership: Venus (Key 3 the Empress)
Exaltation: Saturn (Key 21 the World)

Alchemy:
Sublimation – (Stage 7) - Changing a Solid into a Gas by applying Heat (Analysis). Also the raising of kundalini energy from a lower center to a higher one.

Theurgy:
the discipline of Simplicity

Tarot:
Key 11, Justice
Key 21, the World
Key 3, the Empress

"No servant can serve two masters; for either he will hate the one and love the other, or he will be devoted to the one and despise the other. You cannot serve God and mammon."
Luke 16:13

For the purposes of this work I am associating the discipline of Simplicity with alchemical Sublimation. Psychologically, Sublimation changes unproductive and impure patterns of thoughts or actions into more positive ones. This is an accurate description of the aims of the discipline of Simplicity. We tend to think of living simply in terms of an uncomplicated lifestyle; eliminating what is not needed, or what is wasteful, or what is environmentally unsound. It is all this and more. We also need to enrich our lives with responsible choices that enhance both our inner and outer worlds. Simplicity helps us to more clearly recognize the consequences of our choices.

We have already mentioned the process of Sublimation in our investigations of several of the other disciplines. This underscores the importance of Sublimation for our spiritual development. The raising of kundalini is a natural process that occurs when certain conditions are met. It should be obvious by now how dangerous this would be if the body was not first prepared for the influx of higher consciousness. It is analogous to running 220 volt electricity into a house that is only wired to accommodate 110 volts. The results would be disastrous.

For this reason it is appropriate that the alchemical process of Distillation should come before Sublimation. We saw that the discipline of Service helps the body to assimilate more spiritual essence and thus speeds up the body changes that must occur before Sublimation takes place.

In the science of chemistry, Sublimation is the process of converting a solid by heat into a vapor. When cooled, the vapor becomes solid again without assuming a liquid form. In psychology, Sublimation is identified with a diversion of undesirable natural trends or impulses into more desirable types of behaviors or activities. This can be done by education and by conscious effort.

Paul Foster Case tells us that alchemical Sublimation is a combination of its chemical and psychological definitions. Also included is the concept of exaltation or elevation. For this reason, Case tells us that the exaltation of a planet in a sign of the zodiac serves to magnify the influence of that planet in alchemical work associated with that zodiacal sign. [tt]

The Hebrew letter Lamed is associated with the sign of Libra, and thus with Sublimation and Simplicity. About Lamed, the Sepher Yetzirah tells us that:

> *"The twenty-second path is called the Faithful Intelligence, because by it the powers of the Life-Breath are caused to multiply, and all dwellers on earth are merely under its shadow."*

Paul Foster Case tells us that to be *'under the shadow'* of the Faithful Intelligence is to be bound to the wheel of Karma. This is the cosmic law of cause and effect. Case says that *'Dwellers on earth'* refers to people whose consciousness and judgments are bound by the half-truths and illusions presented to them by their physical senses. [tt]

This is the state of the vast majority of the human race. There are always a few individuals who are able to know the Reality behind the illusions of physical existence. [tt] Case tells us that their numbers are increasing with each new generation. These individuals have absolute faith in the perfect law of the cosmos, and that faith manifests as *the Faithful Intelligence.*

Today's exoteric science is based on laws that are largely derived from observing nature. Inferences are made about causes and effects manifest in the natural world. The laws of science are modified or replaced when they no longer offer a satisfactory explanation for our observations. Cosmic law was established at the beginning of time and is undeviating and just in all circumstances. Ultimately the laws of the natural world have their genesis in cosmic law but the exoteric sciences have yet to adequately acknowledge this.

Upon learning that our inner consciousness is subject to the same laws that apply to the physical world, some incorrectly conclude that we are under the influence of forces beyond our control. Everything that happens on the personal level is the result of pre-existing causes. But there exists in each of us something above the personality, above the continuous series of cause and effect. This is the *One Source*, that center of the world of causes. The goal of practical occultism is to teach us to become consciously aware of our identity with the *One Source.* This will lead us to freedom from seemingly endless cycles of Karma. [††]

This release is also under the reign of law. We cannot hope to attain higher levels of consciousness until our bodies and our personalities have ripened to the point where they can safely become a vehicle for our Higher Souls. We discovered this in our exploration of Distillation and Service.

We can see now that the faith of the occultist is primarily faith in cosmic law. To establish this faith we must become aware of the working of cause and effect in our inner realms.

This takes time and effort. Paul Foster Case asserts that It is just as difficult to change our thoughts as it is to change our actions. He asserts that we will build our faith if we work with Tarot Key 11, Justice. [tt]

Key 11 and Lamed are assigned the 22nd path on the Tree of Life, connecting the sphere of Geburah with Tiphareth. Qabalistic analyses of the numbers 11 and 22 yield results that are similar. 11 is the expression of 1 - the outpouring of the limitless Life-power through the initiative, specialization and concentration of the *One Source* – using the vehicle of the archetypal 1 itself. This carries much of the same significance of the Rosicrucian grade of Ipsissimus, he who is most himself. 22 is the expression of 2 – Wisdom - the reflection of the perfect self-consciousness of the *One Source* through the vehicle of itself. Both 11 and 22 reflect the perfect balance of universal forces pictured in the Justice Key. Balance is again emphasized by the fact that Key 11 is the middle, or balance point of Keys 1 through 21. [tt]

The number 11 can indicate a new beginning, but one that can benefit from the wisdom and experience gained in traveling the previous 10 letter-paths. Libra is cardinal air and so our guiding principle here is primarily mental. Balance, poise, and peace are characteristic of Libra. Balance is illustrated in Key 11 by both the sword and the scales. [tt]

Paul Foster Case tells us the sword in the woman's right hand is made of steel, the metal corresponding to Mars. He says the red color of the woman's robe in the Justice Key is one indicator of the importance of the active Mars energy on the processes of Sublimation (and by association, Simplicity.) A sword has two edges and can represent a number of dualities. A sword can be used to build up and protect, or it can be used to destroy. It can be used to take action or it can be used to eliminate waste and the hesitation that prevents us from taking action. Case further tells us that the sword is a reference to the discrimination of Zain in Key 6, the Lovers. [tt]

Paul Foster Case tells us that the scales in the woman's left hand are made of gold. This represents solar energy or light. Gold may therefore be used to weigh and measure action. The speed of light and its mass are scientific constants used to demonstrate the electromagnetic nature of all that we call "matter." He tells us that future discoveries based on this knowledge will undoubtedly present humanity with new standards of action and make possible a manifestation of the "undeviating justice" represented so eloquently by the energy of Geburah. Justice, as the title of Key 11, implies the active administration of law. It is also reminiscent of the ideas of balance, poise, exactitude, accuracy, impartiality, and equity. [tt]

Paul Foster Case writes that the position of the sword and the scales tells us much about the position of the path of Lamed on the Tree of Life. Note that the sword in the woman's right hand points upward toward the sphere of Geburah. The scales in the woman's left hand represent the balance of the sphere of Tiphareth. [tt]

An archetypal figure for the woman with the scales is the Egyptian goddess Ma'at. Among other things, Ma'at is the goddess of truth, justice, and law. One of her roles is to weigh the hearts of the dead to determine their fate in the afterlife. The heart is weighed against the feather of Ma'at. If the heart is too heavy, the soul will be sent back for another round of incarnation. If light enough, the soul will be sent on to enjoy the rewards of the afterlife. [tt]

The woman in Key 8 has blonde hair and is wearing a green cape.. Case tells us this identifies her with Venus and makes her an aspect of the Creative Imagination of Key 3. We may also identify her with the woman who tames the lion in Key 8. In some exoteric Tarot decks, Key 8 is Justice and Key 11 is Strength. This is a blind, as can be seen if one considers the attributions of the Hebrew letters to the signs of the zodiac. [tt]

Paul Foster Case tells us that the fact that Key 8 and Key 11 can be interchanged shows us that they are two aspects of the same power. This power is Creative Imagination, symbolized by the Empress Key. All imagination is based on memory, and so the women in Keys 3, 8, and 11 are all aspects of our subconscious mind. The subconscious mind is represented by the High Priestess in Key 2. [tt]

The fact that 11 is the balance point between 1 and 21 suggests that with Key 11, we begin a new phase of our spiritual journey. It is fitting, therefore, that we use Simplicity at this point to help us jettison anything that might slow or impede our future progress. We now embark on a higher cycle of manifestation equipped with all the knowledge and experience gained during the previous sequence of ten Keys.

Purified and disciplined, our personalities are now able to recognize the *One Life* manifesting itself throughout the material universe. We now have the ability to discriminate between "right" and "wrong." Case tells us that being the spiritual descendants of Adam and Eve, we are now able to make productive use of the fruit of the Tree of the Knowledge of Good and Evil. [tt]

The 22nd Path of Wisdom on the Tree of Life is attributed to Lamed, and to Libra. Libra is an air sign and is ruled by Venus. On this 22nd path of Lamed, we experience a temperate and mediating influence between the radiant light of Tiphareth and the fiery power of Geburah. Lamed translates to ox goad. The ox of Aleph is the symbol of Air and of Ruach, the Life-breath. [††]

Lamed is not only associated with airy Libra, but itself has an airy purpose. Lamed multiplies and distributes the powers of Aleph in ways that are harmonious with Divine justice and perfect equilibrium. Paul Foster Case tells us that the 22nd path is related to the entire tree because of the totality of the 22 paths that connect the ten Sephiroth. [††]

Again citing Paul Foster Case, Aleph and Lamed form the word "Al" or "El" which means *"God the Mighty One."* Together we associate them with the idea of the airy power of the primal and undirected Life-breath being controlled by direction and purpose. Lamed can be thought of as a teacher whose instruction and correction guides us through all of the cycles that comprise the grand cycle of birth, death, and rebirth. Case points out that when we add up the letters of Lamed (Lamed-Mem-Daleth) we get 74. He tells us this is the number of *sabib* (Samekh-Beth-Yod-Beth) which means "circle or circuit." It is also the number of *od* (Ayin-Daleth) which means "eternity," which brings us back to the Lamed as the "Faithful Intelligence." [††]

Amen (Aleph-Mem-Nun) is the Hebrew word for "faithful." The sum of its letters is 91. Case tells us that the sum of Tetragrammaton (Yod-Heh-Vav-Heh , 26) and *Adonai* (Aleph-Daleth-Nun-Yod, 65) is 91. *Adonai* can mean "Lord of Manifestation" and is frequently used in the Hebrew Bible as a substitute for Tetragrammaton in order to prevent taking the name of God in vain. [††]

Amen is also a name of Kether. Case tells us that Amen is associated with the idea of the original motivational impulse from which everything else proceeds. In Lamed we have the maturation of discrimination. This discrimination is then translated into motives for action. [tt]

The meaning of Aleph – the ox – in relation to Lamed - the ox goad - is that education, in the form of the ox goad, has balance as its purpose. This requires us to discard our unnecessary and outworn forms. This education is followed by action and work. This work is alchemical Sublimation and the discipline of Simplicity. [tt]

As we saw earlier, Sublimation is the largely physical process of raising the energy of the Saturn center with the aid of Venus (desire and mental imagery). In other words, this is the raising of the kundalini energy to higher levels of consciousness through the use of mental images during meditation.

The element of Air is involved, as breath control is essential to the work of Sublimation. We have seen previously that breath control is an effective means of increasing our ability to concentrate. A simple and balanced (and therefore safe) method is to slowly breathe in, holding, and then slowly releasing the breath. Increase the time for each cycle as you become more accustomed to it.

Paul Foster Case writes that the imagery of the Justice Key suggests that elimination is a part of the Sublimation process. Libra rules the kidneys, which are organs of elimination. During Sublimation, we eliminate the mental imagery that we do not wish to see manifested. Discrimination and imagination are needed in order to choose the proper images for elimination. We need to define what it is that we do want. This is a type of limitation and is associated with Saturn. The handle of the sword is shaped like a T, our English equivalent of the Hebrew letter Tav (Key 21, the World). In the B.O.T.A. Tarot deck, the woman in the Justice Key wears a collar that bears the shape of the letter T. The path of Tav is the path of Saturn.[††]

Elimination is also a function of Simplicity and should not be a negative or painful process. If the elimination process is unpleasant, we are not doing it properly. We focus on mental images – ruled by Venus – of what it is that we do want to manifest. Concentration is part of the elimination process because we focus on what we want to the exclusion of everything else. In Simplicity we choose a desirable personal goal and exclude anything which does not contribute to the manifestation of that objective.

When we focus our attention on something, we increase the intensity of the light available through our consciousness. Plants love light! Whatever we plant in our interior gardens will grow even faster when we focus on them. Unfortunately, any weeds that are present will also grow. It is much easier to control them if we focus only on what we desire to manifest.

Must we diligently focus on what is that we want? Must we always have this work on our minds? Not at all! Eliphas Levi wrote, *"The way to see is not always to be looking."* But we must choose recreation that really does re-create, refresh, and renew us. And keep that sword of discrimination handy to cut off any thoughts that interfere with complete rest and relaxation.

To what degree should we simplify our lives? That is a decision that each one of us will make. We need to take stock of our lives and make note of what is serving to bring us closer to our goals and desires. Is there something missing that would help us reach our goals? Conscious retention and acquisition of those things which serve us should be our primary goal. After that, we can narrow our choices to those things which also serve our environment, our world, and all creatures everywhere.

Duane Elgin, in his book *Voluntary Simplicity*, proposes five qualities that describe a lifestyle of Simplicity.

Elgin's first quality is Material Simplicity. The American Friends Service Society defines simple living as *"a non-consumerist lifestyle based upon being and becoming, not having."* In other words, our external possessions and our internal thoughts and beliefs must serve our goals and purposes. We were not created to be servants to our possessions.

Simplicity does not always equate with monetary savings. High quality, non-mass produced items can often cost more than their higher-in-demand counterparts. Each of us will need to determine our level and pattern of consumption in our daily lives. The cost of any item or service is not always reflective of its suitability. Material items need to become supportive of, rather than central to, our personal growth.

His second quality is Human Scale. Whenever possible, we need to orient our lives according to a personal, human scale. Corporations and large cities tend to be antithetical to Simplicity. This theme touches many areas of our lives. Our living and working environments as well as the institutions that support them should be decentralized into more understandable and manageable units. Our efforts should be on a scale where we can know our contributions to the whole. Doing this gives us a sense of shared rewards and responsibility.

Elgin's third quality of Simplicity is Self-Determination. Simplicity requires us to be consciously aware of our choices and their effects. This leads to a greater control over the direction of our lives and to be able to disconnect from control by others. It will also be possible for us to be able to place less value on the expectations of others.

His fourth quality is Ecological Awareness. Simplicity acknowledges our interconnection and interdependence to all of Humanity and to all of Nature. We recognize that the Earth provides a finite quantity of resources, some of which are renewable and some of which are not. If allowed to proceed uncontrolled, our capacity to destroy and to pollute the environment far exceeds Nature's capacity to regenerate and cleanse itself. If we develop a sense of global citizenship we become more aware of the effects we have on others. If we nurture this sense of global citizenship we become better stewards of Nature and more compassionate about the welfare of all of our brothers and sisters on this planet.

The fifth quality Elgin proposes is Personal Growth. While not necessarily a spiritual objective, some level of spirituality plays an integral part. As students of the Western mysteries, we are able to put Simplicity into perspective as a tool for spiritual growth. When we focus on interior and exterior Simplicity, obstacles that impede our spiritual growth are removed. The quality of our life is raised just as the Saturn force is raised in our bodies during Sublimation.

Technology in each generation continues to produce improvements in the quality of our lives. In the last hundred years, many diseases have been cured, transportation and communication have been vastly accelerated, and the quality and variety of our food supply has increased. Today human nature has turned many of the benefits of technology into' too much of a good thing." It is easy to see the negative side of technology. The "back to nature" movement is one of those that believe the negatives of technology outweigh its positives. It is easy to see why some would be willing to eliminate technology in an effort to heal the planet. But let us not forget all the good that technology has accomplished. Discrimination allows us to find a balance so that technology can continue to be a valuable servant.

The spiritual discipline of Simplicity is not about sacrifice. Sacrifice is giving up of something which holds value for us in order to receive something we value even more. Practitioners of the Western mysteries recognize that Simplicity is not just eliminating unnecessary waste and practices from their lives. It equally involves acts of conscious retention. We don't have to get rid of things that we love, use or need. We just have to be intentional about what is kept. Retain what is joyful and get rid of what is not. Be aware of what fills one's life. Fill it with what brings joy and empty from it what brings stress.

We are free to retain those things which make our lives comfortable and familiar – so long as they do not interfere with our relationship with the inner realms of consciousness or with friends and loved ones. We have come to rely on electronic media and conveniences. When used in a balanced way, they free up time for us to engage in other activities. When we become overly reliant on them or when their use insulates us from personal contact with others, we need to reconsider how we use them.

Knowledge that there exists cosmic law that can be observed and understood by carefully studying the natural world fills us with a sense of peace and empowerment. When we understand that there is order and control in the Universe, we are able to take control of everything in our life. What a marvelous gift!

Simplicity brings Unity with higher planes of consciousness. It works in both the inner and the outer along with the discipline of Fasting to rid our lives of clutter. Remember that the discipline of Fasting is not just about regulating our intake of food. It is also about establishing control over what we see, hear, think, read, write, and speak. Unity is freedom. Duplicity brings anxiety and fear. Unity is an inward Reality that manifests outwardly in how we live. We speak truthfully and directly. We no longer crave status and position. When we achieve the inner center we are no longer distracted by the psychotic and fragmented outer world. Without the Unity within, covetousness is called ambition; hoarding is called prudence; greed is called industry. The consumer society feeds insecurities and thrives on what it feeds.

Asceticism and Simplicity are not the same. Asceticism renounces possessions. Simplicity puts them in proper perspective. Simplicity reorients our priorities so that possessions can be enjoyed without becoming a burden.

The practices of Simplicity set us apart from others in our society. This can invite derision and scorn from segments of our society whose vested interests are threatened by our refusal to think and act in accordance with the group mind. As independent thinkers, our actions cannot be easily predicted or influenced. Simplicity makes us identifiably different because it brings freedom from anxiety without being irresponsible. We give of ourselves without expectation of recognition or reward. We stand firm when the world appears to be collapsing. It is not surprising when Simplicity makes the people around us uncomfortable.

In summation, Simplicity is transformation through the power of discrimination. Discrimination directs Ruach, the Life-breath, into a specific action. Simplicity is consciously choosing options that will direct us toward the manifestation of our desire. If that desire is compatible with the *One Will*, we find it easier to make progress on our spiritual journey.

The work we do in Sublimation and Simplicity actually stimulates physiological processes in the body and creates physical changes. Solids in the blood are converted into gases through specialized brain cells employed in the Work. The gases then condense into solids that facilitate spiritual development. These solids, in the words of Paul Foster Case, are "the solid conditions of external circumstance." Case tells us that   without any effort to conceal, we can say that this is what really happens. [tt]

Paul Foster Case further tells us that one function of our human brain is to provide mental matrices which are used to create our physical world. These matrices are made up of mental images. This imagery has its origin in certain solids of the blood. The mental images are taken up by the processes of our imagination and are then solidified into physical forms of the images. Adepts who are well practiced at this process of manifestation can create at great speed; so much so that their works appear to be miracles. We may not get our results so quickly, but as we gain experience, we too can be thought to create "miracles." [tt]

After looking at the discipline of Simplicity with its exalting nature, we now take a look at Solitude with its disintegrating nature. The experience of Solitude can often be uncomfortable. It is a largely subconscious process and a very necessary one. Once again we are faced with the removal of certain thoughts and beliefs, but only those which impede our spiritual unfoldment.

[tt] Paul Foster Case, *Hermetic Alchemy Science and Practice.*

Chapter 8
Solitude

Correspondences for Solitude

Qabalah:
the Hebrew Letter Nun, meaning "Fish"
the Imaginative Intelligence
Transformation
the function of Motion
the South-West edge on the Cube of Space
the 24th Path of Nun on the Tree of Life

Astrology:
the sign of Scorpio (8th house, fixed water)
Rulership: Mars (Key 16 the Tower)
Exaltation: Uranus (Key 0 the Fool)

Alchemy:
Putrefaction – (Stage 8) - Disintegrating into constituent parts

Theurgy:
the discipline of Solitude

Tarot:
Key 13, Death Key
16, the Tower

"But whenever you pray, go into your room and shut the door and pray to your Father who is in secret; and your Father who sees in secret will reward you."
Matthew 6:6

In the discipline of Simplicity and the alchemical stage of Sublimation, we engage the self-conscious mind to reorder our priorities according to our spiritual needs. With the alchemical stage of Putrefaction that follows Sublimation, we disengage the self-conscious mind while spirit transforms our subconscious mind. The Mars energy is directed at the personality, breaking it down – but not destroying it – and a new vision of the meaning of personality flashes upon us like the lightning bolt in Key 16 of the Tarot.

If we are wise, we anticipate this period of subconscious transformation following our experience of Sublimation and create the time and space for this to occur, even if we only have a short time to break away from our busy outer lives. It is far better to devote time to solitude than to experience the effects of this transformation while attempting to carry on with the usual routines of our lives. Practically speaking, of course, this is not always possible.

In the Putrefaction that follows Sublimation it is though someone has turned out the lights and moved the furniture. For a time we go stumbling about in the dark bumping into things. We are disoriented and forget that we can call upon our Higher Soul to help us navigate through the darkness and search for the light switch.

In those times of psychological upheaval following our experiences of Sublimation the practice of Solitude is essential to properly dealing with the upheaval and confusion brought on by the breaking down of our old personality. This is why I am associating Solitude with the alchemical stage of Putrefaction and the astrological sign of Scorpio.

During Putrefaction much of what we thought we knew about our lives is strewn around us like the ruins of the Tower in Key 16. The resulting confusion can throw us into a psychological state called '*the Dark Night of the Soul*'. The self-denial involved with Putrefaction is the loss of the old life so that new life may rise like the phoenix from its ruins.

Putrefaction is the loss of a false interpretation of life, and this loss is absolutely necessary in order that a more accurate interpretation of life may be found. We know that life is continuous. What appears to be a death is only a transformation. In the same instant as the lightning flash, a new personality begins to appear as is depicted on Key 19 of the Tarot, the Sun. We exchange our limited (and essentially non-existent) personal power for the limitless and truly existent Life-power of the *One Source*.[††]

The function associated with the letter Nun and the discipline of Solitude is motion. All motion is change. With Solitude we are dealing primarily with *interior* motion and the associated idea of transformation. According to Paul Foster Case, Nun is associated with the ideas of cause, origin, source, mainspring, groundwork, and leaven. Combining these ideas, Case tells us we may deduce that change is the basis of manifestation. One lesson that must be learned at this stage is that physical death is not the end of existence. It is appropriate that Key 13, Death, corresponds to this discipline of Solitude.[††]

Paul Foster Case writes that the Hebrew letter Nun means 'fish.' A fish represents a power that lives in the Waters. It knows the rhythm and pulse of these life-giving waters. The letter Nun has a value of 50 which reduces to 5. 5 is the number of Heh, which is the archetype of universal life. The Hebrew word for death is *maveth*, spelled Mem-Vav-Tav. The letters of *maveth* total to 446, which reduces to 14 and further reduces to 5. [††]

Case tells us that Nun written in full equals 756. 756 reduces to 18, and further reduces to 9. The Hebrew word for life is *chai*, Cheth-Yod. *Chai* totals to 18, which reduces to 9. Nun can mean *to sprout* or *to generate*. Case says that this associates Nun with the procreative power of Scorpio, the sign of the Mars or creative energy. All of these associations of Nun revolve around the idea of life, death, and transformation through generation and regeneration. [††]

The Dark Night of the Soul, the spiritual experience famously described by St. John of the Cross, is a part of the experience of alchemical Putrefaction. The meaning of this experience harkens back to the meaning of Tarot Key 13, Death. Key 13 is about transformation, not physical death. Again, the function attached to Nun and Key 13 is movement. Death is transformation, a type of movement. Death is not an end to life. The Life-Force continues on in another form. As dark and hopeless as the Dark Night experience may feel, it is not a permanent condition.

The experience of the Dark Night is similar to that of depression. We may experience it for prolonged periods. We may even experience it more than once on our spiritual journey. But if we recognize that it is a natural part of our growth process, we may summon the strength to persevere through it. We may even unfold the Wisdom we need to make the process easier and shorter.

Paul Foster Case writes that we must think of the Dark Night as being a part of the cosmic cycle of birth, death, and rebirth. This cycle is found everywhere and on all levels of existence. This cycle is present wherever the Life-breath of Aleph is active. Wherever Life creates new forms, old forms must first be swept away to make room. The Dark Night is part of the sweeping away of the remnants of our old personality in order for our new personality to function. [tt]

Sages tell us to rejoice when we have the Dark Night experience. As it is written in Matthew's Gospel:

> *"Blessed are ye, when men shall revile you, and persecute you, and shall say all manner of evil against you falsely, for my sake."* - Matthew 5:11

Paul Foster Case tells us that if we apply this verse inwardly, we see that we will meet with internal resistance and hostility when we see the Truth revealed by the higher planes and begin to live our lives according to this Truth. But as we persevere through these trials, we will receive assistance from these planes and our lives will be enriched both inwardly and outwardly.

There are many things that can trigger a Dark Night of the Soul. It can be triggered by an external event, perhaps a natural disaster. It can be triggered by the death of someone close, especially if that death is premature or unexpected. Perhaps we have built up our life and given it meaning based on our achievements, our activities, and our sense of who we are. Suddenly the things that gave our life meaning collapse around us. [tt]

The Dark Nigh can occur if something happens that we can't explain away, something which deeply contradicts what we thought we knew about life. What has actually collapsed is the collection of illusions and half-truths that were created by our old personality. [tt]

The result is that we come to a dark place in our life, with no immediate explanation of how we got there or where we will go from there. When we do emerge from our Dark Night experience, we will possess a transformed state of consciousness. During the Dark Night our subconscious has been busily working below our range of perception and our personality has been transformed. Life has meaning once again, but often it is an abstract meaning that cannot be easily put into words. [tt]

From this point we awaken into something deeper, something which is not based solely on the perceptions of our personality. Paul Foster Case tells us that when alchemical Putrefaction has done its work, we emerge with a greater sense of purpose and a deeper connection with our inner teacher and the other inner planes of consciousness. We experience a kind of rebirth. What dies is our personality based sense of self. A new personality is formed that understands the Reality beyond the reach of our physical senses. Again, this rebirth of our personality is pictured on B.O.T.A. Tarot Key 19, The Sun. [tt]

On the Cube of Space, the letter Nun is assigned to the direction South-West. This edge of the Cube joins the South face (Key 19, The Sun) to the West face (Key 10, Wheel of Fortune, Jupiter). Qabalistically, Keys 10 and 19 are linked because both 10 and 19 reduce to 1. Case writes that psychologically, alchemical Putrefaction involves a combination of the ideas symbolized by Keys 19 and 10. When false conceptions of Reality are eliminated, a personality with true conceptions of Reality arises. This is symbolized by the figures of the two children on

Key 19. They represent our newborn self-conscious and subconscious minds. [tt]

This is an application of the idea pictured in Key 10. Paul Foster Case tells us that, *"Any particular event is really a manifestation of the cyclic transformation or rotation of the One Thing through the various phases of its self-expression."* Each event is analogous to a point on the rim of a turning wheel. All events are continuous with all other events, just as there is no break in the Life-breath's manifestation. [tt]

We fear death because we misunderstand the forces of transformation involved. Case tells us that these are the subhuman forces of the Mars energy that are involved with sexual reproduction. These forces are depicted as the red lion in Key 8, Strength. We see in this Key that through love and the correct use of the mental imagery of Creative Imagination, these forces may be tamed and harnessed for use in creating on higher planes of consciousness. This is the idea behind the title for the letter Nun, *the Creative Intelligence.* [tt]

Paul Foster Case asserts that physical changes will occur in our bodies, and we can prolong our life-spans indefinitely if we rightly understand and utilize the laws of the cosmos. Understanding of these laws will not come until we overcome our fears of death and dying by right knowledge, and by the proper interpretation of the phenomena involved in physical dissolution. [tt]

Because the transformations associated with alchemical Putrefaction are largely internal, it is desirable for us to seek to minimize outer distractions. Great spiritual avatars from traditions around the world did this by seeking solitude combined at times with Prayer, Meditation, and Fasting. We would profit by following their example and allowing our inner transformation to occur in solitude.

We must not cultivate the idea that Solitude is somehow superior to being with others. We need times for both in order to function as balanced individuals. In particular, we need to cultivate a sense of intentional community. We need to choose people who can give value and meaning to our life. This creates a vibrant and living organism of individuals, each of which draws sustenance from the whole and contributes to the functioning and health of the whole. In those times when we do withdraw to recreate ourselves and strengthen our bonds with the *One*, we return to our community refreshed and better able to participate. In *Life Together,* Lutheran Pastor Dietrich Bonhoeffer wrote:

> *"Only in fellowship do we learn to be rightly alone and only in aloneness do we learn to be rightly in fellowship."*

There are a few things we can do to make our times in Solitude more productive and bearable.

First, we need to pay attention to the things that seem to distract us and cause discomfort. What is it that bothers us? Do we have desires that would tempt us away from our spiritual path? Solitude is a perfect time to address these challenges. Suppressing or denying these feelings is not productive. It would be useful during our time of solitude to make a record of the things we need to address. Also make a record of the positive things about ourselves that we would like to reinforce.

It would be profitable for us to make the practice of Solitude a regular part of our life. Most of us do not need to go out into the wilderness and fast for forty days. We should make an appointment with ourselves to spend a few moments each day in silence and solitude. This will send a clear message to our subconscious that Solitude is important to us.

This may be incorporated into our daily practice of Prayer and Meditation. We need to make ourselves physically comfortable and mentally alert. We may choose to remain seated in our meditation posture or do a walking or moving meditation. If we make Solitude enjoyable, it will be easier for us to make it a regular practice.

Inertia can be a problem for us until Solitude becomes like an acquired habit. We can find all sorts of excuses not to do the work. This applies not just to Solitude, but to all spiritual practices. This is a real test of our readiness to make spiritual progress. Inertia can be encountered anywhere along our path. The remedy is to consciously focus on our spiritual goals, make a plan for achieving them, and then carry out the plan. It is our actions, not our intentions that make the most impact on our subconscious mind.

The demands of our daily lives can quickly exhaust us physically, mentally, emotionally, and spiritually. It is important to incorporate rest and recreation into our times of Solitude. Let us not allow ourselves to become so busy that we don't notice ourselves becoming tired. The still, small voice of our Holy Guardian Angel cannot be heard until we make the effort to still the other voices competing for our attention. Let us make a regular practice of giving our bodies the rest, exercise, nutrition, and water that they need to maintain its health. If we enter into Solitude with relatively sound bodies, we will have more time to focus on our inner health.

Allow the emptiness we feel to be filled with an awareness of spiritual Reality. Let us not deny or suppress our feelings, but deal with them squarely. The dark night of the soul can be a shattering experience if we have not made a connection with our higher realms of consciousness. Solitude is a time for going within and strengthening this connection. We will find that the space once occupied by our feelings of emptiness can now be filled with the joy of communing with the consciousness of the *One*.

Solitude is a time for personal honesty. Let us face ourselves as we truly are, so that we may not delay the work that most needs to be done. Let us remember that each of us is a unique expression of the *One Source* and we cannot conceal ourselves from its sight. Let us make a confession and ask for forgiveness and healing. Let us use this time for becoming more familiar with the qualities of our new personalities that are able to hear the voice of our inner teacher and are willing to respond to it.

> *Then Jesus said to them all, "If any want to become my followers, let them deny themselves and take up their cross daily and follow me. For those who want to save their life will lose it, and those who lose their life for my sake will save it."* – Luke 9:23-24

We examined one meaning of this passage in the introduction. Again, when the Mars energy is active in the alchemical process, our old personalities, along with their illusions and misconceptions, are deconstructed into their constituent parts.. This deconstruction is part of alchemical Putrefaction. We immediately create new personalities and new understandings of our personalities are revealed to us like a flash of lightening. [tt]

The self-denial referred to in the passage above is not a punishment. It is not the denial of anything that brings us true happiness such as something we like to eat, or an activity that gives us pleasure. Self-denial is the rejection of a personality that bases its ideas of self-hood on lies, illusions and half-truths. It is a complete reversal of our former philosophy of life. [tt]

This reversal is pictured in Key 12 of the Tarot, the Hanged Man. Key 12 corresponds to alchemical Water, and alchemists tell us that moist heat is needed to stabilize our understanding of our new personalities. This' moist heat' is the combined actions of Keys 16 and 12, the Mars energy and Alchemical Water. [tt]

Continuing our look at the passage quoted above, 'to take up' can also mean 'to keep the mind in suspense.' Both 'take up' and 'cross' have definitions that are specific to the Mysteries. We are told to 'take up our cross daily.' The cross pictured in Key 12 is a gallows. This gallows is shaped like the letter Tav, corresponding to Saturn. [tt]

Putting this all together, this passage from Luke's gospel is telling us to raise the Saturn energy at the base of the spine to the higher centers of energy. This activates the energy of the Mars center, which then becomes available to the higher centers as well. This is alchemical Sublimation and we are told to make this a daily practice. It should be practiced regularly until it becomes second nature. [tt]

Sublimation is accomplished when we totally reject the idea that anything we may feel, think, say, do, or experience is the result of our own personal effort. Spiritual inspiration can only originate in levels of consciousness above our personality. [tt]

The 15th century English alchemist George Ripley states that Putrefaction takes 90 nights. This is part of an allegory. Paul Foster Case tells us that 90 is the total of Mem (Water) spelled out as Mem-Yod-Mem. 90 is also the value or power of the letter Tzaddi (Key 17, The Star). The function of Key 17 is meditation. Ripley states that Putrefaction results in a black powder. [††]

Case tells us that this is no allegory. When we meditate on the fact that nothing in our life originates from the personality, we rightly perceive that everything is the manifestation of the *One Thing* that appears to our personality as *No Thing*, or darkness. This darkness is the Ain Soph Aur, or Limitless Light. [††]

Being separated from it by the Abyss below the supernal triad on the Tree of Life, we are unable to perceive the brilliance of its light and we call it darkness. It is written in the Gospel of St. John, *"And the Light shineth in darkness; and the darkness comprehended it not."* This light has been described by mystics as having a grainy texture, like a powder. [††]

In Key 13, Death, the reaper is a white skeleton. In astrology, Capricorn, ruled by Saturn, rules the bones. This tells us that the Saturn energy is also active here. We have already stated that the Mars energy (ruler of Scorpio) is active in Putrefaction. However, the Mars force cannot be sublimated until it is roused into activity by the rising of the Saturn energy from below. Paul Case points out that In Key 13 the reaper's scythe has a blade of steel (Mars energy). The Handle of the scythe is in the shape of a T (Tav, Saturn energy). [††]

On the Southern edge of Key 13 in the foreground is a rose bush bearing a single white rose. The rose, sacred to Venus, has long been a symbol of desire, and a white rose   represents purified desire. Intentions are important, but without desire, we would have nothing to manifest. Purified desire is achieved when we are able to bring our self-conscious and subconscious minds into balance.

The Fool in Key 0 holds a single white rose in his left hand. The Fool is associated with the energy of Uranus, one of the modern planets. Uranus is exalted in the sign of Scorpio which is associated with alchemical Putrefaction and the discipline of Solitude.

Holding a white rose, the Fool is telling us that the way for us to achieve perfection in our physical body is to control and balance the forces of desire that originate as sexual energy in our Mars center. Again, our desire is purified when our self-conscious and subconscious minds are in balance. It can be said that the main purpose of all of the Keys of the Tarot major arcana is to instruct us in the process of balancing these two aspects of ourselves so that our desire nature may be purified.

Comparing Keys 0 and 13, we see that the cut white rose in Key 0 has taken root in Key 13 and will continue to grow and to thrive. This tells us that when we focus on the proper mental imagery during the process of Putrefaction, our self-conscious and subconscious minds will rise out of the black residue of our Dark Night of the Soul, balanced and purified.

We are like plants which draw from the earth the nourishment that will enable us to grow according to our own unique patterns. In Western initiatory systems, new initiates are often called Neophytes, or 'new plants." Initiates and non-initiates alike need to use the fullness of their minds to create a mental image of what we desire to manifest. We should choose the highest and most detailed desire that we can possibly imagine.

Desire is the engine of our human evolution. No matter what it is that we desire in any moment, there is always a higher desire drawing us to the next horizon. For the present, we must focus solely on our current desire. Let us think carefully about whether our latest acquisition is truly our highest desire. If it is not, we still learn from it. Sometimes we insist on learning through pain and hardship, but we do learn.

Many of the folklore and fairy tales of today have their origin in the wise men and women of the ancient race that gave us the Ageless Wisdom. Many of these tales are about wishes that were granted even though the ones who made the wishes could have made better choices. In fairy tales it is often our fairy godmother that grants wishes. Our subconscious mind plays the role of our fairy godmother and grants our wish if we wholeheartedly desire it and focus on it. If we choose poorly, we defer manifesting those things that would truly help us, but it may have been necessary for us to have experienced our lower desires first in order to appreciate our higher ones.

We have been given a formula for manifesting our desires at the highest level. This formula is stated in the words of the Lord's Prayer found in the Christian New Testament. In his aspect as God the Son, we pray to the Christ consciousness that is our own Higher Soul. We pray that his Kingdom (Malkuth) may come, and that his Will be done in earth and in heaven. Earth is our physical existence. We pray that the same Will that manifests on the plane of our Higher Soul will be made manifest in our own body.

A distinction must be made between solitude and loneliness. Many people fear loneliness. Fear of being alone compels one to seek noise and crowds. Television and other media have become surrogate companions and babysitters. Loneliness is a sign of inner emptiness. Attempts to fill this void with anything less than our own true Self will prove futile. Solitude is inner fulfillment. It is inner attentiveness to the voice of our Holy Guardian Angel. In Psalms it is written:

"Be still, and know that I am God! I am exalted among the nations; I am exalted in the earth."
Psalms 46:10

To hear the 'still small voice' of our Holy Guardian Angel requires the practice of several of the Spiritual Disciplines. We must work diligently to eliminate illusion and the chatter of false voices before we can still the mind enough to hear the True Voice. When we hear this voice we can be with others meaningfully. Our words may be few but when spoken they carry weight and value.

The purpose of Solitude and silence is to enable us to see and hear the Reality behind the illusions presented by our physical senses. Silence does not always mean the absence of noise. It also means control over what is seen and heard. It is control over the mental images one focuses on. Let us remember to weed out the negative mental images in our Magician's garden by focusing only on what it is that we desire to manifest. We will know when to speak and when not to speak. Those who are silent when they should speak are weak. Those who speak when they should be silent are fools.

When Solitude is taken seriously, it leads us to the experience called *the dark night of the soul.* Putrefaction is the alchemical term for this Dark Night. Putrefaction is both deeply transformative and deeply disturbing. Putrefaction presents us with gross, repulsive, disgusting, and loathsome 'stuff' from within our deepest self. This is a deeply creative process of being courageous enough to see all of our "stuff" without self-criticism, feeling sorry for ourselves, reverting to infantile need-fulfilling behaviors, or misinterpreting what is really going on. The result is sensitivity and compassion. This is freedom from the fear of being alone and from the emptiness inside us. Ultimately it will free us from the fear of death.

We are now moving through the third triad of spiritual disciplines. We discovered that Simplicity has an exalting nature. Solitude has a disintegrating nature. We are now ready to move into the group spiritual disciplines and take a look at Worship which has a purifying nature. After sublimating our kundalini energy and having our personality transformed, we are ready to purify our new personality.

†† Paul Foster Case, *Hermetic Alchemy Science and Practice.*

Part IV
The Group Spiritual Disciplines

Worship	9th house	Sagittarius	mutable fire
Guidance	10th house	Capricorn	cardinal earth
Confession	11th house	Aquarius	fixed air
Celebration	12th house	Pisces	mutable water

9th house influences*

> collective mind
> broader viewpoint
> travel
> religion
> philosophy
> mental studies

10th house influences*

> public self
> position in world
> reputation
> vocation
> authority

11th house influences*

> group interactions
> friends and associates
> visions
> dreams

12th house influences*

> collective soul
> devotion to higher ideals
> spiritual values
> selfless social service
> karma
> overcoming ghosts or debts of the past

*from *Astrology for Yourself,* by George Demetra and Douglas Bloch

Astrologically, I am associating the four group spiritual disciplines with the 9th through the 12th houses and signs on the wheel of the zodiac. These final four are the most transpersonal in nature. We see from the influences of these houses that they affect our relationships with ever-increasing larger groups. Ultimately we are concerned with ideas on the cosmic level and with clearing obstacles that impede the unfolding of our own cosmic nature.

The group disciplines are the most public of the disciplines. With the outer disciplines our actions sometimes attract attention. The Group disciplines also attract attention, but our efforts are focused on practicing them with others who will be mostly approving and supportive of our efforts. Group dynamics and psychology play a part in our practice of the group disciplines.

Worship has a fiery nature and is the most transformative of this group. I am associating it with the fiery sign of Sagittarius. Guidance has an earthy nature and serves to ground our spiritual practices. I am associating it with the earthy sign of Capricorn. Confession has an airy nature and helps to keep our lines of communications open to Divinity and to our fellow spiritual travelers. I am associating it with the airy sign of Aquarius. Celebration has a watery nature and helps us to maintain our connection to the love of our creator. I am associating it with the watery sign of Pisces.

All of the Spiritual Disciplines, while experienced on the higher planes of consciousness, are put into practice on the material plane. Guidance is experiencing the mind of Divinity and hearing its voice as a group. This is one of the most difficult disciplines to practice and one of the most transformative. Divinity wants to give and to forgive, but Confession must be offered before forgiveness can be given. Celebration is at the center of spiritual life. Freedom from anxiety and care form the basis for Celebration. To Worship is to experience Reality, to touch Life, and to know the Divine in the community.

Chapter 9
Worship

Correspondences for Worship

Qabalah:

the Hebrew letter of Samekh, meaning "Tent Prop"
the Intelligence of Probation or Trial
Testing/Probation
the function of Zeal
the West-Above edge on the Cube of Space
the 25th Path of Samekh on the Tree of Life

Astrology:

the sign of Sagittarius (9th house, mutable fire)
Rulership: Jupiter
Exaltation: none

Alchemy:

Incineration - Inviting the Super-Conscious to remove all traces of impurity; a conscious act (Key 1 the Magician)

Theurgy:

the discipline of Worship

Tarot:

Key 14, Temperance
Key 10, Wheel of Fortune
Key 1, the Magician

With the discipline of Worship we transition into the group disciplines. These disciplines help us extend our spiritual lives into our communities. Group disciplines are practiced in the company of other, mostly like-minded individuals. Thus we are often dealing with a specific group mind or egregore. Depending on the principle focus of the group, the influence of the egregore can be very positive. Unlike the group mind made up of all humans, a group focused on one or more of the group disciplines can produce an egregore that is supportive, uplifting, and capable of influencing us in a positive way as we travel our spiritual paths.

With Putrefaction and the discipline of Solitude we experience the negation of the belief that all of our ideas and all of our activities have a personal origin. This can be devastating to the personality that makes decisions based primarily on images provided by our material world.. We saw that it can be accompanied by *the dark night of the soul*. With Incineration and the discipline of Worship we emerge from that darkness to affirm the *One Identity* as the true origination of all that is accomplished through the personality.

†† Alchemical Incineration burns to ashes the residue of old ways or thinking and acting.. It consumes all the remaining traces of our erroneous interpretations of experience. This is residue remaining in our sub-consciousness even after Putrefaction is complete.

†† Even when we consciously attribute all action to the One Reality, and deny the personal origination of anything whatever, latent tendencies remain which must be purged out. Self-consciousness alone cannot reach deep enough into sub-consciousness to reach all of the fragments. A higher power needs to be invoked. One of the functions of Worship as a

210

discipline is to make contact with higher realms of consciousness for this purpose.

> *"I will look upon every circumstance of my life as a*
> *particular dealing of God with my soul."*
> Rosicrucian meditation

The alchemical stage of Incineration is often called the *Knowledge and Conversation of the Holy Guardian Angel.* "Knowledge" and "Conversation" are technical terms with specific esoteric meanings. Anyone equipped with only exoteric knowledge is not likely to appreciate its ability to transform our lives.

Knowledge is associated with unity. Da'ath is a Hebrew word meaning knowledge. On the qabalistic Tree of Life, Da'ath is often considered to be located in the region where the 13th path of Gimel crosses the 14th path of Daleth. The 14th path of Daleth connects the sephirah of Chokmah (Wisdom) with the sephirah of Binah (Understanding). This implies that Knowledge is the union of Wisdom and Understanding.

> *And Adam knew Eve his wife; and she conceived, and*
> *bare Cain.*   – Genesis 4:1

The exoteric reading of this passage refers to carnal knowledge, the union between a man and a woman. The concept of unity that we just mentioned applies on all other levels of our existence and so this passage has a number of esoteric readings as well.

When we emerge from alchemical Putrefaction, our personalities are much more balanced and unified than they were at earlier stages of the Work. When we arrive at the next stage of Incineration, our bodies are more capable of receiving powerful energies emanating from higher levels of consciousness. Our subconscious is better equipped to interact with our Higher Soul, or Holy Guardian Angel. We become better prepared to achieve *the Knowledge and Conversation of the Holy Guardian Angel.* [††]

To converse with is to form an association with and to communicate. A balanced and unified personality is a clear channel for receiving the voice of our inner teacher, our Holy Guardian Angel. Recall the image of Key 6, the Lovers, which we considered in connection with the discipline of Study. Here we have the proper relationship between self-consciousness, subconsciousness, and super-consciousness.

Self-consciousness is giving a suggestion to subconsciousness, and subconsciousness is receiving the suggestion and listening attentively to the voice of super-consciousness. Having received a response from super-consciousness, subconsciousness communicates it to self-consciousness and/or manifests it into our material world. All three parts of self are acting in unison. This is Conversation taking place between the three.

This Knowledge and Conversation will not be complete unless we take the additional step of applying to our daily lives the teachings received from our Higher Soul.

To sum up, to have *Knowledge and Conversation of the Holy Guardian Angel* is to identify ourselves completely with our Higher Soul, to hear its voice, and to pattern our lives according to its teachings. This is the gift that Worship brings to us.

To really begin to understand Worship and its corresponding alchemical stage of Incineration, it is helpful to make a careful study of the image on Key 14, Temperance. This Key is associated with the Hebrew Letter Samekh and the fiery astrological sign of Sagittarius.

According to F.L.O. tradition, the Angel in Key 14 is Michael. This is because of the solar disc on his forehead, the glory radiating from his head, and the fiery red color of his wings. In the B.O.T.A. and F.L.O. systems, Michael is associated with the sphere of Tiphareth on the Tree of Life. Tiphareth is associated with the Christ consciousness, our Higher Self and inner teacher.

We see the archangel Michael performing alchemical Incineration. With a torch in his left hand, he is pouring fire onto the head of an eagle. With a pitcher in his right hand, he is pouring water onto the head of a lion. The eagle represents watery Scorpio and the lion represents fiery Leo. The angel is seeking to temper or to balance these two energies. [††]

It should be noted that in other systems, the archangel Raphael is associated with Tiphareth for a number of reasons. We in the Fraternity of the Hidden Light recognize these reasons and honor those who have made this correspondence. But we respectfully feel that the fiery nature of Michael is a better fit for the sephirah of the Sun than Raphael who is traditionally associated with Air. On the Tree of Life Tiphereth is placed on the pillar of consciousness and thus also has an association with alchemical Air.

Paul Foster Case tells us that the Lion of Key 14 represents the fiery energy of Leo and our own animal nature. The eagle represents the watery energy of Scorpio and the procreative sexual energy of our vegetable consciousness. Taken together they represent two aspects of our desire nature. Incineration   is shown in Key 14 to be the purging, refining, and balancing of our desire nature. [††]

Case goes on to say that *the Intelligence of Probation or Trial*, associated with Incineration and Worship, is claimed by Qabalists to be the first test that the *One Source* uses to try the faithful. The faithful are those who profess to identify themselves with the *One Source*. Qabalists call these faithful the Chasidim, the Merciful Ones. They exhibit the qualities of Mercy represented by Chesed, the sephirah of Jupiter. [††]

Jupiter rules Sagittarius. This makes Jupiter a dominant force in alchemical Incineration, with the Jupiter center of the body playing a prominent role. The Jupiter center is a large reservoir of subconscious impressions, often called the abdominal brain. Incineration clears the Jupiter center of the dross of *false* impressions and experiences.

Worship allows us to open ourselves to an influx of positive mental images originating in higher realms of consciousness. This frees subconscious energy to become more identified with the cosmic cycles of the Life-power through improved communication with super-consciousness. These cycles are illustrated on Key 10, the Wheel of Fortune, which represents the energies of Jupiter. [††]

Another view of *the Intelligence of Probation or Trial* holds that the basic meaning of this path of Samekh is verification. Through verification we determine the accuracy of our beliefs and theories. When we successfully work this path of verification we attain the philosophical gold of enlightenment which symbolizes verified truth.

This philosophical gold is not yet the Stone of the Wise but represents a vision of what the Stone may look like. Similar to a Phoenix rising from the ashes it begins to rise above gross matter and its illusory images. Temperance takes on the meaning of regulating and measuring the proportions of constituent parts. Our theories are weighed and measured in order to verify their validity. [††]

Paul Foster Case tells us that the letter Samekh has a value of 60 and is thus connected to the Hebrew word bawkhan, spelled Beth-Cheth-Nun which means to try by fire. See the section on Samekh in Paul Foster Case's Book of Tokens for an explanation. Another associated word whose sum is 60 is spelled Mem-Cheth-Zain-Heh meaning 'vision.' [††]

It may be said that the 25th path of Samekh is the mystical Path of the Arrow which is the direct avenue of true vision. Astrologically the path of Samekh is the path of Sagittarius the Centaur archer. The body of the horse represents our animal nature while the human archer represents our ability to gaze upward or inward and shoot our arrows of aspiration toward the Sun of Tiphareth.

Zeal is the mental state that corresponds to Worship and Incineration through the letter Samekh. Paul Foster Case writes that the Hebrew word for zeal is ragaz, Resh-Gimel-Zain. Ragaz means agitation or trembling. This ties it with the meaning of movement and vibration illustrated in Key 10. Resh represents the Sun, Gimel represents the Moon, and Zain represents Gemini, ruled by Mercury. Zeal therefore, makes use of the solar and lunar currents of the body in combination with Mercury (self-consciousness). As we have previously seen, the Great Work is said to be completed through the union of the Sun and Moon with the aid of Mercury. [††]

Zeal is also said by Paul Foster Case to be associated with our desire nature. Our personality alone is incapable of performing Incineration. Yet our self-conscious mind initiates this process by giving a suggestion to our subconscious, where the actual work of Incineration takes place through the actions of our super-consciousness. [tt]

Remember that our self-consciousness does nothing but observe after the process has been initiated. In Key 1, the Magician, self-consciousness remains passive as it draws down a mysterious force into its garden. This is the same force that accomplishes the work of Incineration. Case tells us that In the B.O.T.A. tradition, this force is represented by the archangel Michael in Key 14. [tt]

Vibration or radiant energy is important to an understanding of Key 14. All things in the manifested universe vibrate, and all forms of vibration can be modified and manipulated by us once we master the transformation of the Life-force of the imagination (the Moon) into the activity of self-consciousness (the Sun).This transformation is initiated by our self-consciousness (Mercury). [tt]

We see this transformation on the Tree of Life where the 25th path of Samekh leads us from the sphere of the Moon, Yesod, to the sphere of the Sun, Tiphareth. Yesod represents our personality and Tiphareth represents our Higher Self. An interesting point to consider is that the 13th path of Gimel (the Moon) completes the middle pillar by connecting the spheres of Tiphareth (the Holy Guardian Angel) and Kether (the One Self).[tt]

Key 2, the High Priestess, represents the 13th path of Gimel. The High Priestess represents memory, the basic characteristic of Mind. Paul Foster Case tells us that the Great Work we perform on ourselves depends on us remembering our True Self. The Rosicrucian grade of Ipsissimus at Kether translates to 'He who is Most Himself.' To remember who we truly are requires the assistance of that part of us which transcends the physical plane. To remember who we truly are is to identify with Life itself. The function of memory is to perceive ourselves in the unity of the *One Self*. [††]

Worship leads to a direct experience of the Reality of the higher planes of consciousness. This is both a personal and a group experience. As a group experience, Worship is the experience of the Divine in the community. To express our love for Spirit is the natural human response to Spirit's love for us:

We love because he first loved us.   – 1 John 4:19

We experience Worship on the inner, the outer, and the group levels. On the plane of Spirit or super-consciousness, the energy is constant and unchanging. On the plane of material existence, our individual experiences and interpretations will be different. This is a manifestation of the Divine paradox: Every unique manifestation of the Life-force is an expression of the *One Source*.

Different experiences and interpretations of the consciousness of Spirit naturally lead to different ways of relating to Spirit. The group discipline of Worship seeks to look past our differences and celebrate the beliefs and practices that we hold in common as a group.

The English word worship comes from two Old English words: *weorth*, meaning "worth," and *scipe* or ship, which means "shape or "quality." We may say that worth-ship is the quality of having worth or of being worthy. So worth-ship is the quality of having worth or of being worthy. When we worship, we are saying that Spirit has worth and is worthy of our praise and our devotion. When we worship as a group, we speak, sing, and offer our Prayers about how good and powerful is our Creator.

> *"But you are a chosen race, a royal priesthood, a holy nation, God's own people, in order that you may proclaim the mighty acts of him who called you out of darkness into his marvelous light".*   - 1 Peter 2:9

In one respect, the group discipline of Worship is related to the outer discipline of Submission. Certain types of worship involve bowing down, kneeling, or putting one's face down as an act of submission to a Higher Power. Our body language says, "I will do whatever you want me to do. I am ready to listen to your instructions and I am willing to obey." Of course, from our previous discussion of Submission, we understand that this is an acknowledgement of our position within the cosmic hierarchy and not an act of self-debasement.

Worship can also be considered to be an act of Service. As Service, Worship carries the idea of doing something for Spirit - making a sacrifice or obeying its Will. When we serve Spirit and carry out its will we are serving not only Spirit, but are also serving the Earth, humanity, and ourselves.

We may approach worship with three distinct channels of expression – speaking, listening, and doing. This is worship that expresses the heart, a worship that engages the mind, and a worship that moves the body. Speaking is giving praise upward, listening is receiving instructions from above, and actions carry out Divine Will in the world around us. All three channels of expression are integral parts in the effective practice of Worship.

Some worship consists primarily of speaking or singing praise to God. Praise is good, but if we praise Spirit without ever listening to what it is saying to us, we should ask ourselves whether we truly believe the words we are saying. Spirit is all-wise and all-loving and we need to be attentive to what it is telling us.

Talk without action does not give Spirit the respect we say it deserves. If our behavior isn't changed by Spirit then our actions are saying that Spirit isn't important — it's a nice idea. It is tempting to make all sorts of excuses for not getting actively involved. When we truly believe that Spirit is worthy of praise, we will be willing to listen and to change the way we live. Effective Worship will affect our behavior.

Worship is our response to Spirit. We can't know Spirit's worth or declare it until it is revealed to us. Spirit initiates worship by revealing itself to us. The more we grasp Spirit's wisdom, power, and love, the more we can understand its worthiness and the better we can worship.

> *And he answering said, "You shall love the Lord your God with all your heart, and with all your soul, and with all your strength, and with all your mind; and your neighbor as yourself".*   - Luke 10:27

Both the Old and New Testaments tell us that we should love Spirit with every part of our being: body, mind, soul and spirit. In our worship, we should also involve every fiber of our being.

Our belief in a Higher Power speaks to its worthiness. The love and trust that we give to it attests to that worthiness. Our obedience and service to Spirit also says that it has worth. Words complete our worship; the words we say to one another;

the Prayers we offer. Even the songs we sing celebrate the worthiness of Spirit.

We can and do worship Spirit alone. This is a part of our regular spiritual practice. But the group discipline of Worship allows us to share this part of our practice with others. Spirit reveals itself to all of us and each of us experiences its presence in our own unique way. We come together in worship to celebrate the Oneness that creates all of our experiences. Spirit reveals itself to our communities, and through our communities, reveals itself to us. As a community we come together in worship, declaring that Spirit is worthy of all our honor and praise.

This mutual support reinforces our commitment to move forward on our spiritual path. In Solitude we experience the destruction of our illusions about personal power and will. We have a choice as to whether we will remain in our dark night of the soul or to ask for help from our Holy Guardian Angel. If we remain, we will continue to spiral downward toward the region of the Qlippoth as our lives become more and more unsustainable. At this stage of our development, requesting the aid of our Holy Guardian Angel is the only way forward.

> *"I appeal to you therefore, brethren, by the mercies of God, to present your bodies as a living sacrifice, holy and acceptable to God, which is your spiritual worship."*   - Romans 12:1

A number of questions often arise when considering Worship: What form(s) should Worship take? Do we need an intercessor? What constitutes a holy and acceptable sacrifice? etc.

How we answer these and other related questions determines both the inner and outer characteristics of our Worship. Disagreement over these characteristics has led to schisms and wars throughout recorded human history. Perhaps in a population ignorant of spiritual matters, leaders may find it necessary to dictate the forms of Worship. Unfortunately, human nature makes it easy to go from dictating forms of Worship to imposing a spiritual dictatorship.

People with a strong sense of self often rebel at the idea of being told how to worship. Having a well-developed sense of curiosity goes hand-in-hand with a strong personality. Not being satisfied with the theology and practices given to the masses, they seek their own answers. We find ourselves among these people when we look inward to search for answers.

Once we begin to find answers to our questions, we find it comforting to seek out others who are on a similar spiritual path and perhaps have had similar kinds of experiences. Communication with our inner planes of consciousness reinforces our desire to learn more and our subconscious mind often creates opportunities for material world contact with others that might help us to find answers to more of our questions. Our search often leads us from one group to another until we find one that seems to satisfy our spiritual needs.

We do our best to "get it right," but paradoxically, part of the process of becoming "right" is to admit that we don't always hit the target. Most of us have a long way to travel before we become spiritual adepts. We require the aid of our Holy Guardian Angel to clear our personalities of the dross that impedes our progress. We look to our inner teacher to help us see the path ahead more clearly. Often the voice of our Holy Guardian Angel can be found in the voices and the teachings of the groups with which we associate. If we learn to develop our faculty of discrimination, the voice of our inner teacher can be found in the most unlikely places.

It is impossible to lose or become disconnected from our Holy Guardian Angel except in our own minds. We just need to remember that it is always present, accessible whenever we wish. It is there to converse with when we feel lonely. It is there whenever life becomes too dark or heavy. It is a reality. We must remember this even when we can remember nothing else.

At the top of Key 14 is a rainbow. The Hebrew word for bow or rainbow is *qesheth*, Qoph-Shin-Tav. The paths for these three letters form a bow and arrow on the Tree of life. In the story of Noah and the Ark, God places the rainbow in the sky as a sign of his pact with Noah. This represents a promise from our Holy Guardian Angel that we will succeed in the Great Work. Of course, to do this we will need the help of our Angel.

> *"For where two or three are gathered in my name, I am there among them."* - Matthew 18:20

When two or more people gather for a common purpose, a group mind or egregore begins to form. Egregore is a concept representing a thought-form or collective group mind, an autonomous psychic entity made up of, and influencing, the thoughts of a group of people.

The characteristics of the egregore are dependent on the individual personalities involved and their participation within the group. The character of the egregore changes as individuals change. It also changes as people enter or leave the group.

When the purpose for assembling is Worship, the group is influenced by interaction with higher levels of consciousness represented by the spheres of Tiphareth and above. The influence of the higher spheres on the lower ones cannot be overstated. When this higher consciousness enters the level of our personalities below Tiphareth, we are able to accept it and interact with it after the work of Incineration has been completed by our Holy Guardian Angel. The group mind or egregore directs the kinds of interactions with spirit that are experienced by the group.

It is important that a group of worshippers have leaders who are advanced far enough on their own spiritual path to be proficient with the process of the Knowledge and Conversation of the Holy Guardian Angel. A good leader will be able to monitor the health of the egregore and work to keep it balanced. Communications coming from higher levels of consciousness must be clearly understood and passed on to members of the group when appropriate.

The egregore must be maintained in such a fashion that all members experience a loving and inclusive atmosphere in which to work on their own spiritual path. When the egregore becomes focused on one individual it becomes unbalanced and can begin to take on the characteristics of a personality cult.

Forms and rituals by themselves do not produce Worship, nor does their disuse. We cannot react in true Worship until Spirit has touched our soul in some way. This is difficult given the prevalent attitudes of society today. Some would say that Spirit is dead or irrelevant. Others see Spirit as far away and unresponsive. Responses to Spirit such as these can make it difficult to worship as a group. Even so, Worship is how we develop a relationship with Spirit and with the Divine in others.

Namaste – "The Spirit within me salutes the Spirit within you!"

In an important sense, to think "rightly" about Spirit is to have everything right. Conversely, to think "wrongly" about Spirit is to have everything wrong. It is vital to our spiritual growth to understand as much as possible about Spirit. It is just as vital to personally experience Spirit's Mercy and Love. Just as a plant dies when it is cut off from its roots, our souls begin to atrophy when we are cut off from the source of our spiritual nourishment.

When we experience Divine Love and Mercy, Worship comes naturally. It is a deep inner fellowship where the Divine in each person touches all. We transform in literal terms from the many to the *ONE*. This transformation is just as complete and mysterious as when the communion wafer and wine are transformed into the body and blood of the Christ consciousness within all of us.

Through the work of Worship and of Incineration, spirit purifies our body, mind, and soul. We take a look at the discipline of Guidance in the next chapter. In the discipline of Guidance we will see that in us spirit now has a fertile garden to perform its work. Through the group discipline of Guidance spirit can reach us not only individually, but through participation in a group.

†† Paul Foster Case, *Hermetic Alchemy Science and Practice.*

Chapter 10
Guidance

Correspondences for Guidance

Qabalah:
 the Hebrew letter of Ayin, meaning "Eye"
 the Renewing Intelligence
 Bondage/Freedom
 the function of Mirth
 the West-Below edge on the Cube of Space
 the 26th Path of Ayin on the Tree of Life

Astrology:
 the sign of Capricorn (10th house, cardinal earth)
 Rulership: Saturn (Key 21 the World)
 Exaltation: Mars (Key 16 the Tower)

Alchemy:
 Fermentation - The inspiration of spiritual power from Above that reanimates, energizes, and enlightens

Theurgy:
 the discipline of Guidance

Tarot:
 Key 15, the Devil
 Key 10, Wheel of Fortune
 Key 21, the World
 Key 2, High Priestess
 Key 17, the Star
 Key 16, the Tower

Guidance, when practiced as an inner discipline is an important part of every other discipline. We must be willing and able to hear the voice of our inner teacher and to heed its instruction. We have already touched on many of the practices necessary to receive inner guidance.

With *Prayer*, many of the illusions of material reality are swept away. With *Fasting*, our bodies and our personalities are prepared for an influx of higher consciousness. With *Study* we begin to understand the mechanism that allows us to hear the voice of our inner teacher. With *Meditation*, we learn how to listen to that voice. With *Submission* we discover that the source of our authentic power is our own Holy Guardian Angel. With *Service* we are able to ground our power and integrate it into our daily lives. With *Simplicity* we begin to consciously raise our power from our Saturn center to our higher centers. With *Solitude* we disengage our conscious mind, allowing Spirit to transform us at the level of our subconscious. With *Worship* we invite Spirit to remove all remaining traces of illusion and impurity. With *Guidance* we are now able to hear the voice of Divinity individually and as a group, and with greater clarity. Shortly we will see why the leaders of any spiritually centered group must be able to hear the voice of Divinity.

As we enter into the practice of Guidance, we have prepared ourselves individually to be a functioning member of a group. At this point on our path, we are beginning to develop our relationship with our inner teacher through *the Knowledge and Conversation of the Holy Guardian Angel.* This enables us to receive spiritual insight and share it with the group.

In the system we are considering here, Capricorn and the Hebrew Letter Ayin correspond to the alchemical stage of Fermentation and to the discipline of Guidance. Tarot Key 15, the Devil, is the card associated with these correspondences. Paul Foster Case tells us that the word Ayin can mean 'eye' or 'the visible part of an object'. Thus the Devil Key represents the state of bondage in which we find ourselves when we interpret the physical appearance of our world as the only reality. [††]

This condition stands in stark contrast to the reality we perceive when we develop the ability to communicate with our Higher Selves. This is an apparent paradox that can be resolved when we understand that we can choose between Freedom and Bondage when we change the way we think, interpret reality in a different way, and make better decisions. Hence the Rosicrucian mantra, *"Change your mind and change your life."*

"For where two or three are gathered in my name, I am there among them." — Matthew 20:18

Jesus is telling his followers that the spirit from whence he came will always be among them when they gather in its name. In these words he is giving his followers both assurance and authority. In the Western mystery tradition we recognize Jesus of Nazareth as an Avatar that embodies the archetype of the Christ consciousness symbolized by Tiphareth on the Tree of Life. The words quoted above tell us that if our earnest desire is to discern the Will of Spirit, we will be successful. A consensus can be developed as a group from the input of individuals and the guidance of its leaders. This assurance allows the group to move forward and act with authority. The unity of a group determined to discern the *One Will* bestows this authority.

There is something about the dynamic of a group and its group mind that magnifies and clarifies the guidance we receive from Spirit. No matter how clear a channel of communication we might be individually, our information is always filtered through our preconceptions and beliefs. If enough people in the group are able to receive and interpret the voice of their Holy Guardian Angel, the effect on the group will be positive and the voice of Spirit may be heard more clearly.

The Christian New Testament contains a number of examples of Guidance as a group discipline. In the book of Acts we learn that the issue of circumcision had deeply divided the early followers of Jesus. Some were advocating the necessity of circumcision for all Christians. Paul saw this as a Jewish cultural takeover of the Church, giving non-Jewish converts no alternative.

Appointed representatives of the early churches met, not to assert the will of one faction over another or to jockey for power, but to attempt to discern the Mind of Spirit. After much debate, Simon Peter rose to tell his story of the conversion of the Roman Centurion Cornelius, a Gentile or non-Jew. When Peter finished speaking, the entire assembly fell silent. Then, acting in unison, the Spirit led group rejected the requirement of circumcision and embraced Jesus' teachings as they understood them.

This was more than the resolution of a divisive issue. It was a victory for the method the early Church would use to resolve many other thorny issues. As one people, they had determined to live under the direct guidance and rulership of Spirit. This was not anarchy or totalitarianism or even democracy. This was Spirit-directed unity. And as long as this unity held, it worked well.

Spirit-given unity goes beyond mere agreement. It is the perception that we have heard the *Kol Yehovah*, the voice of God. Eventually the early Church lost its sense of unity and rejected this Spirit-led governance. In the time of the Roman Emperor Constantine, the Church rejected the authority of its leaders in favor of a leader that took on all the power and trappings of a king.

This is what happened to their Jewish forefathers in Old Testament times when the Jewish people became dissatisfied with being led by prophets and demanded to be ruled by a king. The secularization that followed led to the decline of Jewish society and may have contributed to their captivity. Today we would do well to heed these lessons.

The band of men and women that became Jesus' followers was not transformed from spiritual seekers into spiritual leaders overnight. Neither will we be transformed quickly. We will move in that direction one step at a time. Sometimes it will be two steps forward and one step back. Some of us will not be called to become leaders, but will express our talents in other areas. A Spirit-led individual will exude an aura of leadership and authority no matter what position they hold.

In the middle ages the Christian Church encouraged the idea of a spiritual advisor for individual priests, monks, nuns, and other religious offices. In the Irish Church this advisor was called *Anam Cara*, or Soul Friend. Even the greatest of saints did not attempt their inward journeys without the counsel of a spiritual advisor.

A spiritual advisor would be of great value to anyone on a spiritual path. Today we hardly know about such things, much less practice them. This is a great loss because spiritual direction is so much needed in society today. A spiritual director can be a beautiful expression of Divine guidance through our brothers and sisters in spirit. In the next chapter we will discuss the role of a spiritual advisor as confessor.

An Anam Cara is much more than a spiritual advisor. This person is trusted with the secrets of our soul. We bare ourselves to an extent not possible with anyone else. In the medieval Church, one's Anam Cara was usually a religious cleric. Today, we are indeed fortunate if that person is our spouse or life partner. How much deeper that relationship would be if we could bare our souls to the person we care about most deeply!

The purpose of a spiritual director is to be a guide that introduces us to our inner teacher. This director must not be swayed by his or her own personal biases and beliefs. The director is there only to lead us to the source of our own spiritual nourishment. If our director is connected to their own source of nourishment, we can be sure their guidance comes from that source. The relationship is as an advisor to a friend, or as a friend to a friend. We and our director are both growing as we move forward on our spiritual paths.

In today's secular world people are looking for spiritual guidance to bring more meaning into their lives. People are leaving mainstream religions in large numbers to seek answers in other traditions. Many look to a spiritual guide or guru for guidance. Caution and discrimination are needed when looking for guidance.

Anyone who wishes to be a spiritual leader must first make significant progress on their own spiritual path. Spiritual guides must first transform themselves before they can assist others in their own transformation. Such a person must be an effective instrument for the will of Spirit so that they might lead others to the experience of knowing the Mind of Spirit.

In the Western tradition, many schools of the Mysteries claim to be fully contacted. This means that the leaders of schools in this outer physical plane are in spiritual contact with a school or a group of teachers on the inner planes. The validity of this claim may be tested by the quality of their teachings.

As the New Testament tells us, we can know an effective spiritual guide by their fruits. Anyone with an authentic link to higher planes of consciousness can be calm in the midst of life's storms and chaos. They can absorb and transmute the selfishness, aggression, fear, uncertainty, mediocrity, and apathy that surround them. They will be compassionate and steadfast.

As all of us can attest, the human condition is filled with cycles on all levels of being. Our connection to our Holy Guardian Angel can wax and wane. This is true for spiritual leaders as well. Communication can be better or worse in any given period. Seeking a consensus of the group can negate individual dry spells and magnify the response from Spirit. Wise spiritual leaders will have a trusted group of spiritual advisors that they can turn to when they are in doubt or when important decisions need to be made.

Chemical Fermentation is the work of yeast on milk to produce cheese or on grapes to produce wine. In ancient times these processes were seen as magical or as the work of Spirit. Ordinary foods were allowed to rot and were transformed by unknown agents into products that enhanced the range of our diets. Alchemists saw similarities between the fermentation of wine and the spiritual transformation taking place at this stage of the Work. Something invisible had intervened to create something new. What had become lifeless and repugnant in Putrefaction had now become reanimated and full of life and enlightenment. [††]

The alchemical process of Fermentation allows us to see the Reality behind the phenomenal world of appearances. The phenomenal world piques our curiosity. What most thoroughly excites our wonder is the discovery that things are by no means what they seem. This discovery is the seed of science and the leaven which transforms our consciousness. [tt]

The state of mirth and playfulness associated with Fermentation and Tarot Key 15 is important in seeing beyond the phenomenal world. Mirth and joy break up the energy of the illusions that bind us. When this happens we become more receptive to guidance from higher realms of consciousness. [tt]

We see the playfulness of adepts in the word-play they incorporate into their writings. They are fond of using words that sound alike to incorporate many levels of meaning into their teachings and to confound the uninitiated or the merely curious. For example, the *ros-* in Rosicrucian can be said to be derived from a *rose* or from *ros* which means dew. There are other meanings of *ros* as well. This is an example of the spoken Qabalah.

The amplification of the effects of the Life-force at this stage brings us to a discussion of the *Renewing Intelligence,* the title given to the consciousness of Ayin by the Sepher Yetzirah. The Renewing Intelligence is said by the Sepher Yetzirah to be so called *"because by it the Holy God renews all that is begun afresh in the creation of the world."* Paul Foster Case tells us that the 'eye' of Ayin is both our physical eye that deceives us into believing that 'what we see is all there is' and is also the 'all seeing eye' of Spirit in the Egyptian tradition that appears today in places such as the Great Seal of the United States and in Masonic symbolism. Through the discipline of Guidance we

begin to see our world through both physical and spiritual eyes.
††

> *The fear of the Lord is the beginning of knowledge;*
> *fools despise wisdom and instruction.* - Proverbs 1:7

This proverb describes the consciousness of Geburah as it is experienced on 3 levels. The first level, *Pachad*, is fear of those things we do not understand. This fear extends to the cosmic law that governs all four qabalistic worlds. When we begin to gain some understanding of Cosmic Law, we experience it as *Geburah*, Severity or Strength. When we unfold the consciousness of an adept, we see this same energy as *Din*, or Undeviating Justice. *Pachad, Geburah*, and *Din* are three names commonly given to the 5th Sephirah on the Tree of Life. ††

Thus we see in the Renewing Intelligence an evolution of consciousness from a fear of the natural world to an understanding of the laws that govern it. We see in this evolution the origin of the Devil, The term 'Devil' is derived from the Greek word for hinderer or slanderer. The ignorant ascribe all of their difficulties to this Devil, not aware that there is only one force behind all of Creation. ††

When our fears make life uncomfortable, they become the agents that move us forward on our path of Liberation. We have but to confront them to perceive our error. Paul Foster Case tells us that according to the Ageless Wisdom, *"The Devil is God as He is misunderstood by the wicked,"* Eliphas Levi writes that exoteric dogmatism's Devil is in reality the First Matter of the alchemist.††

On a qabalistic note, it is interesting that the gematric value of both *nachash* or serpent (Nun-Cheth-Shin) and *meshiach* or

233

messiah (Mem-Shin-Yod-Cheth) is 358. The numbers 3-5-8 are also consecutive numbers in the Fibonacci series that incorporates the golden proportion. This leads us to a connection between the Devil and Spirit. Meditation on this will yield many insights. [tt]

Paul Foster Case tells us that the connection between the Devil and Spirit can also be seen in a comparison between Key 15 the Devil, Key 5 the Hierophant, and Key 6 the Lovers. Add the 1 and 5 of 15 together and the result is 6. This gematria tells us they are connected. [tt]

All three Keys feature 3 figures in the same configuration. The man and the woman in Keys 15 and 6 represent self-consciousness and subconsciousness. 15 is also the sum of the numbers 0 through 5. The Hierophant, as the last Key in the series of Tarot Keys 0 through 5, is also connected to Key 15. [tt]

Case further tells us that the background of The Devil is dark, symbolizing ignorance or the absence of the light of understanding. It is this lack of understanding that creates our bondage. The Devil of Key 15 stands in stark contrast to the angel of Key 6. Case says that it is a gross characterization of that angel. [tt]

The man and woman in Key 15 are caricatures of the two figures in Key 6. The right hands of the Hierophant and Devil give different gestures. The Devi is signaling that "what we see is all there is." The Hierophant is signaling that "what we see is only part of reality." Some of our reality remains hidden. [tt]

According to Paul Foster Case, the white beard of the Devil on Tarot Key 15 tells us that he is indeed an aspect of Spirit, though misunderstood. *Intuition*, represented by Key 5 the Hierophant, and *Discrimination*, represented by Key 6 are human faculties that we need in order to overcome our bondage. [††]

The sign of Mercury at its navel tells us that the Devil is an intellectual concept created by human minds. The Pentagram on the Devil's forehead tells us that Spirit is present in the Devil, but the inverted pentagram pointing down places points of the four elements of physical reality and the human personality higher than the point representing Spirit.[††]

Consider too, that the path of Ayin on the Tree of Life connects the spheres of Beauty and Splendor. This is the 26th Path of Wisdom. 26 is the number of Tetragrammaton, Yod-Heh-Vav-Heh, the four letter name of God. [††]

Paul Foster Case reminds us that the Bible contains many statements that show that for the 'People of the Book' God is regarded as being the author of our troubles as well as being the author of all goodness. Both God and the Devil are how we perceive different expressions of the *One Source*. The image of the Prince of Darkness is just an ignorant conception of the workings of the Kingdom of Light. [††]

Many of us, as we were growing up, didn't know or didn't care about the fact that we could balance and completely transform our personalities. Our personalities were quite satisfied being in control. Our subconscious mind was easily swayed by the messages bombarding us from the media. The result was ignorance, inertia, and an inability to look beyond physical appearance. We failed to see that the Devil is our misunderstanding of the nature of our Higher Soul. Recall that the human function related to Key 15, Capricorn, Fermentation, and Guidance is mirth. The Devil is a joke foisted on us by our own ignorance.

The limitations placed on us by our Saturn energy feel like adversity, but this is a result of a difference between our actual and perceived needs. Our personalities decree that we need something and we react poorly when that need goes unfulfilled. Our real needs are always met *when we ask for them.* The alternative is to go through life in a state similar to sleep because that is what our society encourages us to do. Western culture is overwhelmingly materialistic. [††]

The Hebrew letter Ayin means "Eye." At the stage of alchemical Fermentation we are asked to look at our lives and our realities in more depth. We cannot judge by appearances alone. When we do look at our world with different eyes, we see many of the incongruities that were always there. We see the humor of our situation and perhaps even laugh out loud. We finally get the joke. [††]

It is in the uncomfortable and undesirable messengers of Spirit that Sages find the key to the power of *the Renewing Intelligence* of Ayin. It is in the exceptions to our understanding of the laws of Nature that we find clues to higher laws. In puzzles and paradoxes, difficulties and problems, the wise find cause for rejoicing and mirth. [††]

The sages tell us that they also have difficult problems for which they have yet to find answers. They have solved problems that plague most of us, but have other difficulties. The difference is that they have found the Path that leads from Bondage to Freedom and know how to go about solving their problems. They possess the Universal Solvent that grants health, happiness, and the highest good. The sages tell us that we possess it too and may one day make the Stone of the Wise ourselves through the Royal Art of Alchemy. They stand ready to show us how to unfold the Stone in ourselves. [††]

Paul Foster Case reminds us of the parable in the New Testament of the woman who added leaven (yeast) to three measures of dough. In the morning she found that the entire quantity of dough had risen. Up until this present stage of Fermentation we have been preparing our leaven. Now the woman, our subconscious mind, must mix it with the chaotic mass of sense-experiences typified by the Devil. [tt]

In many cultures, Capricorn is the sign of the zodiac associated with the birth of saviors and Sun deities. Note that between Aries at the spring equinox and Capricorn at the winter solstice is a gestation period of nine months. In Christian lore, the spring equinox was the time of the appearance of the angel to the virgin Mary to announce her pregnancy. In the Northern hemisphere, Capricorn is the sign in which the Sun begins to move northward and the day begins to grow longer. This is celebrated as the birth of the Light. [tt]

Note that Mars is exalted in Capricorn. Mars rules Aries, through which the letter Heh is associated with sight. Remember that the letter Ayin means 'eye.' Mars rules Scorpio which is associated with sexual energy. Through the letter Peh, Mars is also connected with the Exciting or Active Intelligence. As a figure of speech, Fermentation means movement, excitement, and agitation. This is a good description of how alchemical Fermentation affects us. [tt]

Dangers do exist in the discipline of Guidance. One danger is the misuse of the leadership role by our spiritual leaders. If unity becomes fractured or if we do not treat each other with a spirit-led attitude of Grace, Guidance can degenerate into a tool to prevent or eliminate what the group considers to be deviant behavior. Leaders can be tempted to impose their will on individuals as well as the group. Guidance can become an effective mechanism for stifling individual expression and for suppressing different opinions when they conflict with the views of the leader.

Manipulating expression within the group stifles the vitality of the group and quashes spiritual growth and vitality. The prophet Isaiah tells us of the Messiah:

> *"a bruised reed he will not break, and a dimly burning wick he will not quench; he will faithfully bring forth justice."* - Isaiah 42:3

Spirit will not harm the weakest person or snuff out the dimmest hope. Mercy, tenderness, and compassion must be the hallmarks of all of our group discussions.

Then there is the danger of divisive and calculating persons gaining the ear of the group. Becoming a voice competing with the voice of leadership, they become a real burden and hindrance to Spirit-inspired leaders. Leaders need both the input and the discernment of members of their group. They also need the freedom to hear and to transmit the living word of Spirit.

Western society is predominantly democratic, but in a spiritual group there exists a hierarchy as we noted in our look at the discipline of Submission. This hierarchy exists not as a tool to 'keep people in their place,' but as an acknowledgement that spiritual growth is a process and spiritual seekers can range anywhere from a neophyte beginner to an experienced adept.

Another danger exists when spiritual leaders allow the group to drift away from the spiritual foundations upon which their teachings are based. These spiritual foundations must inform and shape all of our thought and actions. The *One Source* will never lead us contrary to the teachings it inspired. The written teachings must agree with the inward authority of Spirit which inspired them.

We must also understand that Guidance itself is restricted by our own limitations. As human beings we have our limitations, faults, and misperceptions. Sometimes our fears, doubts, and prejudices keep us from maintaining a spirit-led unity. Sometimes, we just have differences of opinion.

When our unity falls apart, we must remember to be kind to one another. People can and do disagree. Sometimes these disagreements progress to the point where we go our separate ways. We must do whatever we can to make our parting as gracious as possible. We should do prayers and meditations to seek the guidance of the *One Source*.

Practiced as a group discipline, Guidance is hearing, experiencing, and knowing the Divine Mind. As we have seen, practicing this discipline as an individual can be difficult. Feedback from others puts into place a system of checks and balances that can help to eliminate errors. The egregore of the group assists us in contacting higher realms of consciousness. When we participate in formal group activities such as rituals or worship services our collective attention is focused on one common activity. Our ability to safely receive and utilize potent spiritual energies is enhanced.

Because knowing the Mind of Spirit is so important in illuminating our spiritual paths, effective Guidance requires the knowledge and practice of the other disciplines. Group guidance is not the result of majority rule. It requires unanimity. Every member of the group must be committed to experiencing guidance from Spirit.

The dynamics of a group of close and dedicated individuals can accelerate the development of all those individuals when the group as a whole moves forward under the direction of an effective spiritual guide. Guidance is one of the most transformative of the spiritual disciplines. When practiced effectively, one establishes a permanent contact with the voice of Spirit.

With the discipline of Guidance we are able to become inspired by the will of the One Source. With the discipline of Confession in the next chapter we will find that a heartfelt confession will make our hearts lighter and will free much of the energy blocked by negative emotions. This energy will then be available to take action now that we have been inspired by spirit.

†† Paul Foster Case, *Hermetic Alchemy Science and Practice.*

Chapter 11
Confession

Correspondences for Confession

Qabalah:
the Hebrew letter Tzaddi, meaning "Fish Hook"
the Natural Intelligence
Revelation
the function of Meditation
the South-Above edge on the Cube of Space
the 28th Path of Tzaddi on the Tree of Life

Astrology:
the sign of Aquarius (11th house, fixed air)
Rulership: Saturn (Key 21 the World) and Uranus (Key 0 the Fool)

Alchemy:
Dissolution – (Stage 11) - The rousing of living energy (chi or kundalini) in the body to heal and vivify

Theurgy:
the discipline of Confession

Tarot:
Key 17, the Star
Key 0, the Fool
Key 21, the World
Key 19, the Sun

In the last chapter we learned that when we take the phenomenal world of appearances too literally, we become enmeshed in physical reality by the lie of materialism. This state of Bondage to the material world is eloquently illustrated in Key 15 of the Tarot, the Devil. The free flowing energy coming from higher planes of consciousness becomes blocked or frozen and we find ourselves unable to make changes. With the alchemical stage of Dissolution and the discipline of Confession we have the means to change this energy back into its free-flowing state.

When we make our confession to another person the level of communication is the same as if we were meditating. We must rely on our intuition and discrimination in choosing who we may confide in and how we might approach them. The one hearing our confession must also use these faculties in choosing how to respond to our confession. When we open ourselves to another person we open ourselves to guidance from our Higher Souls. We also open ourselves to the possibility of healing and release.

Confession releases the energy we have invested in errors and illusions back into its original state as the First Matter of the alchemists. The First Matter has been described by those who have experienced it as a flowing, semi-solid substance falling to earth in droplets like dew. Once the energy has been returned to this state, it is freed up to form new mental images that can be accessed through meditation.

I am associating the discipline of Confession with the Hebrew letter Tzaddi, the sign of Aquarius and the alchemical stage of Dissolution. Dissolution is summarized in Tarot Key 17 the Star. The Hebrew word Tzaddi means *fish hook*. A fish hook is, of course, used in fishing. The physical function assigned to Tzaddi and to the zodiacal sign of Aquarius is meditation.

Paul Foster Case compares the process of meditation to fishing. He calls it *"fishing for truth in the depths of subconsciousness."* He tells us Tzaddi also translates as *'conception'* and refers to the germination of ideas. Meditation, then, is concerned with the birth of ideas. Elaboration and implementation of these ideas is accomplished elsewhere by the other disciplines. [tt]

The letter Tzaddi has the number or power of 90. Consulting our handy qabalistic dictionary, we learn that the Hebrew word *Domem*, Daleth-Vav-Mem-Mem meaning *profound silence*, also adds to 90.Qabalists tell us that 'Mem is mute like water.' 90 is also the value of the letter name Mem – Mem-Yod-Mem meaning *Water*. [tt]

Tzaddi, the fish hook, symbolizes the physical function whereby one investigates the unseen. Symbolically this represents meditation, by way of which we *"fish for truth"* in the depths of the cosmic stream of consciousness.. Tzaddi is the hook as well as the door and the outstretched hand which guides the aspirant through the door. [tt]

Paul Foster Case tells us we see this line of reasoning in the spelling of Tzaddi, Tzaddi-Daleth-Yod, which translates to hook, door, and hand. Tzaddi is symbolic of our attraction to spirit which draws us completely out of our illusions about physical "reality." [tt]

Meditation is a human ability that partakes of an extraordinary Divine power. This power is available to us as a gift from the Great Goddess herself. The Great Goddess is personified by the naked woman on Tarot Key 17, the Star. Here she is shown as Nature revealing herself to us. Qabalists tell us that the Life-power itself meditates our physical world   into existence. The figure of Nature on Key 17 invites us to experience the eternal meditation of Life along with her. [††]

Paul Foster Case calls meditation *"the only safe regenerative method"* because it draws force up from the Saturn and Mars centers without fixing our attention on the centers themselves. This avoids an unintentional increase in blood flow and other physiological changes in these centers. Unwanted physiological changes may interfere with the flow of nerve energy and alter it in unintended, undesirable, or even unhealthy ways. [††]

The symbol for Dissolution is the symbol of Aquarius, two parallel wavy lines. This symbol is found along with the symbols of the three alchemical essences on the wheel pictured in Tarot Key 10, the Wheel of Fortune. These four symbols hold a clue to the inner meaning of this Key and to the operations of the Great Work. This symbol is also one of several symbols representing the idea from the Emerald Tablet, [††]

> *"That which is above is as that which is below and that which is below is as that which is above, for the performance of the miracles of the One Thing."*

It may seem odd that the airy sign of Aquarius should be represented by waves. The confusion is resolved when we consider that it is the force of wind blowing across the water's surface that creates the waves. This is in perfect agreement with alchemical Dissolution during which the Mars force interacts with our physical bodies to vivify and to heal them. [††]

Confession is often viewed as a private matter between ourselves and Divinity. Why is it placed among the group disciplines? It can be seen as a grace bestowed by Divinity and not as a discipline. Both of these assumptions can be understood more clearly if they are recognized as both/and propositions and not either/or. Yes, Confession can be a private affair, but the memory of our errors often remains even though we may be convinced that we are forgiven. We may still harbor guilt or shame over having committed them.

Dietrich Bonhoeffer writes in Life Together:

> *"A man who confesses his sins in the presence of a brother knows that he is no longer alone with himself; he experiences the presence of God in the reality of the other person. As long as I am by myself in the confession of my sins everything remains in the dark; but in the presence of a brother the sin has to be brought into the light."*

Confession is difficult for us because we all too often compare ourselves to others. We may feel that others are superior to what we believe ourselves to be. We may see others as being more devoted or more spiritually advanced than ourselves. Of course, the reality is that others are just as human and just as fallible as we are. It is helpful to see ourselves in the company of others whose struggle for perfection is every bit as difficult as our own.

Chemical Dissolution is the mixing of a substance with another liquid or solid. Dissolution keeps the components of that substance in suspension until acted upon by another agent. In the same way, the components of our mental images are mixed with the watery astral substance where they can be reconstituted into other mental images.

The agent of this Dissolution is the Mars energy which has been activated by the rising of kundalini energy. The physical function that initiates Dissolution is meditation. As we have just noted, the function of meditation is associated with the airy sign of Aquarius and also with the discipline of Confession. [††]

Saturn and Uranus are considered to be co-rulers of Aquarius by many Western astrologers. This is indeed an odd couple. Saturn traditionally is associated with limitation, order, and discipline. Uranus brings with it a new way of looking at things and its approach is best met with an expanded consciousness. The two planets hardly seem to be compatible. We see this same tug of war in our attitudes about confession. Hiding our short comings from the world keeps us in bondage while the act of revealing them to another is intimidating but liberating.

We may initially be wary or even afraid of freeing ourselves from the chains that bind us, but at the same time, we think longingly of freedom from restriction and pain. This internal struggle continues until our pain compels us to seek change. If we are wise, we listen to the voice of our Higher Soul and seek the release that Confession can bring to us.

In the introduction, we saw that Saturn can be either limiting or liberating depending on the nature of our thoughts. We can choose to hold on to the illusions of the material universe, or we can give free reign to our curiosity and investigate the unseen Reality that gives rise to the material world. Perhaps Uranus with its new way of looking at the world is just what we need to motivate us to accept change.

Saturn represents the necessity and also the ability to create and maintain order. With the aid of Saturn we can be logical and truthful. Saturn demands that we learn to deal with authority, both our own and others. A proper relationship with authority allows us to both teach and learn. We learn to respect both ourselves and those who have legitimate authority over us or have more experience than we. Saturn demands the performance of necessary work, no matter how tedious or mundane. Self-discipline and a realistic sense of our limitations and abilities are also demanded.

Uranus represents expanded consciousness, originality, inventions, computers, and cutting-edge technologies. It is innovative thinking. Uranus is no respecter of the status quo. It prefers to break with tradition and create a new world. Freedom and creativity are valued Uranian qualities. Uranian energy is not subtle. Uranus encourages behavior that may be erratic and bizarre by our society's standard. Utopian societies and humanitarian ideals become possibilities.

Are Saturn and Uranus a compatible couple? As we approach the dawn of the Age of Aquarius, we embark on a grand experiment to answer this question. Hermetic philosophy teaches us that in the highest of qabalistic worlds, all paradoxes and all duality are resolved. Perhaps the answer will come from those who are able to access and work in this world. In the meantime we have the discipline of Confession to help us release the energies of our bodies and minds.. We can free ourselves to work out our own resolution to this question.

Every solid has its own unique melting point where it is transformed by heat from a solid into a liquid. This liquid can be transformed by additional heat into a gaseous state. It is the addition or subtraction of heat that accomplishes the transformation from one state to another. We are accustomed to seeing physical gold as a solid and mercury as a liquid, but each of these has a melting and a freezing point. Physical gold and mercury correspond to mental concepts that are worked with as mental images on the level of the astral substance.

Meditation takes our mental images and places them into the stream of the universal subconscious where they are dissolved and reformed into other mental images. This is *solve et coagula* at the level of Dissolution – dissolve and reform.

Therefore confess your sins to one another, and pray for one another, so that you may be healed. The Prayer of the righteous is powerful and effective.   - James 5:16

When we make a confession to another, we are bringing all of the mental concepts related to our confession into the physical world of Assiah. Once out in the open, these mental images are available to be worked with. If our confessor is understanding and compassionate, he or she will help us to place them in the proper perspective so that they can be dissolved and thereby freed to be transformed into useful mental images that promote forgiveness and healing.

We discussed the role of a spiritual advisor in the last chapter. The medieval Irish Church called this person *Anam Cara* or Soul Friend. An Anam Cara is much more than a spiritual advisor. This person is trusted with the secrets of our soul. We bare ourselves to an extent not possible with anyone else.

The role of spiritual advisor can be performed for one spontaneous act of confession or for a lifetime. In choosing someone for this role, we are looking for someone who we believe is deserving of our highest trust. They must be someone who has demonstrated to us that they are aware of their own shortcomings and are open to the counsel of spirit and to that of their spiritual brothers and sisters. They will have already begun the process of making the changes needed to transform their lives. We will not need to tell them to keep our disclosures secret. We will   intuitively know that they would never betray a confidence. They know intimately the deep sorrow and pain that drives our need for confession.

Of course, there may come a time when our confidence in such a person is betrayed. Some people struggle with keeping a confidence. The person we choose may not be as open to their own growth as we believe. They may not be able to respond to us in a compassionate and loving manner. Such is the human condition. We may greatly diminish the likelihood of misplaced confidence if we develop the faculties of intuition and discrimination. When these inner senses are developed, we can be led by our Higher Souls to a person in whom we know we can place our trust.

If there is a particular offense that we believe is too terrible to reveal, we need to summon the courage to declare to someone, "I need to confess something, but I cannot find the strength to do so." They will then find a method to put us at our ease and proceed to gradually coax us into confession. Perhaps a series of yes or no questions will begin the process of revealing the issue that is causing us such pain and sorrow. Once the Light of truth has been revealed, the grace of spirit returns to our consciousness and peace of mind settles over us like the warm embrace of a loved one.

Alchemically speaking, the process of Dissolution takes the portions of mental images that were broken down during earlier stages of the Work and makes them available to produce new mental images that are consistent with Reality as we now understand it. [††]

Mental images come to us through our subconscious mind in a fluid state. They are brought to the attention of our self-conscious mind. Here they may be accepted, modified, or rejected. The accepted mental images are then applied to our outward, physical existence. Allegorically, their fluid state is transformed into a solid one. This idea is represented pictorially in the ice present in Tarot Keys 0, 9, and 20 – the Fool, the Hermit, and Judgement. We must not allow these images to become so solid in our consciousness that they cannot be easily liquefied and transformed by the heat and light brought by newly unfolded knowledge. [††]

Paul Foster Case writes that higher adepts working with alchemical transformation are capable of altering the forms of solids in the material world of Assiah. They are said to transmute metals by means of the Stone of the Wise. Lesser adepts are also capable of working with this process, but the transformations come about less rapidly and seemingly occur by natural means. The techniques and abilities to achieve the transmutation of physical objects through the use of mental images vary among adepts. [††]

All practitioners of alchemy begin by transforming the structure, function, and chemistry of their own bodies. Paul Foster Case tells us that the alchemist, having transformed his physical body, goes on to produce changes to his animal nature or vital soul. He or she then extends the work to vegetable consciousness and finally to mineral consciousness. The mineral work is illustrated by the mountains in Tarot Keys 6, 8, and 17 – the Lovers, Strength, and the Star. The process of Dissolution is associated with meditation as it is represented by Key 17. [††]

Key 17, the Star, depicts a naked woman kneeling with one knee on land and her other foot on water. This woman represents Nature as she reveals herself to those who earnestly desire to know her secrets. This revelation is done through the process of meditation. Paul Foster Case points out that we do not unveil nature. It is Nature who unveils herself to us. When we meditate, we place ourselves into the stream of the universal consciousness that is ongoing and eternal. [tt]

In the Hindu tradition, the Mother principle, seen in Key 17 as Mother Nature or Isis, is called the Savioress or Illuminatrix. She is also known as "She who carries the Divine revelation." Revelation in Key 17 is seen as a beautiful naked woman. Nature reveals herself to us whenever we pay attention to it. As shown in this Star Key, Nature can be both informative and beautiful[tt].

Paul Foster Case tells us that the physical function of meditation is seen in Key 17 as the flow of water from the two pitchers that Isis is holding. The pool of water represents the reservoir of cosmic mind-stuff that begins to vibrate at a certain level when acted upon by meditation. The stream of water flowing into the pool represents the direct modification by meditation of the pool of universal consciousness. The stream flowing onto dry land divides into five smaller streams, indicating that meditation also modifies physical sensation and unfolds the inner senses. [tt]

Paul Foster Case continues by saying that the function of meditation continuously flows from the two pitchers. In the same sense, Case sys that "Raja Yoga describes meditation as an unbroken flow of knowledge on a particular subject or idea. . . The Qabalist focuses on the symbols involved with a particular path or Sephirah until one discovers its "Silent Source."[tt]

When we make meditation a part of our spiritual practice, we become more amenable to accepting revelations. Not all revelations are earth shattering or dramatic. We receive from meditation exactly what we need. Our spiritual needs in any given moment are not without limit. We may need   certain things, but not others. Through meditation we receive certain information that is helpful to us. Usually our revelations are self-directed and not meant to be shared with others without discrimination. Sometimes we err in mistaking personal revelation for a spiritual directive intended for everyone. Our faculty of discrimination helps us to know the difference. ††

On the Cube of Space, Key 17, representing the Hebrew letter Tzaddi, is placed on the South-Above edge of the Cube. Meditation is begun by self-consciousness, represented by the letter Beth and Tarot Key 1, the Magician, on the top face of the Cube. Self-consciousness is represented on Key 17 by an Ibis bird perched in a tree. The Ibis is the bird of Mercury. Mercury is the planet and the human energy center associated with Key 1. ††

Meditation produces the consciousness pictured on Key 19, the Sun and the letter Resh. Key 19 and Resh are placed on the South face of the Cube. Key 19 represents fertility and regeneration. In Key 19 the Sun is yellow to represent the physical Sun of our solar system. Our Sun collects and distributes energy which gives us Light and Life. That is one reason why the *Collecting Intelligence* is attributed to Resh by the Sepher Yetzirah. ††

Meditation reveals to us the inner essence and significance of appearances in our material universe. This agrees with the chemical definition of Dissolution as the process by which two or more substances are combined to form a single heterogeneous mixture. Meditation can be used to overcome appearances in our world of duality. Pairs of opposites are shown to be two ends of a continuous spectrum, and are therefore composed of the same essence. ††

Meditation takes our theories of Reality and compares them to our experience of that Reality. Our theories are then confirmed, modified, or discarded. Key 17 shows us that nature reveals herself to us. We learn that Nature is always, an ally and never an adversary. Paul Foster Case writes that meditation "transforms the appearance of Nature from the grisly terror of Key 15, and from the cataclysmic disaster of Key 16, into the peaceful, beneficent Mother of us all, shown in Key 17." [tt]

Key 17 is a natural progression of the upheaval in our lives brought about in Key 16 by the destruction of our man-made tower of half-truths and false ideas about Reality. The Star represents the calm after the storm. It is the feelings of joy and freedom that follow cathartic experiences. It is a new beginning once our obsolete or distorted beliefs are eliminated by the Tower's fall. It is also the catharsis we feel after a heartfelt confession. [tt]

With the fall of the Tower, we recognize that when we do not live in accord with our new vision of Reality, we struggle against the prevailing currents of the cosmos. Hardship, pain, and suffering may be the result of not heeding the wakeup call of our Tower experience. If we act wisely, we begin to live our lives in closer alignment with cosmic laws, truth, and principles. The discipline of Confession helps to clear away the remnants of our Tower and make our path easier as we seek to reorient our lives to conform to our new vision. [tt]

Gazing in meditation into the rippling pool, Isis on bended knee is supported by both the water and the earth. This image suggests that when we sincerely seek to base our lives upon spiritual principles, our efforts produce fruit in abundance. [tt]

The position of Tzaddi and Tarot Key 17 at South-Above on the Cube combines Mercury, Above, with the Sun, South. The two interior stars or energy centers associated with Mercury, the upper brain, and the Sun, the heart. Meditation establishes a subtle flow of energy and consciousness between these two centers. ††

The true essence of our own nature is reveled to us by meditation. Meditation also reveals that our essential nature is also the essence of all things in the created universe. We ourselves are the objects of all of our work. Our essence is both the First Matter and the Stone of the Wise at both "ends" of our journey. Like the Ouroboros, they are united in one continuous and eternal process. ††

Alchemical Dissolution reveals to us, through our own nature, the essence of any object of our meditation. We discover this essence to be the mind-stuff of the astral plane, the water which will not wet the hand. We also discover that the ultimate essence of our true being is this same substance. We remind ourselves that the subject of our investigation, the discipline of Confession is the work we perform in the here and now that puts us onto the path of Dissolution. ††

We see from the above discussion that alchemical Dissolution is also a psychological process. This psychological aspect is what concerns us most in our quest to understand the discipline of Confession. Dissolution brings the images and energies stored in our subconscious mind into the awareness of our self-consciousness. It stimulates our inner senses and provides us a direct and factual experience of the true essence of all things.

Our physical and nonphysical bodies are transformed in the process of Dissolution. Our bodies and our personalities become balanced and efficient vehicles of expression for the Life-power. Psychological and physiological transformation is the consequence of Dissolution. Confession with its meditation-like state of mind leads to Multiplication, the ultimate stage of the Great Work.

Out of Love for its creation, Divinity demonstrates the desire to forgive. As the children of the *One Source*, we are recipients of this forgiveness. However, forgiveness cannot be bestowed without a genuine and heartfelt confession and repentance. Confession creates observable change in our relationship with Divinity and fundamental change at the core of our being. The transformation of our inner consciousness begins at the level of spirit and extends through all levels until it reaches the world of physical manifestation.

Confession is problematic in this modern age. Society is largely based on secular values. Some have declared that "God is dead." Spiritual values and guidance have largely been replaced by psychology. It is embarrassing and painful to reveal one's failures and shortcomings to others. We hide behind veils of hypocrisies and falsehoods. Fear and pride prevent our true nature from expressing itself. Paradoxically, the courage to trust enough to confess and to forgive releases and expresses the power to transform and heal. This makes Confession a powerful discipline.

To confess to one another is to communicate at the deepest levels of consciousness. To confess is to remove the barriers of separation and limitation. We no longer feel alone. Divinity is experienced in the presence of another person. We also are able to recognize the Divine within ourselves. Doubts, fears, and self-deceit are removed. Self-knowledge is a great transformer but it will remain an unrealized goal until our true nature and   Divinity

255

are mirrored in the form of another person. When self-knowledge is realized, other people are seen as brothers and sisters in spirit. This transforms all of our relationships from the most private and interior to the most universal.

To be free to express ourselves as the persons we were created to be is real cause for celebration. We will see in the next chapter that Celebration can be a most useful and necessary discipline.

[††] Paul Foster Case, *Hermetic Alchemy Science and Practice.*

Chapter 12
Celebration

Correspondences for Celebration

Qabalah:
 the Hebrew letter Qoph, meaning "Back of the Head"
 the Corporeal Intelligence
 Organization
 the function of Sleep
 the South-Below edge on the Cube of Space
 the 29th Path of Qoph on the Tree of Life

Astrology:
 the sign of Pisces (12th house, mutable water)
 Rulership: Jupiter (Key 10 Wheel of Fortune) and
 Neptune (Key 12 Hanged Man)
 Exaltation: Venus (Key 3 the Empress)

Alchemy:
 Multiplication – (the 12th and final stage) - The Projection
 of finer consciousness into grosser bodies

Theurgy:
 Celebration

Tarot:
 Key 18, the Moon
 Key 12, Hanged Man
 Key 10, Wheel of Fortune

Come, let us sing for joy to the Lord; let us shout aloud to the Rock of our salvation. Let us come before him with thanksgiving and extol him with music and song.   - Psalms 95:1-2

With Confession and the alchemical stage of Dissolution, our bodies have begun to be transformed and our personalities have been cleansed of much error and illusion. Our hearts immediately feel much lighter. We are comforted by an overwhelming sense of Grace. This is a perfect time for Celebration.

In the New Testament book of Luke, chapter 4, we are given details about the beginnings of Jesus' ministry. He is said to have declared a year of jubilee. Two millennia ago the Jewish tradition of Jubilee included such things as the freeing of one's slaves, foregoing the planting of one's crops, the cancelling of one's debts and the return of one's property to its original owners. This was done as a celebration and remembrance of God's goodness, grace and mercy. In remembering that God cares for them, they could cast all of their cares on Him. Regardless of our beliefs and practices today, this exemplifies the true essence of Celebration.

True celebration is possible when we are willing to become free from our cares.. Sadly, the spirit of joyous celebration is scarce in our society today. Social ills such as sexual, religious, and racial discrimination fuel bigotry and mistrust. We see pride, fear, anger, guilt, shame, and other emotions based on the lie of materialism. We discussed this lie in the chapter on Guidance. The lie of Materialism focuses our attention on material concerns and diverts our attention from spiritual concerns. Also, as Harvey Cox writes in *The Feast of Fools,* mankind has been urged "so hard toward useful work and rational calculation he has all but forgotten the joy of ecstatic celebration."

Practicing Celebration as a discipline will bring all of its goodness into our lives until we no longer need to remind ourselves to embrace its joy. Regular practice will make Celebration a habit that will bring us many benefits; physical, mental, and spiritual. Celebration makes us strong.

> *. . . do not be grieved, for the joy of the Lord is your strength.*   - Nehemiah 8:10

Indeed, we cannot endure long in anything without Joy. Women endure the difficulties and pains of pregnancy and childbirth for the promise of the Joy of motherhood. Young couples struggle with building a relationship for the promise of a long and fruitful life together. Finding and keeping the Joy of any experience is important in achieving any goal.

We may begin any activity by an act of will, but cannot sustain it for long without finding Joy in it. The only reason for beginning anything is our belief that its practice and end result will enrich our lives and bring us happiness. Novices in any endeavor understand that mastery brings both fulfillment and Joy.

Celebration is vital to the practice of all of the other disciplines. Without the fruits of Celebration the other disciplines could not long hold our interest. We would see them as boring, tedious, cold, and time consuming. Celebration gives us the strength to persevere in the face of any difficulty. It is said that one way to overcome the influence of the Devil is to laugh. This is one reason why the function of Mirth or Humor is assigned to Tarot Key 15, the Devil.

Joy has long been a part of religious celebration. The Hebrew religion celebrates the goodness and mercy of God in three major annual festivals. These are Rosh Hashanah, Sukkot, and Chanukah. Rosh Hashanah is the traditional Jewish new year celebration where preparations and aspirations are made for the year ahead. Sukkot is the seven day fall harvest festival when thanks are offered to God for the bounty He has shown. Chanukah is a winter festival of the miracle of the oil lamp that burned for eight days. These are celebrations in the truest sense. They give strength to the people of Israel.

Spiritual traditions all over the world from the earliest times have been based on a single Reality; the Reality of the *One Source* that created our world and everything in it. One world created by a single Consciousness is an idea worth celebrating. It helps us to see past our differences to the Reality that unites us. Great men and women of all times and places have known this Reality and have devoted their lives to making this material world a more perfect reflection of this Reality. The spiritual traditions they bequeath to us are all designed to help us to transform ourselves and ultimately to experience this Reality for ourselves. Jack Courtis in Discourse 1 of *"The Quest for the Holy Grail"* writes:

> *"The Quest for the Holy Grail is a system of self transformation that can be reconciled with other similar systems in the Western esoteric tradition. It is a cosmological scheme that is comparable with Tarot, Qabalah and Astrology. There are also hints of a connection with Alchemy. All of these systems or schemes follow a unifying principle that points to one underlying reality. The Holy Grail in its 5 Transformations is one approach to that reality. To achieve the Grail, is to understand reality. To*

understand reality, is to be transformed and to be saved."

The discipline of Celebration and the alchemical stage of Multiplication represent the tingeing of the whole body with the consciousness which is first experienced when the Philosopher's Stone is actually made within the pineal gland. Hence it is associated with the *Corporeal Intelligence* of Qoph. Celebration is the discipline that allows this process to take place. When we celebrate and are filled with joy, our entire being comes alive with a vibration of a much higher rate than that of our normal waking consciousness. Later, usually when we sleep, our bodies are transformed to accommodate these higher rates of vibration on a regular basis.

It may seem odd to think of Celebration as a spiritual discipline, but it is the perfect antidote for the negativity – the apathy, the pessimism, the depression – that is so prevalent in society today. Celebration is much needed. It brings joy to life and imparts the strength to carry on no matter what the adversity.

With Celebration we are presented with the paradox that

> *"For those who want to save their life will lose it, and those who lose their life for my sake will save it."*
> Luke 9:24

This means that if we choose to remain in material bondage, we will not experience the joy of becoming one with spirit. If we choose to relinquish the sovereignty of our personality in favor of our Higher Soul and persevere in the work of self-transformation we will be granted access to higher states of consciousness and will achieve the Stone - the kingdom of Heaven on earth.

Celebration is an integral part of spiritual life. Imagine how much more effective it makes all aspects of a relationship with the Divine. Negative attitudes and feelings only obstruct our communication with Divinity.

Joy spontaneously springs to life when one understands there is an implicit order in the universe and that life is a reflection of that order. Divine Will is then transformed into personal will and the work of the Divine becomes personal work. Genuine Celebration happens when we are transformed by identification with the Will of Divinity.

"The Father and I are One."   – John 10:30

The one true way to produce genuine Joy is to be obedient to the voice of our Higher Soul. The name given to this process by the Western Mysteries is *the Knowledge and Conversation of the Holy Guardian Angel.* To have Knowledge and Conversation of the Holy Guardian Angel is to identify ourselves completely with our Higher Self, to hear its voice, and to pattern our lives according to its teachings. Because we are associating Celebration with Multiplication, the twelfth and final stage of Alchemy, we will be very familiar with this process of the Conversation by the time we arrive here.

We must understand that the process of alchemical transformation is not always linear or sequential. We may encounter the stage of Multiplication more than once on our subconscious and superconscious levels of being before we experience it self-consciously. The Grail knight Parsifal did not achieve the Grail in his first encounter with it. We can experience any of the other stages of alchemy multiple times in the same way before we are ready to consciously work with them.

Many times we encounter the various stages of alchemy in a different order than what is presented to us in alchemical texts. Spirit works however and whenever it finds an opportunity. If we become too concrete in our thinking, we make ourselves more resistant to change. The beauty and power of the spiritual disciplines is that when we work with any of them, we also work with the transformative energies they represent. Each time we do, we are brought closer to our goal of spiritual unfoldment.

Without obedience to the voice of our Higher Soul, authentic Joy is not possible. Our Joy is hollow until the spiritual message of our Higher Soul is put into practice in our daily lives. If our lives are joyless, nothing less than full acceptance and obedience to this voice can change that. The transformative power of this obedience can bring us the Joy we seek. When our family or any other group is filled with love and compassion, and when we demonstrate a spirit of service to one another, we truly have reason to celebrate.

It is important to avoid celebrating when that celebration is devoid of gratitude. This gratitude comes from a deep appreciation for the blessings we receive. Worse is to celebrate when we do not feel like celebrating. What message are we sending to our children or to others when we bless our food and then to proceed to gripe about it? The hypocrisy of our divided minds is immediately exposed.

"Rejoice in the Lord always; again I will say, Rejoice! Let your gentleness be known to everyone. The Lord is near. Do not worry about anything, but

in everything by Prayer and supplication with thanksgiving let your requests be made known to God. And the peace of God, which surpasses all understanding, will guard your hearts and your minds in Christ Jesus."   - Philippians 4:4-7

Apart from the Christian theology in this passage, Paul of Tarsus is telling us that the pathway to a joyful life is to have no anxiety about anything. Do not be full of cares. But this is difficult because we are taught from an early age to be careful about everything. We tell our children to "Be careful," that is, be full of care. We will not be able to truly celebrate until we learn to

". . . not worry about anything."

We will not be free from care until we learn to trust the voice of our Higher Soul.

One reason the Jubilee was so important to the Jewish people was that no one would dare fulfill the requirements of Jubilee without a deep and abiding faith that God would take care of their needs. Faith of such depth and richness today will surely fill our hearts and minds with *"the peace of God, which surpasses all understanding."*

"Finally, beloved, whatever is true, whatever is honorable, whatever is just, whatever is pure, whatever is pleasing, whatever is commendable, if there is any excellence and if there is anything worthy of praise, think about these things. Keep on doing the things that you have learned and received and heard and seen in me, and the God of peace will be with you."   - Philippians 4:8-9

St. Paul goes on to tell us that faith and Prayer and forms of worship alone are not enough to bring us Joy. He writes that what we know to be honorable, just, pure, pleasing, commendable, excellent, and worthy of praise are to be the focus of our thoughts and our lives. Then the peace of living in accord with the *One Source* will be with us.

Our decision to live our lives in accord with the *One* is a conscious act of Will. This is one reason why Celebration is considered to be a discipline. We act as if this is our personal will, but the wise know that only one will exists, the Will of the *One Source*. When we choose this path - or it chooses us - healing and Joy will fill all of our bodies, minds, and relationships. We will have both the inner and the outer experiences of Celebration and alchemical Multiplication.

Paul Foster Case says of Multiplication:

> *"Multiplication is the act or process of increasing in number or quantity. It is the process by which the alchemist, who has succeeded in Dissolution, and the stages of the work preceding it, augments the Elixir. Hence Ripley compares it to fire, from which many other fires may be kindled."* [††]

Paul Foster Case also writes that the main idea behind Multiplication is given in Jesus' parable of the leaven, where a small amount of leaven causes a large amount of dough to rise. Case writes that the words of English alchemist George Ripley tell us that Multiplication is accomplished by repeated, or iterated, Fermentation – a moist type of fire. [††]

Case sums up Multiplication in the following way:

"Multiplication, in brief, is the tingeing of the whole body with the consciousness which is first experienced when the Stone is actually made within the pineal gland. Hence it is associated with the Corporeal Intelligence." [††]

According to the Sepher Yetzirah on the letter Qoph, *"The Twenty-ninth Path (of Qoph) is the Corporeal Intelligence, so called because it forms every body which is formed in all the worlds, and the reproduction of them."* The worlds are the four qabalistic worlds. The import is that in each world there is an appropriate vehicle. The Corporeal Intelligence of Qoph builds the bodies of the mineral, plant, animal, and human kingdoms. This same Intelligence builds all of the vehicles - archetypal, mental, astral and physical - within the created universe. The vehicle used for this purpose by the Corporeal Intelligence is the subconscious mind. [††]

We have no self-consciousness which tells us anything directly concerning the complex processes whereby bodies are built, maintained, and reproduced. All these processes are below the threshold of our waking awareness.

Thus in Tarot and the Qabalah subconscious processes are associated with sleep. During sleep our subconscious mind repairs and transforms the body. It is during sleep that Multiplication does its work. Sub-consciousness has built, repaired, reproduced and transformed all the vehicles of the Life-power. From the sub-atomic level to the cosmic, it has developed all the mineral, vegetable and animal bodies throughout the created universe. [††]

Paul Foster Case writes that the Hebrew word Qoph means "back of the head." This implies that Qoph represents that which precedes the dominion and rulership for which "head" is a symbol. Qoph represents developments that take place under subconscious control. Here all structures transform and evolve. ††

Case adds that on an esoteric level, Qoph can also represent the *"head which is not a head."* This is a name of Kether. It is at the head of the ten sephiroth on the Tree of Life. It is "not a head" because limitless light contained in Kether emanates from the *Ain Soph Aur*, one of the "veils of negative existence." Qoph represents the mysterious Radiant Darkness behind – or above – Kether. ††

Body, soul, and spirit are given distinct identities in Gemini. This is done to emphasize the roles they play in our spiritual unfoldment. Our relationship with our Higher Soul is not yet fully developed in Gemini. Paul Foster Case writes that this relationship is further developed in Virgo where we begin to see that these three aspects of self are in fact unified and were created to act as one. ††

Alchemically speaking, in Virgo we take the elements of earth, water, air, and fire into our bodies as food, water, breath, and light. In our small intestines, chyle is produced that contains the spiritual essence of everything we ingest. Paul Foster Case tells us that in Pisces our relationship with our Higher Soul reaches its fullest manifestation. Our bodies are now ready to accept the higher spiritual energies which quickly transport the spiritual components of chyle to every cell of the body. This is alchemical Multiplication. ††

Paul Foster Case tells us that in alchemical Multiplication every cell of our physical body is charged with higher consciousness. The result is a subtle alteration of our physical vehicle. This produces changes in our finer bodies as well. [tt]

When we master the process of Multiplication our bodies will be so energized that we will be able to accomplish many extraordinary things which the uninformed will call miracles. Our transformed vehicles of consciousness will be able to produce changes in the rates of electromagnetic vibrations of the Life-force. This will create observable physical changes to ostensibly "solid" physical objects. If the transformation serves a higher purpose, we can use this "universal medicine" to reconcile all imbalances and heal all diseases. [tt]

Concerning the transmutation of physical metals, the claims of alchemy are to be understood literally. The instrument of that transmutation is our physical body, changed in subtle ways by the Great Work. By the use of mental imagery we can produce matrices into which the First Matter may flow and take physical form. [tt]

Venus is exalted in Pisces. Venus is the source of our Creative Imagination and the mental images that accompany it. Imagination finds its highest form of expression in the building of bodies, vehicles, and organic structures which we create in order to manifest our desired transformations. The Venus energy is the source from which this desire springs. [tt]

Pisces is traditionally ruled by Jupiter, associated with Key 10 the Wheel of Fortune. Pisces also has a modern ruler in Neptune, linked to Key 12 the Hanged Man. [tt]

Jupiter is guardian of the abstract mind. Its center in the body is in the area of the solar plexus, which is often called the "abdominal brain". Thus its influence is more subconscious than self-conscious. Jupiter rules higher learning and bestows upon us a desire for exploring ideas, both intellectual and spiritual. Paul Foster Case writes that this desire reflects a pairing with the Venus energy. [tt]

Along with Neptune, Jupiter rules religion and philosophy. Jupiter compels us to assess our ethical and moral values and controls our sense of optimism. Neptune rules inspiration, dreams, psychic receptivity, illusion, and confusion. Its influence is more subtle than Saturn. Like the Hanged Man in Key 12, Neptune encourages us to view reality from a different perspective than the majority of humanity. Neptune is associated with intuition and spiritual enlightenment[tt].

Jupiter never does things in a small way. Thus the effect of Jupiter on the imagination and on mental imagery is to energize and expand them. This will greatly influence the energy and the speed associated with the Multiplication process. The effects of both Jupiter and Neptune may engender a sense of euphoria for which Celebration provides an outlet. [tt]

Astrologers tell us that today we are on the cusp between the Piscean age and the Aquarian age. For approximately the past two thousand years we have been suppressing and rejecting our physical appetites and emotions in an attempt to evolve spiritually. And during this time, we have discovered that suppression of our animal nature is a poor way to accomplish this. [tt]

The Age of Aquarius is upon us along with changes in our consciousness. Self-denial is waning. We note that just as the Moon reflects the Sun, our human consciousness reflects the Divine. We discover that every created thing is spirit, including our bodies. Our bodies are instruments of spirit. Our bodies and our world mirror the realm of spirit.

Better health care and preventive medicine are on the rise. More people are focused on personal and planetary healing than at any time during the last two thousand years. Observed from a higher perspective, this translates to service to Divinity, to our planet, and to our fellow human beings. [tt]

In the Tarot major arcana, Pisces and Qoph are represented by Tarot Key 18, the Moon. Paul Foster Case tells us that according to Qabalah, the number 18 is the manifesting archetype of the 8 acting through the agency of the 1, self-consciousness. This makes 18 the number of conscious spiritual evolution. Case goes on to say that the sum of 1 and 8 is 9. Nine is the number of the Hermit Key, the consciousness of the person who has attained enlightenment. The Hermit on Tarot Key 9 stands atop the peak at the end of the path depicted on Key 18. The Hermit offers us the tools to succeed in our own quest for enlightenment and provides the light for us to find our way home. [tt]

The light of the Moon also shows us the way, but it is variable and provides ever changing degrees of light and dark. From this we can deduce that our pathway home will be filled with sorrows as well as joys, with lows as well as highs. If we persevere, Key18 also shows us that our lows will eventually become higher than our previous highs. Paul Foster Case tells us that the 18 Yods, or hands, falling from the sky remind us that we have arrived at our present place on the path as a result of assistance from spirit. [tt]

18 is the value in gematria for the Hebrew word for life, Chai (spelled Cheth-Yod).. Case adds that the 18 Yods falling from the

sky tell us that the light of the Life-power descends from upper realms to help us find our way through the darkness. [††]

In Key 18 all phases of the Moon are shown. Case writes that this is telling us that we must each develop through all phases of consciousness before we reach a sustained state of enlightenment. If we try to alter or circumvent this natural process we will fail. The waxing, fullness, and waning of the Moon bring to mind the three aspects of the goddess, the maiden, matron, and crone. These aspects represent stages of human development. The phases of the Moon and human development are natural processes. Together they underscore the futility of fighting Nature's cycles of ebb and flow. [††]

In the final phase of our personal maturation, events can enslave us as easily as they can free us. This is a characteristic of Saturn that oversees the unfoldment of cosmic consciousness. Our conscious and subconscious agendas are examined and reconciled. We know what we must do to accept responsibility for our lives. The frailties of our human nature often keep us from doing the things that we know must be done. [††]

Case says that Key 18 shows us we can choose to follow the path that has been laid down for us or we can continue to wander through the wasteland. Some wandering may be useful as we explore old pains, illusions, denials, and other cast-off memories carried by our shadow selves. Ultimately, we must find our way back to the path and continue our journey back to the source of our being. [††]

When we practice Solitude we do not fear being alone. We understand that we have never been alone and never will be. We will also never fear being with others because they have no control over our beliefs. We must focus our attention on the

271

good things in our lives and express our gratitude for them. Doing this, we will become joyful and will find reasons to celebrate. Once we learn to focus on these things, they will fill our conscious mind. We will find that most of what previously bothered us is now small and insignificant.

†† Paul Foster Case, *Hermetic Alchemy Science and Practice.*

Epilogue

The discipline of Celebration completes our look at the twelve traditional spiritual disciplines. The system of correspondences that I have applied to them was constructed to demonstrate their connections to Astrology and Alchemy. Only after much experimentation and dialog can we know how well these correspondences work.

If these correspondences interest you and appear to show some merit, I encourage you to try them for yourself and share your experiences with others. Whether or not they prove valid I hope that you have found something in this work that may prove useful to you on your Path of Return.

I also hope that you may have discovered a new appreciation for Hermetic Science and Practice. Astrology, Alchemy, and Theurgy are indeed sciences and are interrelated. One of the reasons that Hermes was called *Thrice Greatest* was his mastery of these three sciences. They should be approached using the scientific method, testing and verifying each bit of information in the laboratory of our own lives.

As we noted in the Introduction, the ancient Greeks had a maxim, *"Know Thyself, gnōthi seauton."* The genius of the ancient Greek civilization was in its advances of the process of individuation. Carl Jung posited that the process of individuation was a crucial one in reaching psychological and spiritual maturity.

The twelve spiritual disciplines we have been examining are techniques for self-exploration and transformation. They help us to achieve individuation. They are also theurgic devices for connecting the *above* and the *below*, our inner and outer reality. When practiced with diligence, the spiritual disciplines take us into places within our souls that we could not otherwise reach.

The science of Theurgy is called by some the *"operation of the Moon."* We have seen that our Moon corresponds to the Hebrew letter Gimel and to Tarot Key 2, the High Priestess. In the Sepher Yetzirah Gimel is given the title of the *"Uniting Intelligence."* The 13th path of Gimel on the Tree of Life unites the spheres of Tiphareth and Kether, the ego consciousness and the consciousness of spirit.

The High Priestess Key represents all levels of our subconscious mind in a state of passivity. Corresponding to the Moon and to the number 2, The High Priestess is thus a symbol of reflection, duplication, (as in a mirror), duality, and similar ideas. The crescent moon is cup shaped, and therefore symbolizes receptivity. The qualities of reflection and duplication are essential to the faculty of memory, which Paul Foster Case tells us is also symbolized by the High Priestess. [††]

The High Priestess is a reflection of the self-consciousness of Key 1 the Magician. However, we are unaware of our subconscious mind and its activities most of the time. Our subconscious is the vessel that receives the creative force of the Life-power and initiates manifestation. It is receptive to the suggestions of our self-conscious mind and that is what makes the spiritual disciplines so powerful. The subconscious mind is the vehicle for attaining spiritual enlightenment and wisdom. The Fool Key represents potentiality and the Magician Key represents Will. Only the High Priestess has the potential power to create. She is the link between the above and the below, the inner and the outer. [††]

The Hebrew word Gimel means *"camel."* On the Tree of Life this path crosses the dark and dangerous desert of the Abyss. As the High Priestess, Gimel is the root source of alchemical Water, which symbolizes consciousness. In the B.O.T.A. deck, this stream of consciousness is shown flowing from the hem of the High Priestess' robe. [††]

The sum of the letters of Gimel, Gimel-Mem-Lamed, is 73. This is the numeration of the letters of the second sphere of Chokmah or Wisdom, Cheth-Kaph-Mem-Heh. From this we know that Gimel, the Moon, and the High Priestess bear a relation to Wisdom. [††]

The 13th path of Gimel unites our human incarnations to the *One Source*. When we are able to safely travel across the Abyss, we receive the ultimate initiation. The *Uniting Intelligence* of Gimel teaches us about the reconciliation of opposites because it challenges us to look beyond the dualities we encounter in our lives. The Hebrew word for unity is *achad*, Aleph-Cheth-Daleth. The letters of achad sum to 13, intimating a connection to the 13th path of Gimel. Once across the Abyss, it is said that we have direct experience of the *One Source*. [††]

Hermetic philosophy has much to teach us about consciousness, evolution, and unity. About consciousness, it tells us that everything in this manifested universe is alive, responsive, and aware. Concerning evolution, it demonstrates to us that everything is striving toward perfection. Hermetic philosophy also introduces us to the reality that everything proceeds from the *One Source* and is its expression and reflection.

These ideas are embodied in the three alchemical Essences of Alchemy; *Mercury, Sulfur*, and *Salt*. A purely intellectual grasp of these Essences may be difficult if not impossible. The spiritual disciplines help us to experience these principles on the inner planes and help us combine our experiences with our storehouse of knowledge to formulate a more complete understanding of Reality.

Theurgy or *high magic* has its origins in the earliest civilizations of humanity, perhaps going back to legendary Atlantis and Lemuria. Theurgy (god-work) is a name coined by Chaldean Platonists in about the second century CE to distinguish it from the speculations of *theology* (god-study) and the manipulations of *thaumaturgy* (miracle-work or lower magic).

Theurgy is based on the belief that humans have a divine essence; that human beings share the same creative and administrative capabilities as the *One*; and that a legitimate use of this power is to participate in the dynamic unfolding and *administration* of the cosmos. Recall that the Sepher Yetzirah calls the consciousness of Tav – Saturn – *the administrative intelligence.*

One example of the science of Theurgy is the use of god-names as well as angelic and archangelic names. These names are not merely signifiers, they are activators. One system uses these names spelled using the twenty two letters of the Hebrew alphabet. These letters represent twenty two types of consciousness. Different names use different letters and thus express different forces and potencies when written, thought, spoken, or chanted. When these names are expressed, we concentrate on the powers they represent and on our intent in invoking them. Other systems use letters of the Greek and Latin alphabets in much the same fashion.

Spiritual disciplines are initiated by our conscious decisions to engage in their activity. Practicing the disciplines brings about changes in our thoughts, beliefs, and actions in all areas of our lives. Our attention is turned from the mundane to the Divine. Perseverance in the work of the spiritual disciplines leads us to the replacement of unwanted habits with ones that support our spiritual goals. These habits engage us in pursuing intentional spirituality that leads us ultimately to intimacy with the *One Source*.

What sets the spiritual disciplines apart from other spiritual activities? A spiritual activity is called a discipline when it does not arise naturally, intuitively, or easily. We must make a conscious decision and set a clear intention when we practice it. It is a developmental activity that opens us up to higher realms of consciousness. Repetition and regularity increase the quality of our results. As we increase our concentration and our confidence, we receive results faster.

Familiarity with the disciplines will ultimately lead us to use them in an almost automatic and subconscious manner. Recall that our self-conscious and subconscious aspects are equally important in the process of manifesting our desires. Our regenerated self-consciousness and subconsciousness is depicted in Key 19 of the B.O.T.A. Tarot. Appearing remarkably alike, their most obvious difference is their gender. Our self-conscious mind must be active in practicing the disciplines to insure that our subconscious mind receives accurate input.

In those times when we do not feel like engaging in our spiritual exercises, the disciplines provide structures and methods that can be relied upon to help us accomplish our work. This carries us through those difficult times when we would prefer to ignore our spiritual health.

†† Paul Foster Case, *Hermetic Alchemy Science and Practice*

Saturn Revisited

When we began our journey, we looked at the role of Saturn energy in the practice of spiritual discipline. We sometimes regard Saturn energy as too limiting and negative. If the lower forces of our subconscious mind are wild and uncontrolled, they will rebel against the restrictive forces of Saturn. Our subconscious minds and the forces they control are not able to comprehend the abstract idea that limitation creates a space in our lives where growth can occur.

The only way we will overcome the resistance that results is to consciously and repeatedly demonstrate this pattern of restriction and growth in our lives. Our subconscious mind will soon take note of the growth and the freedom that results from it. When these advantages have been sufficiently demonstrated, it will become our willing partner in performing the Great Work.

As noted previously, we ourselves are the subjects of the Great Work. It is a voyage of discovery; what Paul Foster Case calls *spiritual unfoldment*. We are creations of the *One* and continue to be at all times and in all places expressions of the *One*. We are all born as children of the *One* and it only remains for us to unfold this Reality and give it expression throughout our lives.

The Saturn center at the base of our spine is the seat of the Life-power in our physical body. It resides there like a coiled serpent where it regulates and maintains the structure, growth, and well-being of our entire body. If the Life-power to some degree is not constantly present in each cell of our body, we could not exist as physical beings. The Life-power remains largely in our Saturn center until it is activated   either spontaneously or consciously. When it is activated this serpent of Wisdom uncoils and moves up our spinal cord to the higher energy centers. This activation or alchemical Sublimation is called the rousing of the *kundalini* energy.

The pervasiveness of the Saturn energy throughout our entire being is vividly illustrated in the Tree of Life diagram. Saturn corresponds to the sphere of Binah in the emanative world of Atziluth. Saturn is exalted in Libra, which corresponds to 22nd path of Lamed in the creative world of Briah. Saturn rules Capricorn which corresponds to the 26th path of Ayin in the formative world of Yetzirah. Saturn also co-rules the sign of Aquarius along with Uranus. Aquarius corresponds to the 28th path of Tzaddi in Yetzirah. The 32nd path of Tav in the world of Yetzirah corresponds to Saturn. Finally, Saturn energy is present at the base of our spine. The physical body corresponds to the sphere of Malkuth and to the material world of Assiah. There is no cessation or interruption in the influence of Saturn.

The physical world of Assiah is the single reality experienced by most of our human brothers and sisters. This is Divine energy acting through form and low levels of vibration. It is the world revealed to us by our five physical senses. The Devil pictured in Key 15 tries to convince us that what we see, hear, touch, smell, or taste is all that exists. As ruler of Capricorn, Saturn plays a central role in this illusion. This is the reality we call Nature or Mother Earth. When we begin to look at Nature and then to observe it closely, we notice that it behaves according to certain laws.

When we make an observation that seems to run contrary to the laws we have noted, our sense of curiosity is aroused. Closer examination and the engagement of our imagination reveal a higher working of these natural laws. A broader picture of

Reality emerges and we are ready to explore it. We are about to begin a spiritual Journey of Return that will ultimately lead us back to the *One Source* whose children we are.

Our Journey of Return to our Creator is symbolized on the Tree of Life as beginning in the material world of Assiah and moving toward the emanative world of Atziluth. Moving from Assiah, Yetzirah is the next world encountered. Yetzirah is the world of mythic reality. It is the world of our imagination and our subconscious mind. Ideas in Yetzirah are expressed through symbols and mental images. In Yetzirah we unmask the lies of materialism, separation, and limitation. Here we encounter the concept of unity and the consciousness of *"we."* The energy of Saturn in Yetzirah is active on the 32nd path of Tav, the 28th path of Tzaddi, and the 26th path of Ayin.

Our physical body and the material universe that is its home are represented on the Tree of Life by the sphere of Malkuth, *the Kingdom*. By the symmetry of the Tree of Life diagram, we see that Malkuth is a reflection of the sphere of Kether, *the Crown*. We see also that 10, the number of Malkuth, can be reduced to 1, the number of the sphere of Kether. This intimates that the material is indeed a reflection of the spiritual. In truth, material reality is the energy of the *One Source* vibrating at a lower level. The rules and orderliness of the Saturn energy allow us to make personal observations that can demonstrate this truth in our lives.

Tarot Key 21, the World, is ascribed to the 32nd path of Tav. This next segment of our path of Return is associated with the planet Saturn. It represents the seventh and final stage of spiritual unfoldment, Cosmic Consciousness. This is the ultimate level of freedom that we are seeking, and yet it also represents union (a form of limitation) with the *One Source*; a Divine paradox.

The 32nd path of Tav is sometimes called the *Serving Intelligence*. It is here that the aspirant learns that Service is the Key that unlocks the door to the temple of the Mysteries. As Dr. Paul Clark tells us, "*It is, indeed the only safe and effective motive for traveling the ancient Path of Return.*" Another aspect is that we cannot learn the more advanced lessons except through service to Divinity, to a higher cause, or to others. When we shift our focus from getting to giving, we learn the occult significance of "*It is better to give than to receive.*"

Saturn brings limitation, discipline, and form It helps us to plan and then execute the work we do on our quest to achieve Cosmic Consciousness. If we are to achieve oneness with the universe we must early in our journey heed the words of Jesus of Nazareth:

> "*Whosoever shall be chief among you, let him be your servant.*"   - Matthew 20:27

The goal setting and the service that accompanies the Saturn energy connects with and activates the powers of our deeper consciousness to bring us the knowledge, skills, and resources necessary for us to ultimately transform ourselves into a new kingdom of beings more advanced than *Homo sapiens*. The lesson of Saturn on the 32nd path of Tav is that in order to achieve liberation, we must rightly understand and implement our powers of limitation.

The 28th path of Tzaddi is attributed to the sign of Aquarius and to Tarot Key 17, the Star. Saturn co-rules Aquarius with Uranus. This is hardly a harmonious pairing. One wonders at the words of the song *"The Age of Aquarius"* recorded by the rock group the 5th Dimension:

Harmony and understanding
Sympathy and trust abounding
No more falsehoods or derisions
Golden living dreams of visions
Mystic crystal revelation
And the mind's true liberation
Aquarius! Aquarius!

The Age of Aquarius that we are now entering will be more about transforming our image of "self" from our individual personality to our higher Self or higher Soul. We will be working on this transformation both individually and collectively. This will be difficult to achieve. Personality will not abdicate its ruling position in our lives voluntarily. This is one reason why Dissolution, the alchemical stage corresponding to Aquarius, is considered to be one of the most arduous stages for us to work through.

The lesson Saturn teaches us here on the 28th path is that the power of the Self does not originate from the personality – the below; it originates from the higher source we label the Individuality or Higher Soul – the above. Through our personality we are given the illusions of separation and limitation necessary for us to deal with an outer reality based on time and space. Problems arise when we mistake these illusions for a reality that does not acknowledge the existence of the above.

On our Path of Return we next encounter Saturn on the 26th path of Ayin. The path of Ayin is also the path of the sign of Capricorn. Saturn is the ruling planet of Capricorn. The   Hebrew letter Ayin and the sign of Capricorn are both represented in the Tarot by Key 15, the Devil.

In contrast to the 32nd path of Tav, The 26th path of Ayin represents the first stage of spiritual unfoldment. This stage is called *"Bondage"* because the natural man that has not given thought to his or her spiritual nature is indeed in bondage to the illusion that nothing 'real' exists beyond physical reality.

A clue that materialism is an illusion comes from the number of the path. 26 is the number of Tetragrammaton – the four letter name of God. When the letter values of Yod-Heh-Vav-Heh are added together their sum is 26. Wherever the number 26 appears in qabalistic work, a connection to Divinity is implied.

Aspirants who have made sufficient progress on their spiritual path understand that the condition of bondage is neither malefic nor permanent. The limitations that others call bondage are necessary conditions for manifestation. Every decision we make leading to creation necessarily eliminates other forms of expression.

The Devil pictured in Key 15 is made up of a collection of different animal parts. This is done to show that such a character has no basis in reality and that it is a man-made symbol: a scapegoat for the perceived ills that exist in our material universe. The reality behind its appearance is that it does not oppose Divinity, but represents that aspect of the cosmos that we encounter when we attempt to live our lives in opposition to Divine law. This connection to Divinity is signaled by its white beard, symbolic of the spiritual figure called the *Ancient of Days*.

The horned male figure in the Devil Key is gesturing toward the half-cube the Devil is perched on as if to say, *"This is all there is. Reality is the material universe."* This is the lie of materialism, represented by the half-cube or partial truth of physical existence.

Capricorn is associated with the function of Mirth. Laughter breaks the spell of the absurdity of the lie of materialism or any other incongruity we encounter. Energy generated by our sense of humor can break through and destroy any illusion. This is one of the many reasons laughter is called the best medicine. In ancient Egypt, the priests of Ra are described:

> *"Thy priests go forth at dawn; they wash their hearts with laughter."*
> The Egyptian Book of Coming Forth by Day

The 26th path of Ayin is called the *Renewing Intelligence*. Our lower natures are focused on desires for acceptance, wealth, and fame. These desires must be controlled. They are actually created by our fears that we are alone, limited, and mortal. Again, our sense of humor can help us to conquer our fears. We are then free to love ourselves and others unselfishly. We are also free to think in new ways. Paul of Tarsus exhorts us:

"Do not be conformed to this world, but be transformed by the renewing of your minds, so that you may discern what is the will of God - what is good and acceptable and perfect."
Romans 12:2

The next encounter with Saturn on our Path of Return is on the 22nd path of Lamed. The 22nd path also corresponds to the sign of Libra and to Key 11, Justice. Venus rules Libra, and Saturn finds its astrological exaltation here. This exaltation greatly magnifies the influence of Saturn on this path. Looking at the image of the woman on the Justice Key, we see the image of a blue-violet tau cross on a yoke around her neck. This is a reference to the letter Tav and to Saturn.

Balance is an important lesson of the Justice Key. It is said that equilibrium is the *arcanum* of the Great Work. As we discussed earlier in the chapter on Simplicity, both the sword and the scales represent balance. The metal of Geburah is iron or steel and thus the Sword is a reference to the Mars energy of the sphere of Geburah or Severity.

The 22nd path of Lamed connects the spheres of Geburah and Tiphareth. The metal of Tiphareth is Gold and thus the scales represent Tiphareth. Note that the raised sword in the woman's right hand and the lowered scale in her left hand are in proper orientation to the positions of Geburah and Tiphareth on the Tree of Life. Also note that Key 11 is at the center of Keys 1 through 21 and is the balance point.

If we are to succeed in our plans and see our desires come to fruition, the universal forces of the macrocosm that interact with us in the microcosm must be balanced. This can only happen if we seek to bring about a balance in our personalities. Once balanced, they become useful vehicles for cosmic forces.

The meaning of Aleph – the ox – in relation to Lamed - the ox goad - is that education, in the form of the ox goad, has balance as its purpose. This is one use of the Saturn energy. Unnecessary and outworn forms are discarded. New images are created. This education is followed by action and work. This work is alchemical Sublimation, the raising of the kundalini force to higher energy centers in our bodies.

Sublimation raises the Saturn energy to higher energy centers through the use of mental images during meditation. Thus the

Venus center (Creative Imagination) is active during Sublimation. Libra rules the kidneys, which are organs of elimination. During Sublimation, we eliminate the mental imagery that we do not wish to see manifested. Using the Saturn energy, we limit our focus to those images that help to manifest what we do want.

The highest placement of Saturn on the Tree of Life is the 3rd sephirah, Binah. Binah is called the Great Mother, the Dark Sterile Mother, the Great Sea, and the Archetypal Womb. All life comes into manifestation through her. But she is also restricting, binding, and limiting. She is the root of Water and head of the Pillar of Severity.

The immense energies of Kether, the Crown, and Chokmah, Wisdom, are boundless and timeless. In the magnetic and attracting energies of Binah we have the beginnings of form and time. The great cycle of birth, death, and rebirth begins here as everything that comes into manifestation is subject to aging, death, and rebirth. Binah is thus intimately associated with the Saturn energy. Saturn has become associated with the figure of Father Time, from which nothing in the manifest universe can escape.

Saturn energy promotes the Understanding of Binah, but only when we offer our patience, efforts, and time. Only then will it reveal its secrets. Saturn demands much from us, but it never asks for more than we are capable of giving. Binah appears black because our material selves are not capable of perceiving the immense radiance of her light. Also, in our material world, the color black contains all of the other colors. Black veils the glory of Binah until time and understanding reveal it to us. With enough time and effort, we will one day cross the Abyss and unite with The Great Mother in cosmic consciousness.

Endings are Just New Beginnings

One of Saturn's lessons is that beginnings and endings exist in our lives to help us move forward from one stage of life to another. If we remain conscious of this fact, we can make the decisions and take the actions that allow us to eliminate those things in our lives that no longer serve us or are detrimental to our growth. We can focus on positive mental images and take those actions that will manifest what we truly desire. The spiritual disciplines are techniques designed to help us accomplish this.

We can transcend the limitations of our material awareness. When daily life begins to weigh on us, we can rely on our sense of humor to point out the incongruities and absurdities that arise from a limited picture of Reality. We can rely on our senses of wonder and curiosity to open our minds and our hearts to the possibilities and the adventures that await us on the inner planes of consciousness. The spiritual disciplines open doors for us in the higher worlds.

Ultimately questions about our true nature such as "Who am I?" and "What is my purpose?" can only be answered by exploring the inner dimensions of consciousness. Seekers who have experienced the spiritual realms before us tell us that treasures await us that transcend our human capability to describe them. Even if they could be described, that would take from us the incredible experience of discovering them ourselves. Spiritual discipline helps us find our way through the labyrinth of illusions to the Reality at the center.

If we accept the proposition that we are all sons and daughters of The *One Source* that created us and our world, why do we continue to live as though we are not connected to our world or to each other? To continue to live in this manner would deny us our birthright as spiritual beings. As children of Divinity it is our birthright to become co-creators and co-administrators of our universe when we reach spiritual maturity.

If we deny that we are children of Divinity, we contradict the words of generations of spiritual masters whose experiences have convinced them that we are, in fact, Divine creatures. Worse, we place ourselves in opposition to the powerful currents of cosmic law. We can continue this opposition only for as long as we have the physical and mental strength to do so. Once we make the choice to turn toward the light of Spirit, we can find the strength and the courage to tread the Path of Return by practicing the spiritual disciplines.

Using the 12 signs of the zodiac and the 7 planets associated with them, we use the 3 operations of the Sun, Moon, and Stars to help us find our way back to our spiritual home. We find that we never really left home but had accepted the illusion of separation. The journey home is not one of becoming, but of unfolding what was, and is and always will be. Our roadmap for this unfoldment is made up of the 22 letters of the Hebrew alphabet and the 22 major arcana of the Tarot that represent them.

We are all prodigal sons and daughters whose fondest wish is to someday return home to be united once more with our spiritual Father. Our illusion of separation will continue for as long as it serves the process of our spiritual unfoldment. At the end of our journey when we at long last return to our spiritual home, our father will say: *"These sons and daughters of mine were dead and are alive again; they were lost and are now found!"*

This reunion may take several lifetimes for many of us, but the spiritual disciplines can help us to learn our lessons faster. We will one day arrive home laden with such treasures as Wisdom, Understanding, Knowledge, and Compassion. As the Master said in the Parable of the Talents: *"Well done, good and faithful children; you have been trustworthy in a few things, I will put you in charge of many things."*

We have reached the end of this part of our journey into the spiritual disciplines. My hope is that you have learned something along the way that will be useful to you in your own spiritual quest. Perhaps some of you will be inspired to add your own thoughts and lead us through the next part of our journey. I conclude now with this wish – **May Light be extended upon you!**

Bibliography

Andrea, Raymond, F.R.C. *The Technique of the Disciple*. San Jose, CA: AMORC, 1999.

Bond, Frederick Bligh, F.R.I.B.A., and Lea, Thomas Simcox, D.D. *Gematria: a Preliminary Investigation of the Cabala*. London. Research into Lost Knowledge Organization, 1977.

Bonhoeffer, Dietrich. *Life Together: The Classic Exploration of Faith in Community*. New York, NY, HarperOne, 2009.

Case, Paul Foster. *Occult Fundamentals and Spiritual Unfoldment: Volume 1 - The Early Writings*. Covina, CA: The Fraternity of the Hidden Light, 2008.

_____. *Esoteric Secrets of Meditation and magic: Volume 2 - The Early Writings*. Covina, CA: The Fraternity of the Hidden Light, 2008.

_____. *The Book of Tokens: 22 Meditations on the Ageless Wisdom (14th ed.)*. Los Angeles, CA: The Builders of the Adytum, 1989.

_____. *Hermetic Alchemy Science and Practice*. Los Angeles, CA: The Rosicrucian Order of the Golden Dawn, 2009.

_____. *The Tarot: A Key to the Wisdom of the Ages*. Los Angeles, CA: The Builders of the Adytum, 1990.

_____. *The True and Invisible Rosicrucian Order: An Interpretation of the Rosicrucian Allegory and an Explanation of the Ten Rosicrucian Grades*. York Beach, ME: Samuel Weiser, Inc., 1985.

_____. *"An Address to Neophytes 0=0."* Hermetic Order of the Golden Dawn. Outer Order of the Rosicrucian Academy of Alpha Omega, 2015. Retrieved 29 July 2016 from http://www.golden-dawn.com

Clark, Paul A. *The Hermetic Qabalah*. Covina, CA: The Fraternity of the Hidden Light, 2012.

_____. *Paul Foster Case: His Life and Works*. Covina, CA: The Fraternity of the Hidden Light, 2013.

Coleman, Wade, *Sepher Sapphires: A Treatise on Gematria The Magical Language – Volumes I and II*. Covina, CA: The Fraternity of the Hidden Light, 2008

Coogan, Michael D. (ed.), et. al. *The New Oxford Annotated Bible with Apocrypha: New Revised Standard Version (4th ed.)*. New York, NY: Oxford University Press, USA, 2010.

Courtis, Jack. *Disciplined Action* - Rosicrucian Archive. The Confraternity of the Rose Cross. 1998. Retrieved February 15, 2015, from http://www.crcsite.org/Discipline.htm

_____. *Secret Symbols of the Rosicrucians - Tabula Smaragdina Hermetis* – Rosicrucian Archive. The Confraternity of the Rose Cross. 1998. Retrieved February 15, 2015, from http://www.crcsite.org/Tabula.htm.

_____. *Quest for the Holy Grail p1* - Rosicrucian Archive. The Confraternity of the Rose Cross. 1998.. Retrieved February 15, 2015, from http://www.crcsite.org/grail1.htm

Cox, Harvey. *The Feast of Fools.*Cambridge, MA: Harvard University Press, 1969.

Daskalodos, Ramose. *A Letter of Introduction to Theurgy.* The Divine Science, 2015. Retrieved March 11, 2016, from https://www.thedivinescience.com/a-letter-of-introduction-to-theurgy

David, Marc. *Nourishing Wisdom: A Mind-Body Approach to Nutrition and Well-Being.* New York, NY: Penguin Random House, 1994.

Demetra, George and Bloch, Douglas. *Astrology for Yourself: How to Understand and Interpret Your Own Birth Chart.* Newburyport, MA: Weiser Books, 2006.

Duquette, Lon Milo. *The Chicken Qabalah of Rabbi Lamed Ben Clifford: Dilettante's Guide to What You Do and Do Not Need to Know to Become a Qabalist.* Newburyport, MA: Weiser Books, 1991.

Elgin, Duane. *Voluntary Simplicity: Toward a Way of Life That Is Outwardly Simple, Inwardly Rich.* New York, NY: HarperCollins, 2010.

Foster, Richard J. *Celebration of Discipline (3rd ed.).* San Francisco, CA: Harper & Row, 1998.

Fox, Emmet. *The Sermon on the Mount: The Key to Success in Life.* New York, NY: HarperOne, 2009.

Godwin, David. *Godwin's Cabalistic Encyclopedia: Complete Guidance to Both Practical and Esoteric Applications.* St. Paul, MN: Llewellyn Publications, 1999.

Hauck, William Dennis. *The Emerald Tablet: Alchemy for Personal Transformation.* New York, NY: Penguin Books, 1999.

Huxley, Aldous, *The Perennial Philosophy: An Interpretation of the Great Mystics, East and West.* New York, NY: Harper Perennial Modern Classics, 2009.
Iamblichus, Porphyry, Thomas Taylor. *On the Mysteries of the Egyptians, Chaldeans, and Assyrians.* Somerset, UK: Prometheus Trust, 1999.

Jayanti, Amber. *Living the Qabalistic Tarot.* Newburyport, MA: Weiser Books, 2004.

Kaplan, Aryeh, *Sepher Yetzirah: the Book of Creation.* York Beach, ME: Samuel Weiser, Inc., 1997.

King, Robert, Rev. "The Christian Mysteries." Servants of the Light. Servants of the Light, 2016. Retrieved 14 Feb. 2016 from http://www.servantsofthelight.org/knowledge/the-christian-Mysteries/

Levi, Eliphas. *Transcendental Magic: Its Doctrine and Ritual.* York Beach, ME: Samuel Weiser, Inc. 1968.

Lotterhand, Jason C. *The Spoken Cabala: Tarot Explorations of the One Self.* Covina, CA: The Fraternity of the Hidden Light, 2010.

Merriam-Webster. *The Merriam-Webster Dictionary.* Springfield, MA: Merriam-Webster Mass Market, 2004.

Nouwen, Henri J.M. *The Way of the Heart: The Spirituality of the Desert Fathers and Mothers*. New York, NY: HarperOne, 2009.

O'Donohue, John. *Anam Cara: A Book of Celtic Wisdom*. New York, NY: Cliff Street Books, 1997.

Parfitt, Will. *The New Living Qabalah: A Practical Guide to Understanding the Tree of Life*. Rockport, MA: Element Books, Inc., 1995.
Reidy, Richard J. *Thomas Norton's The Ordinal of Alchemy*. Oxford, UK: Early English Texts Society, 1975.

Schneider, Michael S. *A Beginner's Guide to Constructing the Universe: The Mathematical Archetypes of Nature, Art, and Science*. New York, NY: HarperPerennial, 1995.

Smith, Hannah Whitall. *The Christian's Secret of a Happy Life*. New York, NY: Merchant Books, 2013.

Starkey, George. *An Exposition upon Sir George Ripley's Preface*. Ann Arbor, MI: University of Michigan Library, 2011.

Suares, Carlo. *The Second Coming of Reb YHSHWH: The Rabbi Called Jesus Christ*. York Beach, ME: Samuel Weiser, Inc., 1994.

"The Emerald Tablet of Hermes." B.O.T.A. Builders of the Adytum. Retrieved 16 Apr. 2016, from https://www.bota.org/resources/emtablet.html.

Three Initiates. *The Kybalion: A Study of the Hermetic Philosophy of Ancient Egypt and Greece*. Chicago, IL: The Yogi Publication Society, 1940.

Wang, Robert. *Qabalistic Tarot: A Textbook of Mystical Philosophy*. York Beach, ME: Samuel Weiser, Inc., 1987.

Willard, Dallas. *The Spirit of the Disciplines: Understanding How God Changes Lives,* San Francisco, CA: Harper & Row, 1988.

Wirth, Oswald. *Tarot of the Magicians*. Newburyport, MA: Weiser Books, 2013.

www.ingramcontent.com/pod-product-compliance
Lightning Source LLC
Chambersburg PA
CBHW031559110426
42742CB00036B/248